GOODBYE
TO ALL THAT

WRITERS ON LOVING AND LEAVING NEW YORK

GOODBYE TO ALL THAT

EDITED BY SARI BOTTON

*Leslie Jamison, Roxane Gay,
Ada Limón, Emma Straub, and more*

SEAL PRESS

New York

Seal Press
Hachette Book Group
1290 Avenue of the Americas, New York, NY 10104
www.sealpress.com
@sealpress

Printed in the United States of America

Originally published in trade paperback and ebook by Seal Press in October 2013

Second Trade Paperback Edition: April 2021

Published by Seal Press, an imprint of Perseus Books, LLC, a subsidiary of Hachette Book Group, Inc. The Seal Press name and logo is a trademark of the Hachette Book Group.

The Hachette Speakers Bureau provides a wide range of authors for speaking events. To find out more, go to www.hachettespeakersbureau.com or call (866) 376-6591.

The publisher is not responsible for websites (or their content) that are not owned by the publisher.

Print book interior design by Amy Quinn

Library of Congress Cataloging-in-Publication Data

Names: Botton, Sari, 1965– editor.
Title: Goodbye to all that : writers on loving and leaving New York / edited by Sari Botton.
Description: Second trade paperback edition. | New York : Seal Press, 2021.
Identifiers: LCCN 2020038592 | ISBN 9781541675681 (paperback) | ISBN 9781541619883 (ebook)
Subjects: LCSH: American literature--New York (State)--New York. | Women authors, American—New York (State)—New York—Biography. | Women—New York (State)—New York)--Biography. | New York (N.Y.)—Biography.
Classification: LCC PS549.N5 G66 2021 | DDC 810.8/03587471 [B]—dc23
LC record available at https://lccn.loc.gov/2020038592

ISBNs: 978-1-58005-494-2 (paperback); 978-1-5416-7568-1 (paperback reissue), 978-1-5416-1988-3 (ebook)

LSC-C

Printing 1, 2021

All I mean is that I was very young in New York, and that at some point the golden rhythm was broken, and I am not that young anymore.

—Joan Didion, "Goodbye to All That,"
Slouching Towards Bethlehem

For Clarisse

CONTENTS

FOREWORD TO THE SECOND EDITION

When I began updating this book in the fall of 2019, it seemed the most dramatic change to New York City since 2013 was the acceleration of a mechanism that was already in place: gentrification. Powered by racism, sexism, classism, and other engines of inequality, it had warped into what *Vanishing New York* author Jeremiah Moss has labeled "hyper-gentrification." New York City has always had a bewitching, intoxicating effect on people, especially those who arrive with big aspirations in publishing or any of the myriad other creative fields of which the city is the unofficial capital. Often, though, at some point, the magic wears off. For some, it happens after their artistic dreams are dashed one too many times. For others, tiny living quarters come to feel too confining. For many, many more, time and time again, the cost of living skyrockets way beyond their means. In recent years, the number of people who could no longer afford to live in the five boroughs increased exponentially. Left and right, people were saying "goodbye to all that."

But just a few months later, in the winter of 2020, a global pandemic would alter New York City in even more immediately obvious ways. What makes the city special would disappear. Hundreds of thousands of restaurants, shops, Broadway shows, museums, book shops, movie theaters—every "nonessential" business that had been essential to making New York the rich cultural tapestry it has always been—would be shuttered. Midtown Manhattan and other business districts would become ghost towns, as workers were either laid off or sent home indefinitely. The population density that has always made this place feel like a teeming, nonstop-happening-now city worked against it, allowing the novel coronavirus to rapidly spread from resident to resident. New York became one of the pandemic's worst hot spots in the United States.

Ninety miles north, in my adopted home of Kingston, New York, I feel an irrational pull—an urge to get in my car and return, to applaud each evening at seven for essential workers, to find my place there once again, even though, especially now, it makes absolutely no sense for me to go back. When will I get to visit it again? What will the city be like then? It's now sixteen years since I left, and I've never missed the place more.

THIS IS A VERY DIFFERENT TIME FROM WHEN THE FIRST EDI-tion of *Goodbye to All That* was released, eight years after I left New York City.

In 2005, after we were evicted from our undermarket loft in the East Village and couldn't afford even a studio at the going rate, my husband and I felt strangely relieved to leave a city that seemed to be changing more rapidly than we could keep up with and where living had become completely unaffordable for us. We moved to New York's Mid-Hudson Valley, just under two hours from the city.

It was only a short time before we met a slew of other expats. Many of them were fellow writers and editors struggling to stay afloat in the new, shrinking publishing economy, just as I was. Trading the high cost of living in New York City for the significantly lower cost of living in a depressed rural area helped. I'd cross paths with them at cafés (often cafés established by yet other expats), and as we got to know one another, we'd compare notes on what prompted our respective exits from the city.

In time, I started to notice a recurring theme. Regardless of the particular circumstances that finally led to each person's departure, they had all, after once being enamored with the city and excited by its literary scene (populated by some of the world's most celebrated writers), over time become largely disenchanted with both. Enough so that they left.

It's a common narrative arc, but nowhere is it related more evocatively than in Joan Didion's iconic essay "Goodbye to All That," included in her 1967 essay collection, *Slouching Towards Bethlehem*. In telling the story of her own eight years in New York City, from her starry-eyed arrival at twenty to her bleary-eyed departure at twenty-eight, Didion inimitably captures something universal and timeless about coming of age as a young person in New York, particularly if one had literary aspirations. It is considered by many to be the gold standard of personal essays, the one that so many writers count among their favorites and that many aspire to replicate. Didion somehow makes the specifics of her own experience recognizable to even those who lived in New York thirty or forty years after she had.

"Goodbye to All That" seems to remain relevant to one generation after another no matter how far in time we get from 1963, the year Didion left Manhattan for Los Angeles. It feels even more appropriate to revisit it now, given the effects of Covid-19 on the city and how the pandemic is forcing more and more New Yorkers to consider leaving.

Back in the days when my departure from the city was fresher, Didion's essay came up so many times in conversations with my upstate colleagues that it occurred to me it might be interesting to get a bunch of writers I admire to write their versions of "Goodbye to All That," their stories of loving and leaving New York City and how the time passed before them in between. At first, I was going to reach out only to writers who had left New York City permanently, as Didion had, and as I seem to have— "permanent" being a relative term. Didion lives there now, again, and if I win the lottery, you can bet the first thing I'll do is get an apartment there, as well. But as I shared my idea with city-based writer friends, many of them asked to be included, too. They wanted to write their versions of Didion's famous essay—about how they left New York for a time, thinking they were done with it, but then, like Didion, eventually returned. Or about their love-hate relationship with literary life in the city, and how the challenges make them frequently contemplate saying goodbye.

And so you have before you an updated version of the personal essay collection that initially emerged from those conversations. In addition to existing essays by writers like Cheryl Strayed, Roxane Gay, Dani Shapiro, Marie Myung-Ok Lee, and Melissa Febos, there are seven new pieces. In "The Assistant's Loft," Leslie Jamison writes about her time working as an assistant to a famous writer (with an amazing apartment) whom she admired and feared in equal measure. In "Eleven True Things," Ada Limón revisits her early days in Williamsburg as a broke graduate student, living among a "family" of friends, before her native California called her home. In "Shelter in Place," Emily Raboteau considers the effects of Covid-19 on life in New York. In "Homemaker," Rosie Schaap pays homage to a South Slope apartment she initially thought was just temporary but then settled into for twenty-three years. In "Fondly, Marie," Lisa Ko recalls first leaving New York for San Francisco and then later returning to Brooklyn. In "Goodbye, Hello, Goodbye," Carolita Johnson writes about getting tossed amid various waves of gentrification from Queens, to Paris, to Kingston, and back to Queens again. And in "Brooklyn Summer," Danielle A. Jackson looks back at her move from Memphis to New York and the events that eventually sent her back to the South.

With their very personal New York stories, these writers all join me in paying homage to one of the most resonant and memorable personal essays ever published. I count myself lucky to have wrangled them all into the reissue of this passion project and to join them here.

—Sari Botton

HOMEMAKER

Rosie Schaap

Brooklyn? I didn't want to live *there*. It was 1996. I was twenty-five. Brooklyn was where my parents came from, and for all their oozy nostalgia (*Ebbets Field! The Wonder Wheel! Ebinger's Bakery!*), it was the place from whence their own parents had fled with them as quickly as they could. Brooklyn was not for me.

But my favorite college professor lived there and liked it, and she knew I had to leave the apartment I shared in lower Manhattan. She also knew there was an apartment open in the building next door to hers, in an unfamiliar (to me) and unloved (so far as I knew) neighborhood that was maybe Park Slope South or South Slope or something. She urged me to come take a look. I could see no harm in that.

To get there, I walked one block uphill from the nearest subway station, past a row of handsome brick townhouses and dignified brownstones. And there she was, without contest the ugliest house on the south side of the street: a squat stunted stump of a building sheathed in bruised white aluminum siding. I considered turning back.

Behind that siding, however, it was a different story. The vacant second-floor apartment had high ceilings and six tall windows, three of which faced north onto 17th Street and the chimneys of the Polish delicatessen around the corner on Fifth Avenue, through which billowed the meaty incense of freshly smoked kielbasy. The other windows faced south onto the pocket gardens and workaday backyards of 18th Street, and sunlight soaked through them, light that stirred my vestigial Dutchness, light that felt like lowlands light, de Hooch light, Vermeer light, clean and generous. But then, this was a borough brimming with Dutchness, at least in its place names: Boerum, Bushwick, Flatbush, Utrecht, Brooklyn itself.

There was a bathroom with a window, a claw-footed, cast-iron tub, a black-and-white tile floor, and a linen closet. What twenty-five-year-old person had her own linen closet? In an alcove beside the kitchen, there was a deep pantry. And, next to the bedroom, a narrow chamber that could make a cozy office. If I moved in, I would need more linens. More dishes, more pots and pans. I'd need office things. Adult things.

The rent for the apartment was less than half of any I'd viewed in Manhattan, none of which I could afford, and the place was easily twice the size—even at no more than 450 square feet.

When Susan, the friendly, chatty landlady, whisked me into her apartment one flight below to talk money and review the lease, I saw a poster of the New York City Labor Chorus on one of her kitchen walls and on the opposite an even larger poster of Nelson Mandela and thought, maybe this place will be all right. I signed the lease and resolved to suck it up for a year, save some money, and then move back to Manhattan, where I was born and raised and rightly belonged.

Unsurprisingly, for all their schmaltzy sentiment about the borough, my parents saw my move to Brooklyn, even if it was temporary, as a sure sign of generational downward mobility. They were not wrong.

I hired an all-woman moving company to shift my small inventory of belongings across the East River: bed, desk, chair, books, rug, some pots and pans. The crew comprised a small, strong forewoman and two gangly, punk-rock Dutch girls on an extended holiday lark. "Never leave this place," one of them said as she deposited the last box of books on the bedroom floor with a soft thud. "It has a good feeling." Her colleagues agreed. I did, too. It did have a good feeling. It would be fine. For a year.

Twenty-three years later, I swept the kitchen floor for the last time. I zipped up three duffel bags and two suitcases, lugged them downstairs, handed Susan my keys, and hugged her. Then I stood on the stoop and waited for a taxi to take me away.

ACQUISITIVENESS IS A BIT OF AN EMBARRASSMENT TO A twenty-five-year-old Marxist, who is supposed to be a Materialist in a big M, dialectical way—not in the contemptible little m way—and not supposed to concern herself with the amassing, collecting, and displaying of stuff. And yet, I could not help myself. Give me a room, even one I might occupy only for a single, fleeting Vermont summer, and I will find things with which to fill it. There is a strain of self-psychologizing I could go into right now—my family moved around a lot! we never really had a home!—but I won't. I think it is more pertinent only to confess that I like things, and I have always liked things, even if this has sometimes created both philosophic and emotional discomfort, seeming as it does to be at odds with other, greater concerns, like social justice and the destruction of the natural world.

When I say I like things, I do not mean expensive, luxurious things, although of course there are some expensive, luxurious things I like very much, just as there are things I have found discarded on sidewalks and things I have rooted around for in curbside trash cans, chancing contact with dog shit and discarded needles, that I love as much if not more.

I'm talking about things that give me pleasure; things I like to look at and touch and think about; things that do not breathe, that are not living, but which nonetheless make life better and more interesting—which is the job of style, which is why style is a good in itself. Those who disagree, who underestimate style, who dismiss it as unimportant, do so, I assume, because they do not have it, and I am sorry for them.

I will take Bad Taste over No Style any day. Bad Taste bestows its own funny kind of joy. No Style is ungenerous: it gives nothing, does nothing, says nothing. Bad Taste tells a story, sometimes even a poignant one. No Style has only the kind of meaning that is against meaning: it borders on the nihilistic; it is sad.

In decorating my Brooklyn apartment, my role models were my aunt Ellen and uncle Bill, bohemian radicals of the old school, who lived for most of my lifetime in a sprawling warren of rooms right where they belonged, one block west of Washington

Square Park, in the heart of Greenwich Village. If they—who had aided the Black Panthers, who had exposed the activities of CIA operatives around the world, who had counseled war resisters at home and abroad—if *they* could love beautiful things and have beautiful things, surely it was okay for me to love and have them, too.

Antique Persian carpets covered most of their creaky wooden floorboards. In the narrow front hall, a gallery of framed portraits of their heroes lined the yolk-yellow walls. Sacco and Vanzetti. Emiliano Zapata. John Brown (about whom a friend has aptly said, "He was crazy. But he was not wrong"). I called their apartment the People's Palace.

Red silk that had aged and softened to persimmon was pinned to the walls of the living room—but to call it a living room is careless. It was a salon, where, save for just a few intrusions of modern life—a television and cable box, a few framed photographs that couldn't have been taken before the 1970s—I could easily imagine Emma Goldman and John Reed arguing the respective merits of anarchy versus Bolshevism, while draining a bottle of absinthe beside the fireplace to which my uncle had painstakingly applied a faux finish resembling malachite, under the Victorian tiger's-eye glass chandelier, the huge Cuban oil painting, the ceremonial masks from West Africa and Indonesia, and the massive, hand-painted old placard picked up in New Orleans that advertised Princess Zina—whose method of divination was "flowerscopes," who might have read your fortune in bougainvillea blossoms and birds-of-paradise from a stall in Jackson Square, for a fee.

In the study a few steps up from the salon, a récamier stretched out in the center of the room, dressed lavishly in cushions and coverlets, under a ceiling from whose center cascaded a tent-like canopy of silk panels. At the back of the room, a glass curio cabinet contained a collection of skulls—wooden, beaded, clay, ivory, metal. "I am fighting a war against minimalism," Bill liked to say, "and winning."

More marvels filled the small kitchen: the massive, brass-hinged, oak apothecary cabinets Ellen discovered on the side of a road in the Catskills, their shimmery, old glass fronts still intact and hardware still in place; the delicate porcelain oyster plates side by side with sturdy French copper pans on the walls; the vintage, industrial Wolf stove with six burners and a salamander at the top, which I long suspected was leaking gas and might possibly kill us all the next time someone lit a cigarette or joint but, fuck it, what a way to go.

I scavenged and bargained and bought and bartered and haunted the local thrift shops for things that would make my little apartment feel like a miniature version of the People's Palace but also entirely my own. I stripped linoleum off the floors and sanded and sealed the wide, softwood boards. I replaced ordinary doorknobs with antique ones, plastic light-switch plates with painted ceramic ones, lackluster lighting fixtures with a beaded Moroccan chandelier here and a Danish paper number there. I painted the bathroom walls delft blue and the ceiling the yellow of van Gogh's sunflowers—the Dutchness I detected before moving in always maintained. I embarked on collections: small floral still-lifes and souvenirs related to Tintern Abbey, a place invoked in the title of my favorite poem. And I came to believe that how one felt about my apartment was a reliable measure of how one felt about me. *Love me, love my home.* Sometimes I brought home the sort of person who resented its repleteness and mistook it for clutter, who disliked its colorfulness and confused it with chaos. That such people were judging me, in the form of my apartment, was self-satisfyingly obvious to them; that I was judging them back—as dull and unimaginative and fearful—well, I doubt they had any notion.

I started to love that apartment so much that it grew painful to think of leaving it so soon. I had no choice but to stay and hope that I would come to love the neighborhood, too. I did.

———

I MOVED IN AS A TWENTY-FIVE-YEAR-OLD SINGLE WOMAN WHO spent most of her time in bars. I lived there when I got to know a good and thoughtful man who loved cooking and loved Wordsworth, and not long after our first date, he moved in.

We lived there together when the planes hit the towers. And when, not long after, my father died. We got engaged there and married. There were dinner parties. Holiday parties. Cassoulets and rib roasts and shrimp boils. So much wine. Too many cigarettes.

Much laughter. Much love. And not the dissolution of love, but its shifts and tempers, its deviations, degrees, digressions.

Jobs in publishing, in social services, in academia, in bars and shops. No jobs at all. Years with plenty of money, years with next to none. At the kitchen table, I wrote a book. In my bed, I wrote another. We raised no children there but the greatest of all cats.

I lived there when we separated, and when he got sick and we unseparated. In February 2010, at thirty-nine, I became a widow there. And that's when it was time to move out, but I couldn't afford it. One year later, still there, I became motherless, too.

My husband and my mother are both buried close by, in Green-Wood Cemetery, where I could visit them, easily and often.

A few years later Bill and Ellen died, too, and I helped to clean and empty and shut down the People's Palace—a dusty, dirty task that took many hands and many weeks. When I was sure I'd cleaned and priced what had to be the last tchotchke, the last pearl-handled demitasse spoon, the last Bakelite brooch, something else materialized from some closet, some drawer, some long-forgotten public-radio tote bag.

So much stuff. There was no end of stuff. And from this stock I inherited my favorite furniture and objects: Bill's scuffed and scarred glass-fronted barrister bookcases, some Persian rugs, the oyster plates, Princess Zina. My apartment became as much like theirs, and as beautiful, as it ever would—but also less my own. It looked exactly as I'd always wanted, but its energies and frequencies had altered. Every corner, every surface, exposed reminders of who was gone, where I'd never noticed anything before. The greatest of all cats—she, too, was gone by then, but the phantom of her jumped on the bed many mornings, as if to wake me for her phantom breakfast.

———

When I was twenty, I spent a summer in Ireland and had, since then, always wanted to live there longer. Almost thirty years later, and after many more visits, a way in which that might happen presented itself. I had by then come to believe that to contend with loss, to grieve properly in a way I had not been able to manage at home in New York, I would have to be in Northern Ireland, and I would have to write about it. It took a few years, with false starts and false endings and other setbacks, to figure out how to make good on this plan. And then, in late August of 2019, I was issued a visa. I would have to arrive in Belfast three weeks later and then proceed to Glenarm, the small coastal village where I would live for the coming year.

That gave me less than a month to clear out my home of twenty-three years. And when I told people—friends, acquaintances, co-workers, family—that, yes, I was finally leaving, the first thing most asked was: *What are you doing with your apartment?* Which is the New Yorkiest possible reaction. Any other details, or questions, or well wishes could come later.

I considered subletting. I considered letting a friend move in. But I knew that, really, I was ready to let it go. And when I told my friends, acquaintances, coworkers, family that that's what I was going to do, most said, in one way or another, *you're crazy.* When and if I returned from Ireland, I was warned, I'd never find such a good deal again. Maybe that's true—but I knew that if I ever wanted to move back to New York, I would find a way.

At the same time, I was surprised, and moved, by how much more sentimental about my apartment, and my stuff, my friends were than I was. In the weeks before I left, many came over to help me pack the small portion of things (I'd crammed a lot of things into those 450 square feet) I had decided to keep: some kitchen gear, a couple hundred books (after I'd donated, sold, and given away on my stoop about a thousand), a few paintings, and small pieces of furniture. They helped me clean. They helped me run moving-out sales. They helped me lug junk to the curb. And although it was strange and stunning to see how quickly what had taken me two decades to fill with things that gave me pleasure, to make a home, could be emptied, it didn't make me sad. I was happy to be leaving, and I was ready. I was more than ready—I was late. It should have happened sooner.

But even though it didn't make me sad, it did make me remember something that had stung me, once, long ago, maybe two years after I'd moved in.

An adventurous friend had come to visit. He had lived in the Amazon rain forest in his youth. He had lived in a village on the Nile as an adult. He had wandered. He had never settled. For someone who was great fun, he had an ascetic streak. Material possessions meant nothing to him. Faith mattered to him and friendship. Not stuff.

He came over for coffee one afternoon. He hadn't seen the apartment since right after I'd moved in—when he had turned up to install a mezuzah on my doorpost, which I had not asked him to do, but I did not stop him—and by now I was proud of the place. I showed him around.

"It's *so nice*," he said, and I was overjoyed. But his expression quickly hardened, and he added: "I find it depressing."

Shame filled me like a cold, heavy liquid, and I was too ashamed to ask him what he meant. But I believed it had something to do with my love for my things—that this was a shallow love and that my attachment to them was wrong. I said nothing but searched in my thoughts for supports and consolations. There were memories of Bill and Ellen, who loved things but who had done so much for others. There was William Morris, whose ideas and productions I relied on to confirm my hope that style *was* substance, not in conflict with it. I had filled my home with things that I knew to be beautiful and believed to be useful. And if perhaps I had persuaded myself that some of those things were useful only because they were beautiful, that was fine.

They are only things, I remember telling myself, after my friend had issued his judgment. *And although I love them, I could live without them.* Afterward, I often wondered if I'd told myself the truth. Two decades later, I discovered that I had.

STRANGE LANDS

Roxane Gay

Recently, after years of avoiding New York City—or, more accurately, not being able to afford it—I traveled there from the small middle-of-nowhere midwestern town where I teach writing. I was going to give a few readings, meet my new agent, and hang out with friends. I was terrified. I knew I wouldn't be chic enough or thin enough. In the car on the way to the hotel, we were stuck in traffic. Radios blared and exhaust filled the air. Certain things about the city never change. My driver was on the phone having a heated conversation in a language I couldn't recognize. He was clearly on the losing end of the argument. I called my mother to tell her I had arrived safely.

In the 1970s, she and my father came from Haiti to New York separately, my father by way of Montreal. They met at a wedding in New York. They fell in love in New York. They married in

New York. I was even baptized in New York, though I've never lived in the city. Back in the day, my parents lived in the Bronx, when the borough still bore the evidence of how it had been ravaged by fire. I remember this detail because they remember this detail, quite vividly. They had little nice to say about the borough, but when they first came here, they were overwhelmed—new place, new language, so much cold and concrete.

My mom asked me how things were going, and I said, "Well, the traffic is interesting." She laughed. She said, "Your father can no longer tolerate that city for long periods of time. He doesn't understand why people would live on top of each other like that."

For a moment, I felt this pang of . . . envy, or maybe wistfulness, because so many of the important moments in their lives happened in New York, because some part of me very much understood why people would live like that.

Throughout my childhood, even though we sometimes visited family in New York, the city seemed more like an idea than a real place—an idea I very much wanted to be a part of—bright lights, big city.

Because of my father's job, we moved often and always lived in suburbs or rural places that bore little resemblance to the sights and sounds of the city. We were in Nebraska or in the suburbs of Chicago or on the outskirts of Denver. We were in the land of sprawling malls and new construction and chain restaurants that advertised with catchy slogans. There was more: we were always the only people who looked like us in our neighborhoods, at school. Not only were we of a different race, but we were of an entirely different culture—Haitians in the middle of America, strangers in a strange world.

My mother has a sprawling family, nine brothers and sisters. My father has four brothers and sisters. When their families immigrated to the United States, most of them settled in New York City, in close proximity to one another. They were determined not to be strangers in a strange land, alone. We'd fly to the city on holidays and cram into my maternal grandmother's apartment, so many of us, my grandmother at the stove cooking Haitian food, making fried plantains in a manner no one else can replicate (the secret is to soak them in salt water before frying), and clucking over her children and grandchildren with great fondness.

Her couches, covered in plastic, the air in her apartment thick with life, us kids always being shushed so we wouldn't disturb the neighbors, as if it were possible not to disturb the neighbors when there were twenty or thirty people in a small apartment. New York was my cousins, who all seemed so sophisticated, who knew the latest slang and wore the latest fashions—Girbaud jeans and leather high-tops and baseball caps. They had sharp haircuts and talked fast, so fast, my brothers and I could barely hold on to anything they said.

New York, then, was Flushing, Queens. It was the 7 train when graffiti flourished—spray-painted bubble words and images stretching from one end of a subway car to another. New York was the Busy Bee market, which was little more than a chaotic swap meet—bright, loud people with thick New York accents selling knockoff bags and shoes, hideous costume jewelry, off-brand toys, cheap electronics—things I had absolutely no use for but considered treasures and embraced, arms wide open. New York was eating real Szechuan food for the first time and understanding that Chinese food prepared anywhere but in New

York was not really Chinese food. New York was Times Square, on the cusp of being cleaned up by an ambitious mayor, still dirty enough to be terribly interesting to a young girl.

Men on corners thrusting squares of glossy paper into my hands, bright shining lights, throngs of people as far as the eye could see. Filthy sidewalks and overflowing trash cans, homeless people asking for money and breaking my tender heart. Broadway, the marquees, the names of amazing performers in shining lights, *The Phantom of the Opera*, a boat floating across a stage filled with illuminated candles, voices soaring through the theater and right into me because tragic, somewhat unrequited love is the best kind of love. There was *Starlight Express* and actors roller-skating onstage.

More than anything, New York was seeing people, so many different people, so many beautiful shades of brown, so many different voices, a place where my brothers and I could actually see reflections of ourselves in others, where we didn't feel so strange in a strange land. New York was everything, and the time we spent in the city was never enough.

In high school, I became determined to attend college there. It was something of an obsession. If I went to school in New York, surely all my problems would be solved. I would learn how to be chic and glamorous. I would learn how to walk fast and wear all black without looking like I was attending a funeral. In adolescence, I was becoming a different kind of stranger in a strange land. I was a theater geek and troubled and angry and hell-bent on forgetting the worst parts of myself. In New York, I told myself, I would no longer be the only freak in the room because the city was full of freaks.

I applied to six or so universities, and one of them was New York University—NYU, the only three letters that existed for me for a time. I was going to go to NYU and major in technical theater and premed. It made no sense, but that was the plan. When I was accepted to NYU, with a merit scholarship no less, I was thrilled. My perfect future was within my grasp. Soon I was going to be in the city. I was going to be part of it all. I was going to find my people.

Alas. My parents had other plans for me. They worried that in the city, I would be distracted from my studies, and the point of college, in their minds, was to study. They were worried about safety. They were just plain worried. I remained in a very deep state of denial even after they made me agree to attend a different university, a fancy one even, that I was damn lucky to attend—a state of denial so deep I still haven't recovered from their denying me the choice to attend college in the city. I feel a pang of . . . something whenever I see an NYU T-shirt or read about the school. I wonder what would have been, though I am fully aware that nothing in my life would be measurably better. The school is my mythical beast, my unicorn. The city is the *one that got away.*

In college, New York was just a couple of hours away by train, Metro North, New Haven to Penn Station. New York was spending the weekend at my roommate's family's apartment and eating bagels from H&H and gourmet delights from Zabar's and reading the *New York Times* (in New York!) and men shouting "Dianetics" and thrusting the books of L. Ron Hubbard into my hands and a Haitian woman mistaking me for a well-known voodoo priestess on a sidewalk while my American friend looked on, bewildered, and Limelight and dancing all night and having hungover breakfast at Time Café and walking through Greenwich Village wide-eyed and Broadway, the performers so glamorous, glittering from the stage, their voices clear and bold, and me, always watching, always wanting desperately to be part of it all, always feeling like "it all" was still just beyond my grasp, wanting so desperately to feel a little less strange.

I wrote my first story when I was four, on a napkin, and eventually advanced to using paper like a normal person, and as my writing ambitions grew so did my fantasies of living in the city, in a lovely apartment with brick walls, lined with books. I'd spend my days in cafés and coffee shops, with a well-worn notebook and my laptop and the latest important book. I would attend readings and rub elbows with the writers I admired most. I'd have cocktails with the editor of the *New Yorker*, and he would be so besotted, he'd ask to see some of my work and I would finally catch my big break. Then I was an adult, or so I was told. I was a writer and finally reached the point where other people knew I was a writer. I was finally more comfortable in my own skin, had finally learned how to feel less strange in a strange land. I had learned the difference between being a writer, which can happen anywhere, and performing the role of Writer, which in my very specific and detailed fantasies could only happen in New York.

New York City is the center of the writing world, or so we're told. New York is where all the action happens because the city is where the most important publishers and agents and writers are. New York is where the fancy book parties happen and where the literati rub elbows and everyone knows (or pretends to know) everything about everyone else's writing career. At some point, New York stopped being the city of my dreams because it stopped being merely an idea I longed to be a part of. New York was very real and very complicated. New York had become an intimidating giant of a place, but still I worried. If I wasn't there as a writer, was I a writer anywhere?

During my most recent visit, I stayed at a hipster hotel, the Ace, because it was the most affordable, which is to say it was not very affordable at all. There appeared to be an unspoken require-ment for all staff to look impeccable in expensive jeans and adorn their bodies in tattoos. The lobby was like a nightclub at all hours of the day, loud music, expensive but delicious drinks, a place to see and be seen, whether you wanted to or not.

Somewhere in New York was my agent's very chic office. It looked like a set for an agent's office on a television show or in a movie. The chairs were modern and fancy, and it seemed compli-cated to even sit. I felt very out of place, though I had a good rea-son to be there. My agent was as chic as her office. I couldn't stop staring because she is very pretty, magazine pretty, and I hadn't realized. I felt that way almost every moment of every day in New York, the writer from the middle of nowhere, surrounded by glamorous and well-dressed people with interesting eyewear.

My agent and I talked for more than an hour as if we were old friends. I left feeling I was a Writer For Real. I felt fancy. And then, I was walking around trying to find a certain street and it started raining, and I was lost and miserable and confused and no cabs would stop for me. The fancy feeling quickly wore off.

That's what New York was becoming now that I could choose to be in the city or not. There were teaching jobs and other op-portunities in New York. I had, just before the visit, turned down an editorial position at a magazine because I couldn't fathom liv-ing in the city on the offered salary. In my thirties, I've found that

I am not as interested in struggling or suffering as I once was, at least not from one day to the next. During that recent trip, I realized I need at least one part of my life to be easy. I may hate living in the middle of nowhere, but there's a lot of wide open space for that hate to thrive in. For every lovely moment with lovely people in New York, there was a deeply humbling moment—getting lost, trying to hail a cab in the rain, dealing with the constant crush of people, feeling desperately out of place among so many sophisticated, beautiful people. These moments revealed just how big and overwhelming the city was. They showed me how New York was always more than an idea, even if I wasn't able to see that. New York was a strange land, and I was still a stranger and would always be one. Overall, that visit was fun. The city was good to me, and I looked forward to returning and soon. But. There was nothing for me to say goodbye to in New York because I never truly said hello. I became a writer without all the glamorous or antiglamorous trappings of New York life I thought I needed.

When my plane took off and I knew I was returning to the middle of nowhere, a different kind of strange land, I realized with startling clarity that my small town in Illinois felt less strange than the city. I was relieved. I was going home.

THE ASSISTANT'S LOFT

Leslie Jamison

She had a name, but in this essay, she will just be *she*. When I started working for her, she gave me a nondisclosure agreement to sign, but she didn't handle any of her own paperwork, so she never knew I'd never signed it. She had a beautiful brownstone and a once-beautiful geriatric dog who peed frequently on the beautiful parquet floor, which was better than when he peed on the expensive Oriental rugs. She was a writer who'd built her empire on self-help books for women, and she'd made a lot of money doing it. Not enough. Shortly after I began working for her, I realized that part of the reason she kept six different phone lines was to keep throwing creditors off her scent. I hadn't known that someone so wealthy could owe so much money. I hadn't known that anyone could earn $75,000 for writing a single magazine article, or that this same person could also care so much about getting refunded for an unused Jitney ticket to the Hamptons that she would pay someone $25 an hour to keep calling the bus company until she got it. That someone was me. I'd been told the job would involve "substantial archival research at the New York Public Library." That happened, twice.

But it seemed impossibly exciting to work for an Actual Writer. Most days I worked as her personal assistant in a loft above her palatial living room, which was full of upholstered couches and heavy brocade curtains. The room seemed to be asking you to call it a parlor. The assistant's loft hadn't been purpose-built. But it had been occupied by an assistant for so long—decades—that she had begun to think of the Assistant, whatever her name was, as yet another piece of parlor furniture. Later, I would learn there was a small group of former personal assistants who still met sometimes for cocktails—like an informal support group—to discuss the harrowing emotional experience of working for this woman. She was powerful but felt powerless. She cared quite a bit about her floral arrangements. She did not like her coffee any way but Very, Very Hot. She yelled frequently at the people she employed. Sometimes it seemed like she employed people so she could yell at them. She had an ill husband who was in a nursing home uptown. In my mind, they were so powerful—by virtue of their careers and their money—that it was hard to imagine the ways they might be suffering. I was twenty-three years old, and it was hard to understand that the people who had the things I wanted most—bylines, long marriages, stature in the literary world—might be lacking other things I took for granted.

When I started working for this woman—for *her*—I'd just moved to New York from Iowa City, where I'd been a student at the Iowa Writers' Workshop, an ostensibly academic experience that involved a decent amount of writing and a *lot* of late-night talking about writing and also a lot of late-night drinking (and early-evening drinking and late-afternoon drinking) and a lot of daydreaming about what the Life of a Writer might look like. Many of these daydreams had involved New York, where most of my friends from college lived. When they spoke about their subway commutes and their local bodegas and even their terrible bosses, it all sounded simultaneously glamorous and *actual*; this was the grit and grain of living. Now I was living it. As a kind of homework assignment, I'd read *The Devil Wears Prada*, a best-selling novel written by the woman who'd been Anna Wintour's personal assistant. My job wasn't at *Vogue*, but it felt *Vogue*-adjacent by virtue of coming attached to a similarly difficult personality.

On a daily basis, my job involved picking up Very, Very Hot Coffee, and also dry cleaning and also gifts for loved ones and also theater tickets for exactly the right seats at Lincoln Center. Occasionally, it involved long lunches that included several bottles of wine. It involved booking car services and Jitney buses and answering the phone and lying about whether my boss was home or even lived there anymore. It involved listening to her rant about documentary filmmakers who had stolen her ideas. It also involved crying. Honestly, it involved a tremendous amount of crying. At the time, I believed this said a lot about my boss— and it did—but looking back, I can see it also said a lot about me.

My boss yelled at me about every mistake I made or anyone else did. When other people came to the house, she spoke about me in the third person as if I weren't there: "I don't understand why Leslie can't seem to get this straight." I was intrigued by the fact that I didn't seem to be developing "a thicker skin." I just crumpled each time, usually escaping to the large bathroom, which always stank faintly of dog urine on marble, so that the flushing toilet could mask the sound of my crying. I flushed it over and over again.

I told myself I liked working for a writer, but eventually I had to admit that the appeal was just as much about the job's proximity to money. Wealth cast a velvety, vaguely soporific spell over my days in the loft, like the lotus flower in the *Odyssey*, seducing its isle of indolent men. There was a tin lunch box in my desk drawer full of "petty cash"—hundreds of dollars that I was allowed to spend each week, was even *supposed* to spend each week, on lunch, wine, and "supplies," defined with a delicious, capacious vagueness. (Could it also include the beautiful camel-colored fur-lined coat hanging in the window of a nearby boutique that probably cost more than the rest of my wardrobe put together?) The petty cash amounted to far more than I would ever reasonably need and seemed like a gratuitous display of excess when it wasn't even clear there *was* excess: all those creditors kept calling on the extra phone lines.

Before I started working for her, I honestly hadn't understood that someone could be incredibly wealthy and carry tremendous amounts of debt. Mainly I just saw the size of her brownstone, the decadent upholstery of her living room furniture, the robust stable of employees that supported her life and felt the second-hand high of getting close to her money, to that expansive sense of ease and possibility that New York can hold, always underwritten by wealth, if not explicitly then implicitly—a wealth that has disappeared its own seams. There can be a sudden, clarifying vertigo to realizing that the seduction that didn't seem to be about money is actually *all* about money, like when Jay Gatsby and Nick Carraway are talking about Daisy's endlessly appealing voice: "'Her voice is full of money,' he said suddenly. That was it. I'd never understood before. It was full of money—that was the inexhaustible charm that rose and fell in it, the jingle of it, the cymbals' song of it."

Which is all to say, showing up at my boss's brownstone each day made me hear the charm and jingle of Manhattan money, its supple siren call. I had grown up middle-class; I went without want. But this money was different. It wasn't that I admired it, exactly. It was more like I wanted to have sex with it, as a friend of mine once said. Even being close to it was thrilling, like inhaling pheromones, that sense of being close to power, being at the epicenter of Where Things Happen. This was even better than being a writer, perhaps. Perhaps. I told myself I'd moved from the place where the stories got written to the place where they were actually lived.

EVERYONE IN NEW YORK WHO WASN'T BORN IN NEW YORK has a story about moving to New York. My story involved a fifth-floor walk-up with an entryway that always smelled like noodles left out overnight. Our kitchen had a skylight that always made out-of-towners say, "Must be wonderful to get this *light*," and city dwellers ask, "Have you ever tried to store your suitcases up there?" If you lived in New York long enough, you got obsessed with space: how to find more of it magically hidden within the limited space you had. I lived with one of my best friends, and our favorite bodega was even called Space Market, as if you could buy more space there. It was right across the street from Washington Square Park, and we got salads there almost every night.

In time this started to feel like the whole of Manhattan held in a single awning: *Space Market.* We were all just looking for footing in the city, trying to find some square of land—some sense of purpose, vocation, belonging—to call our own. It was part of why people were so obsessed with real estate: *Where is your apartment? How did you find your apartment? How much does your apartment cost?* And always, but usually unspoken: *How do you pay for it?* All of these were ways of asking: *What feels like home to you in this infinite city?*

Life in Iowa had been full of parties that lasted until dawn—at an old farmhouse out in the cornfields or else someone's basement studio with shag carpets and a bathtub full of PBRs on ice. New York was probably *also* full of parties that lasted until dawn; I just wasn't getting invited to them. I found myself going through the motions of a tidy parade of time-boxed dinner dates at restaurants where we mainly talked about other restaurants we might go to. Drinks lasted from six o'clock to eight o'clock instead of six o'clock to whenever the cocaine ran out.

If New York was supposed to make me feel like I was living at the center—*supposed to,* as if it had made me some kind of promise—then in actuality it made me feel more peripheral than anywhere I'd ever lived. It made me feel as if there *were* a center—close enough to sense but always out of reach, like the salt smell of an unseen ocean. Everyone else had always just taken the subway to the beach. It all felt like an extended version of the more acute disappointment I'd felt as a little girl visiting my older brother after he'd moved to New York for college, when the hole-in-the-wall vintage stores I'd imagined were nowhere to be found. The outside of the *Seinfeld* diner did not lead to the inside of the *Seinfeld* diner!

It wasn't that I thought the city had failed me but something like the opposite: it felt like I'd failed the city, by failing to have the experience I'd imagined. It felt like trying to locate the secret doorway of a bookcase that might swing open if you knocked on its hollow books three times, revealing the sparkling inner grotto of the city I'd imagined: dim, cavernous shops stocked with paisley jumpsuits from the late 1970s and subterranean speakeasies where people read poetry that wasn't afraid to reach for a shimmery sincerity on the far side of rigor. And also maybe pastry shops full of exotic macaron flavors? So far, I'd only managed to find the exotic macarons. Eating expensive or unusual foods seemed to be the main way aspirational people in New York convinced themselves they were alive—or rather, that they were Living. It wasn't that I judged this—I wanted to Live, too, with capital-letter emphasis—I just couldn't get to that sensation through high-end restaurant culture. I needed to get there by talking about provisional epiphanies in midwestern dive bars through thick clouds of cigarette smoke.

Here in New York, my life was supposed to be iconic and transformative enough to justify the job that made me cry almost daily in the palatial bathroom. But instead, life mainly felt vapid and saturated by money—by both its presence and its absence—a daily grind of morning commutes on subway cars crowded with other people who didn't want to be going wherever they were going and my own futile attempts to wake up at dawn and deepen the inner lives of the characters who populated my novella, or else arriving home from work at 7 PM and trying to rejigger their narrative arcs so that they actually had narrative arcs, except I was too weary and blank-headed to do anything besides binge-watch *Gilmore Girls* on DVD, my brain bleached by the intricate logistical hydraulics of a wealthy woman's life.

The best part of my New York existence was my home: that fifth-floor walk-up on Thompson Street that I shared with my dear friend Charlotte. We had a two-person book club. We had an antique pie chest full of every episode of *Sex and the City*. We had rice crackers and soft Australian licorice in our pantry. We made lemonade pie on a sweltering August night. We threw a South Pole party where everyone decorated pup tents made of gingerbread. We had all these luminous details to share about our lives, but in truth I was lonely. It wasn't really the loneliness of being single, though I was single, or the loneliness of wanting to get drunk every night, though I did want to get drunk every night, I just couldn't really afford to, or even the loneliness of having too many acquaintances and not enough friends. It was the loneliness of wanting to write and not writing. I tried. I tried to wake up early or stay up late. But it all felt perfunctory and dead on the page. It mainly just made me tired. That's part of why I wanted to throw a South Pole party; I wanted to make something. I was trying to make my life into a string of anecdotes, a charm bracelet, because I wasn't making art—the only thing that really felt worth making.

In New York, most of the people I knew seemed to define themselves not by what they made but by what they consumed: the food they ate, the museums they frequented, the movies they saw at Film Forum, the bars they liked, the neighborhoods they preferred. One night I got drunk with an old friend and threw up my hands, exasperated, disgusted by my entire generation. "I see everything they buy!" I said, gesturing at the lit-up city all around us. "But what do they *create*?" As if I were creating anything. And what could I do about it anyway, besides buy another drink?

———

At the end of each workday, I was responsible for submitting something called an EOD, an end of day report. It was basically just a typed list of all the things I'd done. After a few weeks I realized that the primary objective of the EOD was to make it as long as possible. More than my boss actually wanted things to get done, she wanted to *feel* like things were getting done. She wanted to look at a set of stapled pages listing my completed tasks, or even my in-progress tasks, which I included for thickness, and know that things were happening in the Assistant's Loft. These daily ledgers helped her understand herself as the leader of a tiny but prosperous empire.

Part of me wanted to dismiss the entire job as an absurd farce, but it wasn't. In two weeks, I learned more about the world of magazines than I had learned in two years of graduate school. My boss could turn a pitch into an assignment in a matter of hours. We'd cycle through the whole submission process by late morning: researching the pitch (me), drafting it (me), critiquing it (her), revising it (me), and emailing it (her). She had worked with editors for long enough to know things like what time of day was best for sending it to each one. We'd usually have a response by early afternoon. The turnaround astounded me. In my midwestern MFA program, we still tucked our stories into manila envelopes and took them to the post office to mail to literary magazines. We worshipped the people who'd spent ten years on their novels, even if we didn't exactly want to become them. Duration was feared and fetishized. Here was a world where writing happened on another time line entirely. What did they say about a New York minute? Everything could change. Here, the creative process wasn't insular and rarefied. It was expedient and pragmatic, directed toward an immediate concrete end. Writing got *made*. Like a widget. It wasn't conjured, and it certainly wasn't perfected.

I didn't particularly admire my employer's work, but there was something I admired about the way she refused—or leaped across—the very same gap between vision and execution that often got invoked as a kind of holy, impossible threshold in the midwestern bars where I'd been drinking. Of course, leaping across the gap between vision and execution was easier when you had a brownstone, a lot of disposable income, and an entire stable of paid employees to whom you could outsource the elements of your existence that most vexed you. But you *couldn't*, not really. I was starting to suspect that was what so much of my crying was about, on some primal level: she was offloading her pain onto me. It was part of my job to absorb her frustration and her anger, the same way it was my job to chase down her opera ticket refunds.

My boss, like so many employers of Ivy-League-credentialed entry-level workers in the city, simultaneously treated me as someone with intellectual capital (it felt good to say her assistant had gone to Harvard) and someone who deserved to be doing menial labor (it felt even *better* to know her Harvard-educated assistant was picking up her dry cleaning). In the afternoons, I traded emails with two friends who were also personal assistants. One worked for one of the most famous chefs in the city; the other worked for the editor in chief of the *New Yorker*. My boss was tilling the fertile soil of women's conflicted feelings about aging. At least my friends' workplace degradations were in service of acquiring genuine cultural capital. Mine seemed to be in service of getting a few laughs or sympathetic smiles at a bar lit by flickering votive candles. It often felt like I hoarded up horrible moments from my day, ready to share them with whomever I was meeting that night, and then I felt the same hollow comedown after I'd delivered my short parade of anecdotes— what had they been good for? They hadn't changed my life, or excavated any meaning from it, or even brought me closer to the person I was talking to. They felt rehearsed and perfunctory, but underneath them was a desperate yearning—more like a scream and far less possible to express—for another life entirely.

***

ONE FRIDAY MORNING IN NOVEMBER, MY BOSS WAS SCHEDuled to give a talk at a conference that was an easy walk from her house. Still, she wanted me to book her a town car for a half hour before the talk.

Gently, I suggested that if we were going to book a car, we should probably book it for a bit earlier. "There might be traffic," I said quietly. What was my "might" about? There would *definitely* be traffic, *obscene* traffic, in Midtown Manhattan at rush hour on a Friday morning. Maybe it was a strangled, deceptive attempt at generosity—as if to suggest that it wasn't completely misguided to book a town car, simultaneously indulgent and inefficient, because who could truly foresee the whims of the NYC traffic gods?

In any case, my boss didn't want the car booked for earlier. She didn't even want to go downstairs once the car arrived! Or rather, she wasn't ready. She was indignant, even, at the number

of things she had left to do before she could leave—at the audac-
ity of the driver for arriving before she had time to do them.

Sometimes you can foresee every whim of the gods, and the
seemingly endless car ride to the conference played out as I might
have expected: my boss was *livid* we were running late. Why were
we stuck in such traffic? She was yelling at the driver from the
back seat, literally leaning forward and *yelling*, while I tried to
catch his eye in the rearview mirror to tell him with my gaze:
I know this isn't your fault. I know this woman is insane. It was
almost a relief when she started yelling at both of us: This was
an important speech and how had we failed to fully grasp that?
It was clearly my fault because I'd booked the car, but it was *also*
clearly his fault because he was driving. We were running more
and more late by the minute.

Every time I caught the driver's eye in the rearview, he looked
away, and I realized that to him I wasn't an ally at all. How could
I be? I was simply part of the machinery of this woman and her
various shades of monstrosity—another well-paid mercenary
serving the cottage industry of her hybrid journalistic self-help
empire. Something shifted in my molecules that day as new
knowledge took root: whatever you are paid by, you can't get it
out of you. You have to own that it sustains you.

Before my boss went onstage to give her lecture, she screamed
at me in the lobby outside the auditorium about how much I'd
gotten wrong that morning, how I'd almost ruined everything.
Getting yelled at wasn't terrible because it felt personal but precisely because it didn't—it felt utterly *im*personal. It was like I
wasn't even human; I was just a hologram upon which her frustrations could be unleashed—a projection of everything in the
world that had ever failed to understand her needs or honor

them. What happened between us in that lobby felt less like an interaction between two sentient beings and more like the ritual flogging of a corpse. There was frustration, and it needed to hurl itself at something, like water finding its level. I was also funda-mentally unnerved by people who weren't ashamed to get angry at other people in public; and it felt deeply embarrassing to be yelled at in front of strangers—as if some primal vulnerability had been exposed, like I'd peed in my pants and then walked around with the dark stain showing.

While my boss gave her lecture, I called my mom and said, "I don't think I can do this." She said, "You don't have to."

Looking back, I don't think she literally meant, *You don't have to do this for another minute*, but that's how I took it. My boss flew to a speaking gig across the country that afternoon, while I went back to her brownstone and posted an ad for my own job.

Because the job *sounded* great and the pay was decent and there were countless people in the city who were just like me—*young and hungry*, as they say, eager to get close to power and prestige in any form, no matter how compromised—I had about two hun-dred résumés within an hour, including one from the personal assistant of the woman who'd written the best-selling book about being a personal assistant.

After printing ten of the strongest résumés and leaving them on my boss's desk, along with my keys and a note telling her that I was done, I took the rest of the petty cash (severance pay) and walked out the door. On my way to the subway, I used the petty cash to buy the beautiful fur-lined coat.

Nearly fifteen years—and several not-inexpensive tailoring repairs—later, I still have it. I still love it. But whenever I wear it, I feel the smallest twinge of shame. The fact that I just walked out, so impulsively and suddenly, seems to point to some internal deficit: Was I not stoic enough to get yelled at a couple times by my boss? Was I *such* a fragile flower? So convinced I deserved something better? Why couldn't I just suffer through, as her other personal assistants had done, for decades?

But I also feel a deep tenderness for that younger self, who quit so impulsively and irresponsibly. She sensed a great darkness, and she wanted to remove herself from its grip—from its payroll. She was a quitter, and a survivor. She had a coat that all her friends admired.

———

That day at Columbus Circle wasn't the end of New York, but it was the beginning of the end of New York. It was the moment it became undeniable that this was not the city for me. After quitting the loft, and then fielding a series of phone messages from my boss that shifted from apologizing to pleading to berating, I spent a few weeks gloriously unemployed, setting up my laptop at a coffee shop on Mercer Street to work on my novella.

But, rent. Our rice crackers and soft Australian licorice weren't going to buy themselves. So I got a temp job that staffed me at a Citibank office located—literally, honestly—at 666 Fifth Avenue. In my heart, though, I knew that the entrance to the underworld was actually located at the immaculate brownstone I'd left behind.

At 666 Fifth Avenue, I ran the names of high-asset clients through a series of databases meant to determine if they were white-collar criminals, and I also read various Victorian novels that were emailed in discrete chunks to my Citibank inbox. Who knew services like this existed? Clandestine novel-emailing services? You had to spend many hours bored at a cubicle to care enough to discover them. I started fantasizing about moving back to Los Angeles, and on my way home from the office, I'd stop at the internet café near my apartment to exchange flirtatious emails with a journalist out West. He started to show up in my daydreams, cast as My Boyfriend, along with smog-vivid sunsets and strip-mall cigarettes.

Back in Midtown, I ran names through databases and read bite-sized chunks of *Twenty Thousand Leagues Under the Sea* and heard through the grapevine that our office didn't have windows because a temp down in Miami had jumped out of a window and died. The truth at the core of that rumor wasn't its content, which was likely false, but the fact that it gained such traction in the office. We were saying something important about our lives—or at least our jobs—by repeating it over and over again.

In the middle of a bleak January, I left New York to move back home to Los Angeles. The move felt like freedom and failure at once. I'd barely lasted six months.

———

BACK IN LOS ANGELES, I SPENT MY MORNINGS WRITING AND smoking cigarettes instead of pressed up against the bodies of unhappy strangers on the A train. I spent my afternoons tutoring and my evenings working shifts at a bed-and-breakfast near the ocean, stealing bottles of wine that I drank alone on my futon before waking up the next morning to write and smoke and do it all over again. I got tapas with the journalist and then I got naked with the journalist and he never ended up becoming my boyfriend. This life in LA wasn't necessarily a better life than my life in New York had been—and from the outside, I knew it looked a little less mature—but it felt more like it belonged to me. I'd moved to New York because it was A Thing People Did; I left New York because it was something I wanted to do. My LA days were organized more fully around the thing I wanted to be doing—writing—even when I wasn't sure I was writing anything worthwhile. And though I still worked eight-hour days—often, actually, ten- or eleven- or even twelve-hour days, because my shift at the inn didn't end until 11 PM—I had those *mornings*, which felt sacred, each one an offering at the shrine of the novel I was trying to write. No more novellas for me.

Back in LA, there was something grimy and displaced about my life that felt simultaneously isolated and generative. The pure, bracing sensation of loneliness had replaced my frantic efforts to pretend I wasn't lonely. There was relief in that. It felt more solid. More honest. It felt like those ash-speckled mornings could yield some kind of truth. Or at least, they were more likely to yield truth than a windowless hive of cubicles at the devil's address in Midtown. That's what I thought at the time. Now I think truth comes from all kinds of places: the strip mall and the cubicle, the urine stench off the marble. The loneliness that rises up from the smoke of an early-morning cigarette, and the different kind of loneliness that clicks away at Midtown keyboards, typing the names of high-asset clients; the loneliness of all those crowds on the A train, the hidden struggles in everyone. Now I look back and recognize the truths that weren't about loneliness at all but rose from the sudden joy of getting a sentence right or nailing a moment of dialogue before getting in my little red Dodge Neon and driving to another tutoring client, revving the clutch up the big hill, feeling that grind, tasting SAT words under my tongue and hating that work but thinking, *yes*, I got that one sentence right. I left that other city and came to this one and bought this shitty little car to drive to all these mansions so I could raise the verbal scores of all these teenagers. I made all these choices just so I could get that one sentence right.

A FEW MONTHS AGO, I WENT TO A MUSEUM EXHIBITION JUST A few blocks from my boss's brownstone. It was a Wednesday evening, one of my daughter's nights with her father, so I'd brought myself uptown to see the eerie, wondrous, startling creations of people who'd made beauty for decades, often invisibly: the aching, enchanting, often ecstatic drawings produced by a group of psychiatric patients at an Austrian asylum; the dream pictures of a Toronto junk dealer who favored hybrid creatures with bulbous noses; the notebooks of a California draftsman who understood all the buildings he imagined as the architectural embodiments of everyone he loved.

Walking out into the cold clear winter night, I found myself walking past the plaza where I'd sometimes bought an apple cider donut at the farmers' market before work—a small pleasure to steel myself against my boss's demands and her possible fury.

I could remember how much that young woman I'd once been wanted to make beautiful things—wanted to lead a life that mattered *because* she made beautiful things—and I could imagine more easily than before the ways my boss must have been hungry for meaning as well, or full of other desires I couldn't see clearly at the time. Back then, I couldn't fathom anything but how much she hurt my feelings—all the harm caused by her discontent, how her money let her splatter that discontent all over everything like a kind of toxic pain flung across the world.

That night—missing my daughter, awed by all that beauty born of loneliness—I gazed back at my boss across the terrain of all the living I'd done since leaving her brownstone: all those lonely cigarettes in LA, months of teaching in a one-room schoolhouse in Nicaragua, trying to prove myself in graduate seminars in New Haven, trying to make a life with a man I loved in Iowa, trying to make a life with another man I loved in Brooklyn, becoming a mother, becoming a single mother, becoming a teacher. I'd come back to New York at thirty and ended up living some version of the life I'd imagined when I was young—as a writer, a professor, a mother—but not in any of the ways I'd imagined: I was divorced, sober, grateful, well versed in toddler toys, extravagantly lucky in my friendships, often uncertain, often alone.

New York had taught me many times, in many ways, that life never plays out in exactly the ways we imagine. But what we get—in fragments, distortions, faint approximations—has its own beauty. New York kept trying to teach me that a life can look far more coherent from the outside than it actually feels from within—the most obvious truth in the world, I guess, but who ever really grasps it?

Looking back at my boss, it's easy to make her a villain and harder to imagine the ways she must have been hurting. It feels important to salvage the moments of beauty, too, amidst all the hours of bathroom crying. Even ten years into sobriety, fifteen years after quitting that job, I can still remember the magic of coming home drunk from our boozy lunches, how it felt, for those afternoons, as if I were finally living in the movie I'd imagined New York being—buzzed in that hazy late-afternoon light, up there in the loft, at the top of the world.

HOME

Melissa Febos

I.

My first New York apartment was a nine-by-five-foot room on 20th Street between Seventh and Eighth Avenues. It was an all-female boarding house or SRO (single room occupancy), as they were called before my time. The eight women on my floor all lived in cell-like rooms and shared the two tiny bathrooms in the hallway, one with nothing but a toilet, the other with a moldy shower.

My room was the smallest on the floor, just big enough for a twin bed, a mini-fridge, a small sink, and a few hundred books I'd lugged from Boston. I kept my clothes in garbage bags under the bed. If I'd gained ten pounds, I wouldn't have been able to walk the narrow aisle that ran the length of the room. Luckily, that never happened; as a depressed nineteen-year-old heroin addict, food was not my first priority.

During the day, I attended college. After classes, I'd loiter around Tompkins Square Park until I found a junkie I could trust enough to buy for me, since I was too new to the city to have my own dealer. In the evenings, I got high and wept into the phone to my best friend, Ariel, from back home, who hadn't come with me.

I was miserable. And toward the end of my six months in that place, borderline suicidal. Still, I never thought of leaving. New York was the only place I had ever wanted to live. I'd finally made it here, and I wasn't leaving except on a stretcher or in a straitjacket. Thankfully, those possibilities receded with each year I stayed.

Twelve years later, I couldn't believe I was in perfect health, packing those same books, getting ready to say goodbye to the place I'd loved longer than anything else in my life.

When we were kids, Ariel and I would lie in the grass of her backyard in worn T-shirts, the cool earth pressed against our backs. We spent hours fantasizing about the future—a glittering mirage that was always changing but always better than the familiar world of rural Massachusetts. I imagined New York then as a blur of lights and sound. The only thing in perfect focus was the two of us together, grown tall and invincible.

———

IN THE LATE SUMMER OF 1987, I TOOK MY FIRST TRIP TO NEW York alone to visit my father's mother. Technically, my abuela lived in New Jersey, where my father grew up, but she was a New Yorker to the bone—all four foot ten of her. In 1924, her parents had moved from Puerto Rico to Harlem, where she was born and raised. She met me at Penn Station, and as soon as we reached the sidewalk, I saw that she was different here, even her walk had changed, become faster, more confident.

On that first afternoon, we emerged into a rippling current of bodies. I froze, struck dumb by the summer heat, the smells of garbage, cigarette smoke, and roasting nuts. I looked up at the sliver of sky and ahead at the sea of faces and experienced the only kind of love at first sight that I believe in. Abuela tugged me to the curb and showed me how to tuck my money in my shoe.

IN THE FALL OF 2011, WHEN I STARTED APPLYING FOR JOBS OUTside New York, the idea was so abstract as to be unbelievable. Sure, I might leave the city someday, the same way I might become an astronaut or a lion tamer. But in the bedrock of my consciousness, formed back on that Massachusetts lawn, I'd settled on one future: I would live here, and I would be a writer.

And yet, New York City had never been this expensive before, and writing had never paid so badly. I had imagined my dreams coming true, but not what happened after that.

I first realized at twenty that an artist in New York needs two careers to stay afloat. By the time I was twenty-five, I'd exhausted the professions that only a brave and stupid twenty-year-old can sustain. Then I started teaching. To my great delight and relief, I found I loved it. All through graduate school and the publication of my first book, I watched my students grow more alive in telling their own stories. I kept pinching myself. How lucky, to get paid to talk about the thing I love most in the world! For years, I didn't care about how little I was getting paid.

Until I started trying to write another book and realized it was going to be pretty hard to get anything done while shuttling among four different campuses, teaching six classes a semester, and sleeping five hours a night. So, in February 2011, in those melancholy doldrums of late winter, when it seems like nothing will ever change—for better or for worse—I rode a train into the deep middle of the state and spent sixteen hours in interviews for a job I wasn't sure I wanted.

It didn't seem like it had anything to do with me—the scenery rushing past the train, the unfamiliar college town—so it didn't quite seem real. The city, on the other hand, had everything to do with me. By 2005, every neighborhood in Manhattan and many in Brooklyn, too, had been engraved with one personal memory or another. I couldn't use the bathroom in a certain diner on Sixth Avenue after having gotten violently sick there once. I couldn't eat at a favorite vegan restaurant without reliving a Valentine's Day breakup fight. For years, I couldn't really handle Herald Square because the neighborhood made me remember my time working as a dominatrix there. The city was haunted in a way I hated and cherished at the same time.

But it had changed, too. The city I lived in was not the same one to which I'd come. No one smoked in bars anymore. Favorite cafés had been shuttered, and new condos had sprung up in the unlikeliest neighborhoods.

My abuela—who went alone to a Julio Iglesias concert at Madison Square Garden when she was seventy and once told me, "This is my city. I'll never be too old for it"—became too ill with cancer to leave her New Jersey home and visit the city. She left this planet soon after.

Not long before that, Ariel died of an overdose. Our childhood fantasies died with her.

A few days after the interview upstate, the college called to offer me the job. My girlfriend and I drove up to look at places to live.

Then spring arrived. Overnight, it seemed, the trees burst into blossom, and I could smell that dirty, sweet perfume of the city stretching awake. On the first afternoon warm enough for bare arms, I was walking down East 10th Street. I'd just run into a friend I hadn't seen in years and was on my way to meet another. The stack of papers to grade in my bag was heavy but made lighter by the sunshine.

I reached the corner of Avenue A, and in front of me sprawled Tompkins Square Park. Its trees hung heavy with new growth, pollen sifting dreamily over the benches and grass, the dogs and playing children. Buzzing with laughter and motion and birdsong, it seemed more alive than anything I'd ever seen. Smelling the spring that day, and in it my own unearthed history, I wanted to lift my face to the sky and howl.

Leaving things you love is easier when you're younger. You make stupid decisions about the wrong people. You slam the apartment door, throw your lover's clothes out the window onto the sidewalk. Leaving gets harder as you age. You don't leave out of anger or from coming to your senses but because your love is not as strong as your reasons for going.

II.

WHEN WE PULLED UP BEHIND THE MOVING TRUCK IN FRONT OF our new home, my girlfriend and I looked at each other and grinned. I jumped out of the car and led our seventy-pound pit bull out of his nest in the back seat. For a moment, Red stood dazed in the brilliant light, ears lopsided, watching a bumblebee hover over the overgrown lawn.

Next door, our neighbor weeded her garden.

"Hi there!" I called out.

"Hi!" she called back, pulling off her gardening gloves. "I'm Patti."

Patti introduced herself as a college professor and area native. I mentioned my new position and that we'd arrived from Brooklyn. I didn't tell her that before joining the professorial ranks, I'd been a professional dominatrix and drug addict, or that I'd recently published a memoir about my days of spanking and shooting heroin. I wasn't in the habit of hiding my recent success, but it just seemed impolite to mention.

But I had experience with hiding. In my early twenties, I had juggled the life of a junkie dominatrix with that of a successful college student. It almost killed me, so good was I at keeping that secret, at maintaining my manners and appearance. For my first three years of teaching college, I hid all my tattoos. I had been dating my then boyfriend for three years, but in the months leading up to my book's publication, I never even told his parents what it was about. Concealing parts of me that might upset other people was a way of life.

But the year before I moved upstate marked an end to all that. The book came out, exposing me completely. I broke up with my boyfriend. I stopped wearing long sleeves to class in the middle of summer. And I fell in love with someone who gently reminded me that I had nothing to hide. It was the most terrifying and liberating year of my life. After five minutes in the country, however, I remembered how much easier it is being the person you think other people want you to be.

That night, I lay in bed listening to the crickets outside the open window. No sirens, no yelling, no car alarms, no footsteps on the floor above. The breeze drifting in the open window was sweet, but it took me a long time to fall asleep.

——

MY NEW DEAN HAD DESCRIBED THE AREA AROUND THE COL-lege as a "red county in a blue state," but it hadn't sunk in until we were driving around looking for a home. In some of these towns, I didn't want to get out of the car to pump gas. The people looked angry, and I spotted a Confederate flag flapping from one porch. It was difficult not to judge people based on superficialities, even as I was afraid of being judged myself.

Driving through Clinton, we knew it was the obvious choice. Clinton is "quaint." It has bed-and-breakfasts, a health food store, a population of under two thousand, and the highest median income of the surrounding towns. It is the Park Slope of its county, minus any people of color and minus the (visible) lesbi-ans. Until us.

We were pleased to find almond milk in the supermarket, but I started to feel the subtle double takes people made in the produce aisle. I wasn't embarrassed but felt something else. Something I hadn't felt in a long time. The instinctive urge to hide myself, streaked with a defiant preening   let them stare.

On the way home, Sini and I saw a middle-aged man and woman strolling across the village green. "Can we hold hands here?" she asked.

"I *think* it's safe," I said hopefully.

At Home Depot, where I went, alone, to get materials for a backyard fence for Red, people still stared, but only because I was one of few women in sight, and certainly the only one cruis-ing post drivers in three-inch wedges and mascara. I made a mental note to ditch my city heels to avoid looking like an off-duty stripper.

Later that week, our dryer was leaking gas, so I called a local plumber, which turned out to be two men with the same name.

"We tried replacing the tubes," I said, leading them to the basement door, "but it's still not working." They were friendly, but I found myself faintly hoping Sini wouldn't emerge from her office. Being stared at in the supermarket was one thing but having to witness that moment of recognition in our own house made me feel too exposed, too vulnerable. That snarl of contradictory feelings emerged again, protective and defiant at the same time. I wanted to spare Sini any discomfort, any regret in moving here for me, but I knew the answer was not to let people assume that the "we" I referred to included a husband somewhere out of sight.

——

IN MID-JUNE, I DROVE SINI TO THE CITY TO WORK FOR A FEW weeks. As I crossed the George Washington Bridge and sped down the FDR Drive, I felt strangely heartbreaky. Seeing the East River beside us, so gorgeous and contaminated, was like bumping into an ex you're still in love with. The city wasn't mine anymore, and it hurt to see it looking so beautiful and so familiar. Driving down Second Avenue, we saw the usuals: skater kids and college students, queens and models and junkies. My heart hurt more and more. The landmarks of my most troubled memories now tugged at my heart and filled it with longing. I even missed my ghosts.

To distract myself from my growing anxiety, I began obsessing over the fence. I pulled over on country roads to inspect strangers' pickets, their welded wire and split-rails. I googled and watched YouTube videos. I convinced my handy younger brother to drive out from Amherst to help me build it.

A few days before he arrived, I drove into town. Strolling around, reusable shopping bag dangling from my arm, I felt such a powerful surge of loneliness that it almost knocked me over. I fled back to my car and drove up and down the rolling hills outside town, smelling the lush twilit perfume of summer, the smell of my childhood. All of it: the beauty, the chirrup of crickets, even the homesickness was reminiscent of some past self. Change does that. The uncertainty of moving forward jostles the sleeping lions of childhood fears: that I am alone, that I am not seen or seen wrongly. That I have made some terrible mistake. That the loneliness will last forever. "I want to go home," I whispered, not sure what that meant.

The next day, I invited our neighbor Patti over for dinner. At first it was awkward, as I'd feared. But Patti was funny and kind, and we bonded over our mutual love of Middle Eastern food and dictionaries.

"I make a pretty mean baba ghanoush," she offered. "I'll save you some next time."

As I walked her out, she paused by the refrigerator.

"Is this the cover of your book?" she asked. Indeed it was, an early copy of the paperback cover, magnetized to the fridge.

"Um, yeah," I said. I took a deep breath. "Why don't I give you a copy?"

I regretted it almost immediately and worried about it all the next day as my brother and I struggled and failed to build a fence. Had I ruined the only alliance I had in town?

That night I sat alone in my home office and watched the live New York Senate hearing on gay marriage. As it passed thirty-three to twenty-nine, a cheer rose up in the hushed Senate chamber, but our neighborhood was dark and silent. I imagined the celebration on the city streets. I picked up the phone.

"The gay marriage bill just passed," I told Sini, wiping my nose with my sweatshirt sleeve.

"That's amazing!" she said. "Why do you sound so upset?"

"What if we did the wrong thing?" I asked and felt something crack in me. I'd wanted to say that for so long. "I'm so afraid I dragged us up here, so far away—" I deteriorated into sobs.

"You're just scared," she said. "Change is scary, but it doesn't mean it's wrong."

———

THE NEXT DAY, AS MY BROTHER AND I CAME BACK FROM OUR last trip to the hardware store, Patti came running across her lawn, holding a Tupperware container. I pulled over and rolled down the window.

"Baba ghanoush!" she said. "I made it yesterday."

"Thank you so much," I said, accepting the Tupperware.

"I read your book," she said.

"You did?" I fought to maintain eye contact.

"I loved it," she said. "Will you stop by and sign it for me later?"

All I could do was nod.

———

MY BROTHER FINISHED THE FENCE THAT AFTERNOON. Excited, I led Red out the back door and unclipped his leash.

"You're free!" I said, waiting for him to race around, commencing his freedom. Instead, he just lumbered to a sunny patch of grass a few yards away and rolled onto his side, happily panting. I had to laugh. Sometimes, it's enough just to know that we're safe. We don't necessarily have to do anything differently or be anyone but the person we've always been.

People who don't love the city talk about the freedom of the country and its wide open spaces; they marvel at how one could live in so cramped and crowded a space. But I always felt free in Brooklyn. I found safety in its enclosures. The city let me relax into being myself. Being who I am in New York didn't feel like an action I took—it just felt like living.

III.

WHEN THE POLLEN-LADEN WEEKS OF SUMMER DWINDLED, however, so did my certainty that we had made the right decision. First, Sini got sick. Or rather, sicker. She'd been ill before we left the city, but things worsened that fall. With no diagnosis and a debilitating list of over sixty-five symptoms, a current of panic rushed beneath our daily life together, which grew increasingly unmanageable. Her diagnosis of late-stage Lyme disease came with some relief, until we realized that insurance would only cover a tiny portion of the extravagantly priced treatments.

In the cooling months of the fall semester, we settled into a routine. Red paced in the yard, Sini trembled on the couch, and I wept in the parking lot before class, panic and loneliness tearing through me in ragged gasps as I looked out at the balding lawn of the college. "I want to go home," I whispered to myself, mantra-like. "I want to go home."

We didn't fight. Instead, I fought myself, and took comfort in knowing that I would never leave her in such a condition. There were tendernesses—many nights curled in our upstate-sized bed, the dog between us as we stroked his velvet ears and fantasized about the future. But I flinched under her hands and flung myself to the far edge of that great bed in sleep.

She needed me, and that terrified me. I needed help, too, but could not accept it. If I gave in to my own choking fear and loneliness, I feared it might crush me, as our life seemed to be crushing our love. I could not afford to fall apart.

After classes and interminable faculty meetings, I jogged for hours through the farmland and then sifted through bills and claim forms. On better weeks, Sini commuted back to the city to work. The house seemed vast without her, myself a swirling mote, carried by twin winds of relief at her absence and bitter loneliness.

———

A month later, I was on antidepressants. Did it help? I couldn't tell. My hands were drier, and I suddenly became a person who napped. But I still didn't want to be touched. I still felt a caving pit in my chest when I thought about Sini's health, about New York and the possibility of going on as we were for an indeterminate future. Though my eyes stayed dry, I still found myself whispering under my breath when alone, "I want to go home."

———

When, after a grueling series of treatments and astronomical costs, Sini's health took a turn for the better at the end of the spring semester, I tendered my resignation, and we began looking for an apartment back in Brooklyn.

The new apartment was over our budget, and Sini balked at the size, but I insisted, preferring location over square footage, desperately needing to be close by the people I had missed upstate, to feel close to the pulse of my old life.

On moving day, Sini drove the truck while I led in the car full of plants and medical supplies, my new prescription rattling in my purse. For a few moments, crossing the Manhattan Bridge, the river preening below in the dazzling spring sunlight, I felt free again. It felt like coming home.

But before we'd finished unloading boxes, my purse was stolen out of the car. My wallet and medication were gone. My dismay felt tinged with some deeper hysteria. Throat dry and palms damp, I called the bank and canceled my credit cards, the cave in my chest yawning hungrily.

It was a Friday, and my doctor's office was closed. For the next two days, I waited for some sign of breakage, for a panic greater than that I already felt to seep into my hands and heart. Nothing. Just the same old ache in my chest, the same aversion to my beloved's touch. I waited a week, then two, and saw no difference in my mood. Again, relief and disappointment. Whatever my condition, it would not be cured with a pill. Perhaps it could still be cured by coming home.

For the next month, our apartment remained crammed with boxes and the walls bare. Something in me resisted opening those boxes, as if the muted despair of our upstate life might rise in fumes, poisoning our new home. I raced around the city with work and social engagements, breathing in my city, but then went numb when I arrived home.

"What is going on with you?" she finally demanded one afternoon, and I could barely meet her gaze.

"Nothing," I said.

"What the hell are you feeling inside, Melissa?"

I didn't know what I felt inside, only that I couldn't stop moving, couldn't stop trying to outrun the caving feeling inside me.

The next day, a cop pulled me over on Houston Street. When the officer walked away with my license and registration, I stared at the dirty windshield, the ceaseless flow of traffic heading toward the Manhattan Bridge, and burst into tears. Something opened in me, and from that cave came a scorching flood of tears. Once I started, I couldn't stop. My body rocking with sobs, I leaned my forehead on the steering wheel and yielded to the surging waves of grief. I didn't even raise my head when the police officer returned, and he flung the ticket through my open window and fled. Hands gripping my thighs, the steering wheel slick with tears, I wailed for the lost hope that we would emerge from our troubles closer and stronger. I sobbed for my beloved, who had had to suffer alone in so many ways, and I wept for myself, for all the ways I wanted to be more than I was.

There was more between that day and the day Sini moved out of our home. I wish I could say that I recognized the moment when it was over, when I had reached the limit of my love, and that I faced it with some dignity. But I didn't. I could not face the decision to leave while we still loved each other. And we did. But sometimes, love needs more than love to survive. Were we still *in* love? I don't know. I know that I had stepped far enough outside our love that, a few weeks after I got that ticket, I touched someone else's mouth with mine. I know that the day she moved out, when I walked back into the empty apartment and surveyed the pile of dusty wires where her desk had been, the lone fork and mug she'd left me, my chest filled with a terrible sadness and with relief.

THIS MORNING, I WOKE FEELING LIGHTER. RED LAZED IN A patch of sunlight near my desk chair as I sipped my coffee and wrote a little. I've got a new desk, new plants, and a few knives and spoons to accompany my fork. In the kitchen, light streams in, and through the cracked window, I can smell autumn coming. There is more space in here, now, and I am beginning to fill it with words, with forgiveness, with a future that's only beginning to sharpen into focus.

Though my heart is in pieces, I have not found myself whispering for home. Because home is here. Not only New York but this heart that I'm learning to trust, however much it hurts. In these emptier days, I have come to know that my sadness is not a problem to be solved. It is simply my humanity. Sometimes pain is the call of a wound that needs tending, and sometimes it is the sting of its healing. And sometimes you have to break your own heart to be true, and you have to go home to do it.

TRANSPORT

Emily Carter Roiphe

left New York, my twenties, and the 1980s behind at the same time. I was perfectly glad to do so since I had never wanted to be provincial, living my whole life in the same place I was born. New York City was the only thing I had ever felt excitement or affection for, but I refused to believe that the world ended at the Hudson River to the west and the Brooklyn Queens Expressway to the east. The famous Saul Steinberg cartoon in which the world did just that was only funny because it was accurate. In my eyes, this view was not much different from the village idiot's in *Mayberry RFD* who, when asked what lay to the east, replied, "Old Man Johnson's woods, then Kelly's Gas and Go, then . . . th'Atlantic Ocean." I knew that New York, specifically the New York of my family, was in many ways a fine and interesting place, but it was not the only place. Added to this was the fact that in New York there was no place for me, and to continue to throw the jagged shape of myself into a three-generation-deep round hole would only result in the kind of splintering that would leave me yelling tired homilies about yuppies and space aliens outside whatever outerborough group home next to a parking garage I'd be lucky enough to find myself in. I wouldn't miss the culture—New York winnows out a lot of mediocrity—but I was only interested in heroin at that moment in time, of which, I admit, New York did have the very best, and it was cheap, too, its price being only ten dollars a unit, and my integrity. It probably cost quite a bit of my future as well, but that was something I was clearly not constitutionally capable of taking into consideration. I did not, however, want to be associated with the horrid troops of well-off Caucasian poseurs who were using heroin as an expression of fashionable, expensive anomie while thousands of hardworking people had to deal with it as a blight on their neighborhoods and families. I didn't particularly care if I died at that point since I was clinically depressed, but the thought of being associated with the whole heroin-chic thing made me wish I had never existed in the first place. That being the case, I got my wealthy Caucasian family to send me to a fashionable, expensive treatment center in Minnesota. The only thing I would miss, and I missed it for twenty years and still do every day, was the New York City subway system. Keep your dawn-splashed canyons and soaring cathedrals; keep your pyramids, your temples, your gold-domed pagodas rising above ancient capitals. The Metro Underground Transit system is the wonder of the world, and I was in love with it and still am, even though it's going through a "respectable" phase.

I knew right away that I was going to have to deal with transit nostalgia when I was picked up at the Minneapolis airport by a friendly young man who looked like the guitar player at the church I'd gone to once when I was ten with my friend Eleanor out in Scarsdale. He played Cat Stevens songs and invited us to a "rap group" after the service. The Minnesota counselor sported the same dark-blond receding hair pulled back in a ponytail, the same wide-wale, dun-colored corduroys, the same aviator glasses. The guitar player had been transferred for what Eleanor said her parents called "overly fluid boundaries," which meant—she told me in the objective tone kids adopt when trying to scare another kid with a piece of evil news—that the stories of his putting his finger into Nancy Spencer's vagina were true. In New York, when I grew up, there were mashers and molesters all over the 6 train I took to school. You could be assured of running into one at least three or four times a year. They were no threat, however. You learned how to dodge them in a moment, and if it was crowded and you were smushed up against one, you could loudly declare "Take your hand off my leg" and watch their faces crumple in terror. It's true I was frozen with fear the one time during a morning crush that I felt someone's hand scrabbling around my underpants. This was nothing, though, compared to the thrilling infusion of self-reliance I got from discovering he was more frightened of what I could say than I was of what he could do; one word from me and he'd be assaulted by a hailstorm of name calling:

"Fucking perv."

"Swear to God . . ."

"Quit touching the little kids, douche-wad!"

The Upper East Side professionals in the car would remain silent, not willing to abandon their class status to become involved in public theater, but they would look at us. Meanwhile, somebody would use the distraction to pick someone's pocket, and he'd be likely to get accused of that as well. It happened faster than calling 911 on a cell phone, the current method of citizen action.

If I didn't feel like making a scene, I just moved, and they disappeared back into the cluttered background of human flesh and faces that every subway rider learns to take for granted and ignore, like a dirty but comfortable blanket.

But in Minneapolis, in the car with this odd man, whose strange presexual aura reminded me of Mr. Rogers—who had always looked to me like a gentle, delicate cloud of pedophilia—there were no witnesses. Later I learned he was quite a decent sort, but I actually thought, after we headed north on I-35 and turned down a wooded road, of jumping out of the car. Even though it was January, I considered running across the flat white expanse to one of the little homeless encampments dotting what appeared to be a snow-covered field just behind the ragged black tree line. It took me a while to discover that it was not the wind-blasted prairie but one of Minnesota's ten thousand lakes, and what I assumed were squatters' shacks were ice-fishing huts, which is only one example of how growing up in New York makes you ridiculous everywhere else.

The first place I lived when I got out of treatment was a "developing" neighborhood in St. Paul. I shared an apartment right off Selby Avenue in the Cathedral Hill neighborhood and took two buses to my job at an airport gift shop. First, I took one bus down the hill past the dome of the Cathedral of Saint Paul and the capitol building and then transferred to another down on Kellogg Boulevard in an area we called the flats. I didn't think about it much on the first day until I got to the transfer spot and wound up waiting twenty minutes on a windswept, vacant street in front of an auto parts distributor, a closed-up body shop, and the empty acre of a construction site. The wind was so strong that it had ripped the green-and-red soot-spattered plastic pennants around the lot into strips of dirty ribbon. When my shift ended, the last number 4 had already left, and I waited forty minutes for the 7, which connected to another bus in Minneapolis that dropped me off in front of a White Castle on Lake Street—empty streets, nail salons, occasional propositions from passing cars, because who else would be standing on a street in public but someone who was "working"—just after the last 21 had left and three-quarters of an hour before the next one. It dropped me off back on Selby and Dale, where I staggered in my first wet, now-frozen work shoes back to my apartment and fell asleep with my coat on as soon as the insistent pain in my feet turned to numbness. Later on, the airport employees petitioned the Minnesota Department of Transportation for an extra number 7, but until they did, the manager would say "must be nice" as I clocked out five minutes early and ran through the terminal to get there before it left. The trip home, if nothing went wrong, would take two hours and fifteen minutes. When I mentioned this, people looked confused. Why didn't I just drive?

The idea of someone living without a car didn't come up any more than the idea of someone walking around without a head. If you lived, you drove, was the assumption anywhere but the small island where I was born. The only people who took the bus were disabled, like me: by poor eyesight, by Parkinson's or schizophrenia, by deafness, by poverty. Those of us who rode the bus didn't merely look resigned; we looked defiant, staring straight ahead in the kind of square-shouldered so-what attitude most often used to conceal shame about our cheap snow boots and the huge sums of subtraction that showed in our faces.

I hit up my mother for driving lesson money. "Only marginal people take the bus here," I said.

"Well, Sweetie, you *are* marginal."

But she gave me the money, figuring it was but a drop in the bucket of the money I had cost her throughout my life of private schools, privilege, and psychiatrists, all of which had done me no particular good, so much so that it was no longer even a matter of throwing good money after bad but simple harm reduction. The crosstown boulevards and freeway entrances were standing between me and my last chance at a life lived outside an institution.

That being the case, I learned to drive. But I never liked it. Every day for twenty years, I wished that the buses in the Twin Cities would run a little faster.

For green spaces and civic decency, the Twin Cities beat out a great many metropolitan areas on the planet. Like the rest of America, however, they were designed for driving, not walking, and that has made quite a few of its people fatter and more suspicious than they need to be. It was there that I first wondered what really made New York different from the rest of America and why I was finding it hard to navigate. If I hadn't left the city of my birth, I would never have discovered Jane Jacobs, whose books explained to me exactly what I was missing and what made the good parts of a city good. Neighborhoods one can walk in are important, of course, but you need a way to get from one to the other without putting yourself outside space and time, without detaching yourself completely from the communities through which you move. What makes a city a real city? Number one, in my opinion, is a subway system.

When I returned to New York on family visits, I had the usual sense of melancholy. I felt like a foreigner; all the stimuli that had melded into a humming backdrop now distracted and overwhelmed. I had to get my blinders back and build up my audiovisual stamina for a day or so before I could travel reflexively again, but if I took the 2 train out to the Nevins stop to visit my sisters, it would put the spring back into my step twice as fast. It's not the neighborhoods themselves I crave; it's the commute: to go into a cool, dark tunnel and emerge twenty minutes later in a different world that is also, in the most fundamental and invisible way, the same.

Today when I walk around my hometown, I see the obvious changes that money and power have wrought, and I think the obvious sorrowful, angry thoughts of any person made a financial exile from the place of her birth. I'm no longer young, and of course that colors my view of the East Village and Williamsburg, where I lived in 1986, in all the expected ways. If, however, I take the train to any of these neighborhoods, or to Rockaway, or to Dyckman Street in Washington Heights, my heart still starts to beat a little faster. If the train goes elevated, I still get a sting of excitement when it bursts out of the tunnel into the air three floors up, girded on either side with millions of windows topped with water towers, the iron lacework of fire escapes, and glimpses of glittering, steel blue river.

I don't like rush hour any more than anyone else, but sometimes I have to laugh, standing there surrounded by the pressing flesh and odorous breath, at the amazing, manic fact of it all.

Look at us, twelve million little corpuscles pulsing at superhuman speed through the circulatory system of this grungy, grandiose giant. Someone told me, "Ah, New York isn't diverse. People just get thrown together on the subway and at work; then they all scatter home to their separate enclaves." Maybe so, but there are enough exceptions to that rule that the last time I was on the L, I overheard the conversation of a family whose smallest members, twins, were wearing identical Puerto Rican flag T-shirts. They were on their way to a bris, about which they were unnerved— you could tell by the bad jokes—but were nonetheless attending because their son's study partner and friend at CUNY was the father and he'd come to the son's wedding, so they had to reciprocate. Peace on Earth it wasn't, but you have to start somewhere. Rome wasn't built in a day, and the first time anyone tried to build an underground train in New York, Tammany Hall thugs shut it down for lack of kickbacks. Now look: it was an 85-degree day and I was enjoying an air-conditioned ride, traveling in relative comfort, underground, while people hurtled from one microcosm to another at forty-five miles an hour. It would be something to write home about, if people still wrote home, and if I weren't, in fact, home already.

ELEVEN TRUE THINGS

Ada Limón

1. THE PLANTER IN TIMES SQUARE

I hate everything about the moment the city starts to leave me. That's what it feels like. Not as if I am ready to leave but that the city is pulling away from me. Like a relationship you know is over, and still you go on kissing each other on the cheek and silently grinning through your teeth because how can it possibly be over, a love as big as this? I am standing near Times Square by my office and my stepmother has just died and I am putting my hands in an enormous concrete planter and before I know it I am crying from the feel of dirt, the real leaves of something living. I don't want my life anymore, not the way it is. I need more space. More time to think and make things. Someone hits me from behind accidentally while coming out of the subway. They don't apologize. Some part of me is embarrassed because I am stopped in the middle of the sidewalk in Midtown, which feels like the middle of everything; a real New Yorker would know better. A real New Yorker doesn't look up or down; they look straight ahead. They are propelled by momentum. They don't stop.

2. THINGS THAT COST A DOLLAR

WHEN I FIRST MOVE TO NEW YORK, I BEG MY FRIEND T TO meet me at the airport. T has already been in New York for two weeks, and when I call her she says, "No one picks up anyone at the airport in New York." She is already a New Yorker. I know this. I fly a discount airline that no longer exists, and somehow T meets me outside. I have three thousand dollars saved from working as a receptionist for King County Water and Land Resources Division. It's August. I am twenty-three. I start graduate school at New York University in three days. Though I know very little about poetry, I am going to study it. T has short hair and a pager attached to her jeans when she picks me up. No one but drug dealers or medical personnel have pagers back in Seattle. Pagers are fancy. In the cab she keeps talking about the street food you can buy for a dollar. She says a slice of pizza is a dollar, pizza rolls are a dollar for like a whole bag, soft pretzels are a dollar, hot dogs are a dollar. Then, she turns to me and asks to borrow a hundred dollars. The blur of traffic and gray exhaust-filled air, the tall buildings, the rush of pedestrians, the cabdriver who doesn't seem to care where we want to go, I want to remember all of it. Mostly, I remember T showing up. Even though she said real New Yorkers don't show up at the airport.

3. NOTHING COSTS A DOLLAR

DISCOVERING NEW YORK IS LIKE DISCOVERING A DIFFERENT color. Something you've never seen before that's on par with both beauty and agony and looks both terrible and fantastic on everyone. I walk everywhere. One day I walk from Battery Park to Central Park, all while carrying the fat *Norton Anthology of Poetry* in my backpack. It's impossible to look cool wearing a backpack. I don't have a cell phone or a pager. I have an actual fold-out map that is small enough to fit in my pocket. I walk because I want to see the city. I also walk because I am terrified of taking the subway. The subway is a color I recognize. Something like a putrid yellow of disgust and urine and fluorescent lights and warmth and danger all at once. I discover jaywalking in earnest and how it's best done together as a herd. When I get lost, I look downtown and see the Twin Towers. The towers always mean that way is south. A bottle of water is a million dollars. Drinks are a million dollars. I am losing money so fast, and suddenly it seems ridiculous that anyone would go to New York to be a poet and not a banker instead.

4. THE SHIRT

I HAVE ONE NICE SHIRT THAT WAS GIVEN TO ME BY MY FRIEND Diana. It's Pierre Cardin, and it's black, long-sleeved, ribbed. It somehow never fades or stretches out. T and I have to swap this shirt on street corners if either of us has to go to some place nice. We only ever call it "the shirt." I still have it. We hand-wash it, not because we are being delicate with it but because it is needed more than twice a week. If we have to go some place nice together, we are screwed because who gets to wear "the shirt"?

5. THE LITERARY WING

T AND I MOVE TO GREENPOINT, BROOKLYN, IN 2000. Everything is done in cash. We hand over $2,400 and it's more money than we've ever seen. From then on, we pay rent to a twelve-year-old who brings it back to her parents. We give her cash and hope she gets home okay. T says to her while she counts out the hundred-dollar bills, "Well, here's a hundred dollars for every year you've been alive." We get the go-ahead to paint the walls. We stay up late, listen to a classic radio station, take mushrooms a friend has given us, and paint the whole apartment terra cotta. For years you can still see areas where we got distracted and the paint thinned out. I write poems. T writes plays. T's father sends mail to us that is addressed to "Apartment 2L, The Literary Wing." We do our laundry at a laundromat where you can smoke inside and get grape soda out of the vending machine. We don't get many channels on our small television, and one night the lady at the laundromat stays open late so we can finish watching the Academy Awards while we smoke and drink grape soda. We love our laundromat. We love our apartment. We love our deli. We are living the dream.

6. STONE SOUP

THE FIRST TEMP JOB THAT T GETS IS AT GQ MAGAZINE. The first temp job that I get is at GQ magazine. By the time I get my job at Condé Nast, I'm in my second year of graduate school and T has already gone on to a better job. I shop at secondhand stores to get most of my work clothes and supplement with new cheap things from Rainbow Shop. Everything from the secondhand store smells like body odor and smoke and everything from

Rainbow Shop smells like plastic and burnt hair. We cash our small paychecks at a busy check-cashing spot in Midtown and then walk around with hundreds of dollars of cash in our pockets like our twelve-year-old rent collector. The money we don't spend on rent, we spend at bars. That's okay because everyone we know does the same thing. We make a family out of our friends. We are chaotic and unstoppable. We are making stone soup. We are the stones. Our friends provide everything else. We forget where we are from except when it is late and we've been drinking and someone gets a little homesick or wonders whether someplace else is still easier, a little softer. We don't stay too long in that place of our origins. We pay our tabs and go back into the crackling dirty city that has become our home.

7. LAUNDRY AND TREES

I SPEND MOST OF MY TIME IN GRADUATE SCHOOL WRITING POems about California and using words like "eucalyptus" and "bay laurel" and "manzanita." When I sit to write a poem, each time, I return in my mind to a place across the street from where I grew up in Glen Ellen, California, where the Calabazas Creek runs underneath Arnold Drive. I think if I can get to that place of stillness, of curiosity and wonder, I can write a poem. When I look out my window in Brooklyn, I see the square backyards that we can't access and all the laundry looping from house to house like broken kites. I grow tomatoes on the fire escape. A friend of mine in my same poetry workshop introduces me to someone at a bar and says, "This is Ada. She writes poems about horses and rodeos." Which is strange because I have never written about a horse or a rodeo.

8. HARRISON FORD

THE TOWERS COME DOWN. NOTHING IS THE SAME. I BEGIN having panic attacks. No one has ever loved New York more. We cry and lean on each other. There's a fundraiser we volunteer for hosted by our friends who are actors and also own a shop that refurbishes old muscle cars for movies. The fundraiser is for our local firehouse that's lost men. The fundraiser is also a hipster paradise with live music and a kissing booth and I work the bar for a long time. If I am busy working I do not have a panic attack. At one point someone is walking toward me with the light behind him so I cannot see his face but I know him. It is Harrison Ford. He gives an apologetic smile and I try to pretend that I see him every day even though he is my favorite actor of my childhood. I do not call him Han. I do not call him Indy. I ask how many beers and tell him it's donation only. He throws a wad of cash into the bucket and grabs six beers for his friends and two off-duty firefighters. Somehow, now and forever, I associate the terrible grief of September 11, absurdly, with Harrison Ford.

9. THE IMPOSSIBLE GARDEN

WE MOVE INTO A REAL HOUSE ON METROPOLITAN AVENUE between Bedford and Berry. H moves in with us so we can split the whole house, which comes with a small backyard. And for the first time in nearly five years, I make a garden. When it's nice, it's the only place I want to be. I am working for Martha Stewart, and I become a homemaker. I make an herb garden and grow lettuce and tomatoes and an accidental boomer crop of okra that T wanted to plant. That's the same year I discover I don't like okra. T and I try to write a song that starts, "When okra was our cash crop." That's the year we all start to think about ourselves in the past tense. When the furniture is settled and the house is perfect, H lies on the couch we found on the street and says, "I'm already nostalgic for this time right here." This is the house I am most happy in. It is the only place I've had in New York where I can be outside and alone at the same time.

10. THE LAST APARTMENT

I LIVE IN THE LAST APARTMENT I'LL HAVE IN NEW YORK FOR four years. It's a small one bedroom with a good bathtub on Manhattan Avenue between Jackson and Withers in Williamsburg. It's the place where I begin to think about leaving New York for the first time. My stepmother becomes very sick with cancer. I lose my friend who is my same age to cancer. I begin to think about what it might be to live in nature, to stop grieving so much, to be away from concrete, to stop working so hard in jobs I don't love. I try to save a little money for the first time since I've moved to the city. I make a plan for an interim place to live in California. I don't believe that it will really happen, but someday maybe I will leave this place. But leaving New York is impossible. It's as if you are the gum and it is the hair; you are stuck and the more you pull away the more it hurts and tears you apart. T and I begin to prepare ourselves for months before I leave. We make a plan. We cry. Six months before I leave, I fall in love. It is most inconvenient. It feels like a cruel trick New York is playing on me.

11. THE FIRST DAY

I DRIVE UP MOON MOUNTAIN ROAD TO WHERE I AM RENTING a small apartment in my hometown of Sonoma, California. It is October and unseasonably warm. As I am driving, I see so many birds along the road. I see bay laurel and California oaks and manzanitas lining the path. I do not have any place to be and nothing is required of me. There are two things happening. I am grieving. I am untangling myself. I cry the whole way up the mountain, but I feel like I should be happy. I suddenly miss even Times Square. I think I've made a mistake. I don't know what to do with myself. I am nothing without the city, without T. Everything is a new color again, and this time it is something that hurts to look at it because it is as if I have made the color up. A color I haven't told anyone about, a private color. I stop in the middle of the country road and take a picture of the sunset and send it to the man I love and then I send it to T. She says it's so beautiful it makes her want to poke her eyes out. I keep driving. I am propelled by momentum. I do not stop.

HOMECOMING

Mira Ptacin

It's late November and my husband and I are walking down a plain gravel path headed toward the Atlantic Ocean. We pass a tall compost heap, a wobbly wooden tree fort, a nervous cluster of chickens pretending to ignore us, and a baseball diamond where, to no one's surprise, a beige miniature horse is roped to a bench and contentedly mowing the lawn with her mouth.

We live in Maine now, the Pine Tree State. The only state in the country with just one syllable. The state whose motto is *Dirigo* ("I lead") and slogan is "The Way Life Should Be," which, to me, after living in New York City for just over half a decade, Maine is.

It wasn't easy getting here. One day about four months ago, after the air conditioner in our fourth-floor Brooklyn walk-up broke yet again, after our dogs had met the police twice (once for nipping at a Hasidic man's tzitzit and once more for attacking a soda can collector's garbage bags), after we'd drained our bank accounts and accumulated a severe amount of debt, spent more time with strangers on the subway than we did together at our own kitchen table, and finally had enough of New York, Andrew and I quit our day jobs, gathered the dogs and our belongings, rented a U-Haul, and said goodbye to all that and hello to more peace, more quiet, and less distraction.

I had moved to New York six years earlier because I wanted to be a famous writer. I was twenty-five and determined but without a road map. I'd been living a blissful life in Portland, Maine, but felt, like so many young people, I needed a "New York Chapter." So I uprooted myself. My very first night in New York, my car windows got smashed and then the car was towed (I didn't realize I'd parked illegally), and at midnight that same night, my license plate expired. I spent my entire first week in New York trying to find and retrieve my car; each day, the impound lot was charging me fifty dollars. I spent my first six months in New York subletting a room above a sushi restaurant in Carroll Gardens, Brooklyn, with a putty-faced girl my age who happened to be the assistant to a famous and important and powerful magazine editor and who behaved as if, by association or osmosis, she was just as famous and important and powerful. She was rich and intimidating and well dressed and had attended Columbia University. I owned three pairs of shoes and had gone to a public college in Michigan. I was broke and sensitive and naïve and knew no one fancy in Manhattan; I could barely navigate the subway. I felt sorry for the mice in our apartment building that our landlord was trying to poison—*they were just trying to survive*—and I found it painfully unnatural and difficult not to look the people sitting across from me on the train in the eye. I thought that to be a writer in New York, all one had to do was live in New York and write and write well. My putty-faced roommate introduced me to the notion that, to be a successful writer in New York, one must dress the part, act the part, know all the players, and sleep with a good bit of them. It was a game that I just didn't want to play. Within a year, I'd become drearily drained of hope and money. I was walking dogs professionally during the day while moonlighting as a data entry clerk, and to boot, I lost the few belongings I had to bedbugs. But the worse things got, the more determined I became to beat New York at whatever game we were playing: it would place obstacles in front of me, and I'd hurdle over them until I reached the finish line. I refused to give up, no matter what, no matter how hard New York got, until I felt I'd achieved what I thought was success.

Within time, my career started picking up speed. The literary circle opened itself up to me (or maybe the barrier eventually toppled after I'd thrown myself against it enough times), and I started getting published frequently. Then, out of nowhere, I met a man. I hadn't planned on dating anyone, let alone ever getting hitched, but after I reluctantly agreed to go on a blind date with him, Andrew and I hit it off. We were both eyeball deep in our career goals, but we fell in love and soon after got married. The Monday morning following our wedding, we jumped right back into our manic work routines.

With financial security and some material comfort, we thought we had it pretty good, but in reality, we were unhealthy newlyweds. We lived right next to Prospect Park but fought over whose turn it was to walk the dogs and who got to stay home and work. Unless we were sleeping, we rarely spent more than two hours a day together. Andrew would get home from work at night, and I'd be heading out the door to show my face at a colleague's reading. Weekend days were spent getting chores out of the way (Andrew: laundry; Mira: clean apartment) so that we could spend our precious evenings tending to work projects. We saw a marriage counselor, who suggested we pencil in date nights, but by the time date night rolled around, we were always too tired to follow through. We fought all the time, and in time, the threat of divorce slipped into our arguments.

Nothing was irrevocable. Everything was within reach. Joan Didion's words rang true, but what we hadn't considered was that once we reached one rung in the ladder, there was always the next rung above it, and another and another. Our spirits became comatose because our lives revolved around our careers; even our marriage felt like a business arrangement. The day our dog bit that soda can collector in the park (who eventually sued us) and a policeman came to our apartment to file a report—the day we had to defend our pet—was the first time my husband and I had worked as a team in months. That's when we realized it was time to leave New York and save our marriage.

———

ONE OF THE FIRST THINGS ANDREW AND I DID AFTER WE LEFT the city was go to a funeral. Brent, the father of one of Andrew's childhood friends, had been diagnosed with liver cancer a couple of weeks earlier. Days before he passed, Andrew and I brought cookies to Brent's wife, Rosemary, who'd been keeping vigil at her ailing husband's bedside in a nursing home. I remember it was the Fourth of July and nearly 110 degrees outside. In a shared room, Rosemary sat beside Brent, who reclined in bed, sedated with morphine. She'd barely been eating or sleeping and was still coping with her husband's fate. "It feels like a dream," she'd told us. "It feels like just yesterday we even found the cancer." Once diagnosed, her husband had been given about a month to live. As she stroked Brent's arm, Rosemary told us how the doctor had told her husband his fate and left them alone in the exam room; then the couple, who'd been married for thirty-five years, had raised two grown kids, and had three grandchildren, suddenly had to say goodbye.

"That was it," she said. "That's when Brent turned to me, took my hands, and said, 'Well, Rosemary, we've had a good run.'"

The day after we visited him, Brent was gone.

BRENT'S FUNERAL WAS HELD THREE DAYS AFTER HE DIED. After the burial and as the sun was setting, we gathered at Brent and Rosemary's home. We walked there from Andrew's childhood home, too, and we stayed until nearly 2 AM, drinking on their wraparound porch, exchanging stories, eating Doritos, passing photo albums, and handing out tissues. This went on for three nights and kept going even after Andrew and I left town.

Here are some of the things I learned at Rosemary's that first week after leaving New York: I learned that when a widow is crying and smoking a cigarette, you let her cry, and if you speak, it's to ask if you can get her another Diet Coke. I learned that no one cares that much what you do for a living, but they will be grateful if you stay up with a six-year-old and watch *Dennis the Menace* because his grandfather is dead and he cannot sleep. Rather than get into a political debate about the war, you thank an Iraqi veteran for his service. You do not check your BlackBerry in the middle of a toast, and when someone hands you a crying baby, you hold it. I learned that ice cream cakes make grandpas feel really special, and when a neighbor invites you to swing by the food pantry during her volunteer shift so that she can take a look at that nasty poison oak on your shin, you go, and you wait patiently until she can get free to see you. I learned that you don't judge someone's worth based on what they can do for you and that you aren't expected to ask, "How can I help?" Instead, you just jump right in.

Here are some of the things I learned while living in New York: That you shouldn't interpret direct and efficient communication as rudeness. That a sidewalk operates by the same rules as a highway: if you walk slow, walk in the right lane, and if you have to stop, pull over. I learned that once the late June sunshine hits the streets, pretty girls in summer dresses come out of the woodwork. I also learned that summer brings with it the inescapable smell of marinating garbage and human urine. In the city, you can get weed delivered to your front door by a hipster on a bicycle or pick up a screwdriver in the dead of the night at a twenty-four-hour hardware store. I learned that the city has resilience like no other city during natural (or manmade) disasters and that the people of New York generally coexist peacefully, which is impressive, considering there are 27,352 people per square mile. But it's a class-divided society. It's a rich cultural environment, full of galleries and incredible restaurants and museums and shows, but unless you're wealthy, the city requires sacrifice to enjoy those things. Unless you are rich, you struggle every day. You grind. You ride the subway for two hours just to work at Starbucks. But there's also nowhere else to be for professional networking. You can access the movers and shakers. You can *be* a mover and a shaker if you work hard enough. Just plug yourself into the scene, whatever your scene is. But what ends up happening—or what ended up happening to me—is an unplugging from family life, an unplugging from the things that make you feel whole and rooted. While living in New York, I eventually came to realize that for every good thing about the city, there was also a dark side. We go to New York to make our careers, but we end up stepping over homeless people on the sidewalk on our way to work. Successful New Yorkers can ignore those dark sides, but I could not.

However, small towns have their dark sides, too. Small towns can be conservative and close-minded and tacky. People in small towns often like to be all up in your business. Yet I can get over those things. And I can still be a successful writer and not live in a big city. I couldn't be my true self while living in New York. If I had stayed, my spirit would have died. My marriage, my health, my sense of peace—all had been placed on the back burner, and they would have stayed on the back burner. It wasn't the city's fault; it was mine. I was unmoored; my ambition trumped my principles. If I had stayed in New York, my marriage to Andrew might not have survived. Our run would not have been so good.

The morning after our third night on Rosemary's porch, we left Andrew's hometown and headed to Maine. During our drive, I thought about all the hopeful lonely faces I saw when we set foot in the nursing home where Brent stayed. They were all so sad but smiling, so hopeful. They were wearing Fourth of July hats and T-shirts and big bead necklaces. I wished so hard that someone would be coming to visit them that day. We drove, and I thought about the lines in the funeral home, the unsophisticated décor and the casseroles, and how long the friendships had lasted. I thought about who cared about me like that, and I tried to remember the person I was before I arrived in New York City. Driving into Maine, I started to wonder, *Who would visit me on my deathbed? Who would take a rain check or tell me their*

*subway line wasn't running? If I couldn't talk or walk or even go to
the bathroom, who would help take care of me? If I died tomorrow,
who would attend my funeral?*

We kept driving. We passed a public supper, a scarecrow contest, some steeples, and sailboats until we crossed Commercial
Street and drove our car onto Casco Bay Lines ferry and drifted
along Portland Harbor until we reached our little sanctuary on
Peaks Island, Maine. Population: 800.

———

WE WALK THROUGH A PINE TREE FOREST, STEP ACROSS A
homemade bridge, and there, strong like a mother, is the Atlantic. Ahead of us, the tide is coming in. I breathe in the moist air;
I remember how desperately, when living in New York, I wanted
to inhale such things: saltwater, sand, isolation. I didn't want to
smell smog or hear so many signs of life, millions of them, all at
once. I was too soft for New York, too easily saddened or distracted. I didn't want to be callous. I just wanted to remain the
sensitive creature I was, to write, love, and be a little hidden.
Now, here on this small island in Maine, I'm beginning to feel
alive again and unafraid, as if something in the air has taken over
me, as if the water is breathing out the secret to something I'd
been looking for, something I'd been looking for so long that I'd
nearly forgotten what it was. The answer. I'm home now. This is
where I'm supposed to be.

LEAVING MY GROOVY LIFESTYLE

Chloe Caldwell

Although it was only two hours away from Hudson, my small town upstate, New York City seemed like a fictional place until I moved there. My older brother was living in Brooklyn and working at the Strand. When I spoke with him on the phone, it was noisy in the background and there was something new to his voice—my shy, introverted brother sounded almost *joyful*, if not a little manic. I've always been the type of person who sees something she likes and then sets about getting it in her own life. I liked New York. So when there was an open "room" (a couple of feet on the creaky wooden floor without a door for $600 a month) in my brother's railroad apartment on North Sixth

Street in Williamsburg, I dropped out of college and moved in a week later.

Like Joan Didion, I moved to New York in summer, when I was twenty years old. I slept with the sun on my face while my mother drove. But in late afternoon, the sun became too yellow and too hard to ignore, awakening me on the Williamsburg Bridge. I opened my eyes just in time to read "Brooklyn—Like No Other Place in the World," and the juxtaposition of the filthy water and brick apartment buildings and plants on fire escapes and men on construction sites and clear broad sky exhilarated me, made my body tingle. A skittish feeling struck me at my core, alerting me that I was really *going*. This skittish feeling lingered inside me for months. My mother says it was exactly like when she dropped me off on my first day of preschool—I was so amped up that I didn't turn to wave and watch her car drive off. My brother and I skipped off to thrift stores, and he helped me pick out a flowered curtain to hang up as the door to my new bedroom. I thought my room was beautiful.

That first summer—the summer of 2006—I lived on the streets of the city. By that I mean I was only at home for my four hours of sleep. I moved in on June 2, and one night in early August, my brother said to me, "This is the first night we're not out doing something since you got here." Everyone I met during my first three years in New York seemed exceptionally exotic and exciting. The cokehead bartenders, cute baristas, and hipster girls. The guys with long hair and borderline personality disorder. I fell in love with almost anyone who looked my way.

When a friend who was not living in New York City visited me, she watched me get dressed one morning, smirked, and said, "Who are you, Johnny Cash?" Black jeans, black boots, black sweater, black leather jacket. My best New York friends and I wore each other's leather jackets. We were always accidentally wearing the wrong one home. Leather jackets in dark bars tend to get mixed up. We shared our black jeans and lace-up Doc Martens and black riding boots too. The subway in the wintertime always cracked me up: fifty shades of black. My brother left New York for Berlin, and when he came back he was against the all-black fashion statements that he once adhered to. "Color is . . . nice," he said to me on a subway platform after surveying the scene. "It's okay to wear color." But black was slimming, black was enigmatic and ninja-like.

We ran around the city like street rats. A lover once told me not to get in his bed with my "street clothes" on. "You get in here in your jeans and boots and track dog shit and who knows what the fuck else," he said.

I'm not saying we were dirty, exactly, but grooming wasn't too important. We were never home straightening our hair. Grooming was trading leather jackets and jeans. Grooming was going to Sephora and using and stealing their lipsticks that claimed to be the color of "Brooklyn." Grooming was cutting each other's bangs in dark bars. Grooming was stealing the eye cream of a lover's girlfriend. Grooming was buying leggings at that trashy, cheap chain, Strawberry. Grooming was buying a thong at Forever 21 while coked up out of our skulls because we had plans to have anal sex that night. Plus, how clean could you really be when you lived in apartments where you never knew when the hot water, heat, and plumbing would be out?

If I wanted a metaphor for my life in New York in my early twenties, it would be this: in 2008, the opportunity had arrived for me to finally go to the dentist. I worked as the manager of a jewelry store and I now had dental insurance. My boss was on my back about going to the dentist. Not that I had fucked-up teeth— she just always worried about me, pushed me, and mothered me. So she made me this dentist appointment way in advance, and she talked about it every day. I had the day off from selling ass-loads of jewelry to the women of the West Village. I never had days off, not even Christmas. I woke up that morning where I was living, on Audubon Avenue in Washington Heights, put on my Johnny Cash clothes, and marched to the 181st Street station. Hopped on the A train. I was a bit early, so I went to the Strand to see my friend Skye on her break. We went to this hole-in-the-wall bar (that's all people did on their breaks at the Strand—drank, seri- ously—they called it "liquid lunch") and sat outside in the court- yard. I told Skye about my dentist appointment. But instead of going to the dentist, I ordered another whiskey and soda. And when Skye went back to the Strand, I ordered yet another and kept writing in my journal and texting and decided that it was too late to go to the dentist. I left the bar and walked around the East Village. The Lowes Village multiplex on Third Avenue caught my eye. The first *Sex and the City* movie was playing. Next thing I knew, I walked into the theater, buying not one pack of candy but *two* (Milk Duds and Whoppers) I munched as I watched the movie. I lied to my boss when she asked how my dentist appoint- ment went. "No cavities!" I told her.

I had this thing for strangers—the stranger the better—for train wrecks, and for grit. I liked the dirty parts of cities, though I didn't realize that then. I wanted to be as out of my element as I could be. I wanted to talk to everyone and anyone. I sat on bar stools for hours.

My friends from upstate were off at college while I was liv- ing in New York, but I was learning too, just different things.

Plumbing, for example. I learned that there is a website called Fix a Toilet. I learned how to be away from home, how to read maps, how to be lost and find my way home. I learned how to make lattes and how to waitress. I learned what I liked in bed, how to come. How to feed myself, how to pay bills, how to cope with unrequited love, how to work for micromanaging bosses. How to ride a bike in traffic and how to live on thirty cents a day (buy bagels on Grand Street, at the bakery with moldy wedding cakes in the window). I learned that coffee is your friend and cocaine that looks like baby formula is not. I learned how to cope when a lover commits suicide. New York City during my college years was like being enrolled in Heartbreak, Sex, and Death 101.

I was unlearning things, too. Unlearning how to drive, unlearning what was acceptable and unacceptable behavior. Forgetting to look for doors on my bedrooms before signing leases. Forgetting how to keep my voice down. Forgetting how to relax. Forgetting that bathtubs were a real thing. Forgetting what moderation was. Forgetting that I wasn't stuck there, that there were actually other places to live. I moved and moved. I thought I'd stay everywhere forever. I lived on North Sixth Street for one year, moving next to India Street in Greenpoint. After I came home one night to cops and a crumbling fire escape, my apartment condemned, I was left homeless for one week. I moved in with a friend in Washington Heights and ended up in Inwood, the very last stop on the A train. "The girl that never wanted to leave North Sixth Street lives in *Inwood*!" my friends laughed.

NEW YORK PUSHES YOU AND MOVES YOU ALONG, TESTING YOUR endurance, daring you to quit at any time. I moved the same things over and over: My three-pound purple weights and my eight-pound lime-green ones. My sunflower mirror. My pink-and-white polka-dot sheets.

Eventually, I did remember there were other places to live. I was getting tired and I was only twenty-three. The sun was too harsh, yet I became even paler each year. I grew uncomfortable looking people in the eye. I felt paranoid around people, and whenever someone closed their eyes on the subway, I assumed they were insane. I wanted to leave because even after dozens and dozens of times walking into a store and telling myself I would *not* come out with something black, I always walked out of the store with at least fifty dollars' worth of black clothes. When my father visited, he'd look at me and say, "Because black's how you feel on the inside, right?" I remember being at a café in Greenpoint, listening to a Belle and Sebastian song: "The city was losing it's ap-pea-ea-eal . . ."

I was terrified that I would come to hate New York. I never wanted to be like any of the buzz-killing, jaded people I met who hated it. They'd been there too long. I'd thought of Didion's essay "Goodbye to All That" as a how-to. Like *New York City for Dummies* or something. I read into it that Didion advised leaving New York before turning twenty-eight. I was going to learn from her mistake; I wasn't going to be like her and "stay too long at the Fair." I wouldn't be like the guys at the Strand who didn't know how to smile anymore. No way. I was going to get out alive at twenty-three and go experience other fairs.

Part of it was that I couldn't sustain my "groovy lifestyle," to borrow a term Lena Dunham's parents use in the first episode of HBO's television show *Girls*. My lifestyle was definitely groovy and at some points felt unhealthy. Though I'd grown up playing beauty parlor in the woods with berries and playing in the stream behind our house, I'd forgotten about all that. I rarely went upstate anymore and was a slave to the pavement, making choices that sometimes scared me.

"Totally unbalanced groovy lifestyle" is probably a more precise term for how I began to feel in New York. There was a subtle beating, a ticktock in my chest telling me I should probably leave. I began to wonder what my life would be like if I didn't have to jiggle the handle on the constantly running toilet after I flushed. When I took the time to listen hard enough, I could hear the subtle ticking of a clock inside my body, gently telling me to leave.

But I wanted to leave New York on my own terms. So I didn't leave after my apartment was condemned or after the guy I loved hanged himself. I didn't leave when I was unemployed for three months. I left of my own volition, on my own schedule. I chose a random date in late April and moved back to Hudson. I wanted to leave New York on a high note. The night before I left, I sat at Lucy's bar on Avenue A with my best friend. We were both wearing Indian headdresses and drinking whiskey. We were on our way to a sexual adventure—we had agreed to go have a fivesome with the guy I was seeing, his best friend, and his younger brother. We'd just snorted a bag of cocaine at our friend's apartment—a forty-year-old ex-dominatrix, a British cokehead. She lived on Avenue B near Seventh Street, above the Moroccan restaurant Casimir. We went over there to get cocaine and tips and confidence on how to have an orgy. What I'm getting at is this: I didn't feel safe around myself in New York. I never knew what I was going to do.

———

LAST YEAR I MOVED TO PORTLAND, OREGON. SLOWLY HERE I am growing out of my restlessness and finding balance. I'm not sure what it is, but I know I cannot live there forever the way I could live in New York.

"Time passes, that's for sure," Eileen Myles writes in *Chelsea Girls*. I remember when one of my friends informed me that the formula of seven dog years to one human year is inaccurate. "What it is," he patiently clarified, while alphabetizing the dollar carts in front of the Strand, "is that one human year in *New York City* equals seven human years." I suppose that explains why having lived there three years felt like twenty-one.

There's a distinct change, an evolution, that happens between twenty and twenty-seven. In my early twenties, I felt that my life could be one big experiment, and in my midtwenties I am coming to terms with the fact that, no, my life is actually *my life*. Five years after leaving New York City for Hudson, life has taken me to Portland, Oregon. This past Election Day, as I went about babysitting and writing, meeting someone for coffee, the sky darkened and the memory of the Election Day four years prior crept in. I couldn't help but note the ways in which my life had changed. Four years before, in 2008, after work, I took the subway back to my apartment on Seaman Avenue and waited for my lover to join me. I had a large room, windows and walls I'd painted yellow myself. My lover came over. I had this tiny little bed and also a futon. We took both mattresses off and put them on the floor. We had sex off and on for a couple of hours. Then, from the streets we heard the cheering. Obama won! Obama won while we were having sex in New York. We declared it a holiday.

I was not having sex this year while Obama got reelected. I was sitting on the couch in my friend's apartment in southeast Portland.

I moved to Portland because after visiting a bunch of times, I fell in love with it. Not the same love I felt for New York: "The way you love the first person who ever touches you and you never love anyone quite that way again" (Didion). But it was love nonetheless. I moved to Portland because I can afford to work less here and write more, a very important thing for my well-being. I moved to Portland because over time it seemed I had more friends here than in New York. When I visit New York City now, I have nowhere to sleep. We've all moved on, but I don't allow myself to think about it too much because it breaks my heart. New York City gave me everything it had, and greedy as I was for experience, I took and took. I carry with me every day the gift of the lessons New York taught me.

There have been nights when I've clutched the pillow in tears, grief-stricken for New York. The other day I was waiting impatiently for the bus and found myself walking into the street and leaning the top half of my body out even farther to look for the bus. The movement felt so familiar, and then I realized it was what I would do while waiting on a subway platform. I feel New York inside me when I talk too loudly, when I'm in line for coffee and feel rageful and restless, when I ask inappropriate and personal questions of strangers. When I say, "Oh, I walked," and people look at me quizzically and say, "That's a *long* walk."

I can't say if I'll stay in Portland because I'm in my midtwenties and still floundering around. When you tell people you're going to leave New York, they like to tell you, "New York will always be here." But it won't always be there. My insides ache when I think, "I will never be twenty again and moving to Williamsburg with the sun on my face." So I don't let myself think it.

I wear a bright red winter coat this year, and I feel that if I had a dentist appointment, I could make it there. On Friday and Saturday nights, I've traded binge drinking for yoga teacher training. I work at Powell's City of Books, and sometimes I pretend I'm at the Strand because somewhere deep in my gut, I long for my Johnny Cash clothes, my irreverent best friends, the whiskey I could keep down, the hellish sun, and the debilitating snow—the groovy lifestyle that I could once sustain. Now I decline cocaine when it's offered (though I'm tempted) and I wear colorful clothes (but it's a challenge) and I rent apartments that have working locks and doors, but none of them charm me the way my New York City squalors did.

I used to think that every eventful thing that happened in my life would feel as good as moving to New York City did, that my life would be like moving to New York, over and over and over again. I know now that as with falling in love, you're lucky if it happens to you even once.

MISFITS FIT HERE

Marie Myung-Ok Lee

Even before I'd ever set foot on its teeming streets, New York City represented to me the perfect place. As in perfectly opposite of the place I was: I was nine and growing up in Hibbing, Minnesota, a rural mining town where, in winter, snowdrifts could easily engulf cars. I was bookish, introverted, the daughter of Korean immigrants. Everyone else seemed tall, blond, athletic. The center of town was the indoor hockey arena that seated hundreds. My favorite place was the tiny public library. My love of reading and solitude did not make me a particularly sought-after playmate.

The billboard that welcomes you to Hibbing boasts WORLD'S LARGEST OPEN PIT MINE!! There is little preserved to indicate Bob Dylan ever lived here, confounding the pilgrims who've driven two hundred miles straight north from the Minneapolis airport. Any and all locals of a certain age will instead cheerily recount how he was laughed off the stage at the high school talent show or suggest that he hadn't written his own songs. To the town, he wasn't a cause for celebration but a long-haired countercultural freak. My introduction to him as a child was when we sang "Blowin' in the Wind" in music class—with no adults ever mentioning that *the man who wrote it* was from our town. If you're a misfit, either you acquiesce to having your rough edges pummeled to fit the groove of conformity or you leave. Dylan left Hibbing almost immediately after that disastrous performance at the high school and headed for—where else?—New York.

For me, I'd similarly marked New York as my future destination—I'd already decided to become a writer, and that's where the writers went. Logical.

Taking William Saroyan's advice about how to become a writer—"You write, man, you write"—I wrote. In my senior year of high school, my essay "Volunteer Workers Are Not Schmucks!" was accepted by *Seventeen*. "Schmuck" was a word I picked up from *MAD* magazine, unaware of its origins in the word "penis." The lack of Jews in our town (again, Robert Zimmerman's family was one of the few) left me unacquainted with Yiddish, yet here I was already speaking like a New Yorker. My editor gently changed the title to "Volunteer Work Does Pay Off!"

It is strange to think you can have a spiritual home even before you have ever been there. But some places are so iconic—the Taj Mahal, Paris, the moon—it is possible to know them from afar. That was New York for me. When I arrived, everything was instantly familiar. What people are most apt to complain about—the bustle and chaos—both excited and soothed me. I didn't like the urine smells, the near suffocation by crowds, the unbearably hot subway cars covered with lurid graffiti. But that was also a symptom that the place was chockablock with *people*. What it was, I realized, was the teeming number of human stories being pushed right into my face—a cornucopia from the muse, the freedom to observe unobserved. This environment doesn't exist in a small town, where you never escape surveillance.

When I was out and about in Hibbing, curtains would swish aside, Vincent Price eyes peering out. Was it small-town snoopiness or the dreaded invisible letter *A* (being Asian in a white town)? Once, when my sister and I went to play at the house of a little girl we knew from church, she started closing the electric garage door on top of us when she saw us, saying: "My mother told me I'm not supposed to play with you!" *Asian*, I could only conclude.

In New York, being Korean American would be just part of who I was, along with single female writer, recent college grad, cat owner. Ironically, being among such diversity allowed me to seek out others of my various tribes: writers and Asian Americans. I even ended up cofounding the Asian American Writers' Workshop, many of us also former midwesterners. Hating being singled out for being Asian elsewhere, we could choose to identify as such in New York. And, ironically, with Korean groceries starting to dot the Upper West Side, the owners would sometimes chide me for not speaking Korean; in New York, sometimes, I wasn't Korean *enough*. A former premed student who majored in economics, I had a day job at an investment bank. Therefore, I didn't live in a garret or with tons of roommates. A Wall Street salary allowed me one of those 1970s cookie-cutter high-rises, across the street from the Merkin Concert Hall, the name I secretly smiled at every day (look up "merkin" if you haven't read *Valley of the Dolls*). The apartment was a studio sloppily bisected by a fake wall to make it into a one-bedroom. It made the space smaller, but I liked having another room to go into. The "view" was a close-up of the Chinese consulate, a similarly featureless brick building. Tower Records (now defunct) blocked out any aspirational sun, so that even on the brightest days, the best I'd get was a pencil-thin shaft of light moving through the interstice between the buildings, not enough to sustain even an air plant. Instead, I got a cat, who spent all day snoring on the printer.

On weekends, I wrote, often straight through the day. I found I longed to look into the distance while writing. The longest view I had was straight down, six stories into the Chinese consulate's courtyard, where people would be walking in endless circles as if they were in prison.

Something about having that first New York City apartment made suffering fun. Maybe not fun but novel, a sacrificial rite of passage, the way medical residents have to stay up all night for days at a time. It had been almost comical, the logistics of containing the necessities of daily life in two shallow closets, then trying to make the only-in-New-York decisions, such as determining which cleaning supplies were attractive enough to remain out (vacuum) and which needed to be hidden (bucket, mop, and rubber gloves).

I had moved to New York with an inchoate sense that writers went there and then stuff happened. Writing-wise, the straightforward transaction—write, get paid, make a living—that I'd envisioned given my early *Seventeen* success turned out to be more complicated. The alumni contacts at magazines that I'd been given by the college career office all rebuffed me. At the investment bank, I earned ample money with handsome benefits, but the work left me so exhausted I understood the logic of seeking a no-think job like waitressing. I was waking up at 4:30 AM just to get in a solid hour of writing before heading off to my job where a misplaced decimal point could mean disaster. I was a terrible employee but also a stunted writer. While my e-banking peers were applying to Harvard Business School, I continued to write. But on a practical level, while I occasionally did a small nonfiction piece for *Seventeen*, for which I received twenty-five dollars, I couldn't even get journals that didn't pay to take my fiction. During those early years, the highest-paying gig I scored was a free dinner for winning a writing contest at *West Side Weekly*, describing my travails at the DMV. My first short story publication was still a decade away; by then I was so accustomed to rejection, I reflexively threw away the acceptance letter, only later to dig it out of the trash—*Wait, did it really say, "We would be happy to publish—"?*

I still wrote. I even finished a novel. And what had begun as mild distaste for my job at the august Goldman Sachs became full-bore loathing. But it brought in the money and allowed me to stay in New York, where I still held out hope that proximity to the literary world might engender its affection for me. I acquired an unexpected in when my boyfriend (now husband) followed me to New York one year later and won a job as an editorial assistant at a venerable publishing house. To make up for the poverty-line salary ($13,000), assistants often received invitations to literary events. One of my favorites was a book party at the now-defunct Mars Bar in the East Village for a literary journal called *Between C and D*, where we sat in the semidark as an author read, accompanied by a screeching flute.

At a more sedate PEN event, I was standing in line to get a book signed by two authors I loved. The signing broke up before they got to me, and Author Number 1 said the equivalent of "Fuck off, kid," while Number 2 actually took a minute to chat with me. When I tremulously mentioned that I'd written a novel, she said I should send her twenty pages.

As improbable as it seems, that is how I found my first agent. Not only that, Author Number 2 has become a good friend, thus confirming that the daily slog of living in New York—the crowds, my long commute to Wall Street, the lack of space, the heaviness of bags of kitty litter—could pay off.

IN YOUR TWENTIES, YOU ALWAYS SECRETLY THINK YOU'RE THE one person who's never going to grow old, your evidence being that the next day you're not old, or the next or the next—ta-da! But one day, you're thirty, and no matter how well preserved you look, chronological limitations begin to become apparent. At thirty I was a published novelist, had sold an op-ed to the *New York Times*, had done a few teaching gigs—and I was also very tired.

Goldman Sachs had to plunder the US economy without me. I'd quit to write full-time and found my new life still kept me on a frantic treadmill: paying for rent, food, utilities *plus* my own Social Security taxes. And no more luxury medical insurance where I actually *made* money every time I went to see the dentist, no more free Wall Street travel clinic where you could get your shots for dengue fever and prophylactic antibiotics for your trip to Cozumel. Now I had a high-deductible catastrophic plan paid out of pocket that dissuaded me from ever seeking medical help for anything short of losing an extremity. To make up for the inevitable shortfalls, I established a small word-processing and editing business from my apartment, as well as a job reading submissions for *Ladies' Home Journal's* "Helpful Hints" column. Even income from three sources wasn't enough; I returned to work part-time for another investment bank.

My personal life was also starting to shift. The idea I'd had at age nine of life in New York—cat, tiny apartment, lots and lots of writing—turned out to be eerily accurate. But its sustainability came into question. Because my building was a singleton's warehouse—almost all studios and one-bedrooms—as soon as people had children, they moved out, most of them directly to Westchester or Jersey, leaving the child-free to age alone. Given the building's proximity to Lincoln Center and Juilliard, there were musicians and actors who, you could tell, had begun full of youth and potential and were now bittering past the ingenue parts and prodigy stages, realizing that after they had sacrificed space, sanity, fertility, and whatnot in pursuit of their art, New York was not going to keep up its half of the Faustian bargain.

I knew I would always write, but I wasn't sure I wanted to end up like my neighbor, an older man named Vincent, who slowly went batty as his aging brain oxidized: yelling at me for allegedly not saying hi to him moments after I did, leaving his door open at all hours, which also meant I could see he often didn't leave the apartment for weeks. He seemed to have no discernible relatives or friends or outside activities besides procuring the minimum for biological survival. Sun, rain, snow: the days marched on by, his relentless routine—and mine. One day, the clock ran out for Vincent. Nothing violent, just whatever battery that had been animating him ran out.

After a dozen years, I had a hankering if not for open spaces then for something new. The exigencies of my current novel, which was set in Korea, drove me to apply for a Fulbright to do research.

I won the Fulbright and believed my leaving New York to be temporary. My plan was to spend the next academic year in Korea, come back, and resume writing and life as it was before. Life, however, had other plans. My boyfriend (who selflessly agreed to take the cat) was now my fiancé. I was just as adamant about my writing career but becoming less rigid about where to conduct it. We wedged our wedding in between my leaving for Seoul and Karl's first job as a professor at a college in Ohio. Somehow, in this short time, my mother-in-law was diagnosed with pancreatic cancer. I hadn't even fully unpacked in Seoul before I flew back from Korea to take care of her until she died, a few weeks later. Then my new husband had two cats to take care of and no wife. It was a long year, at the end of which we received the wonderful news that he'd been chosen for a job at our alma mater, Brown.

We inherited one of Karl's family cars, an aged but sturdy Jetta, and I remember an odd sense of relief as we drove my stuff from the Upper West Side north to Providence. No more ridiculous humidity in summer! A yard! Being by the ocean! And because we'd both gone to Brown, the place was already familiar and manageable. It was a wonder, the small stuff, like driving to the grocery store and stocking up heedlessly, instead of mentally calculating how much one could stand to carry.

We bought a house. It was a modest four-square, but our New York friends marveled at the size. There was a single-car garage for the Jetta and even a pizza-slice of a yard. This was the early 2000s, when most of our friends had also left New York, either priced out by the beginning of the hedge funders' era or smoked out by the devastation of 9/11. Even our most stalwart friend, Gordon, who lived in a tiny apartment not far from mine, a place so small he slept in a loft and kept books in his unused stove, gave up and went to graduate school in, of all places, Indiana.

It was an end of an era, of my twenties, of my youth, but also of much of my searching anxiety: What would the future hold? Would I succeed as a writer? Would I get married? As I headed into my fourth decade, I finally realized what would happen would happen, whether I worried about it or not. I enjoyed my new outlook in the easy yet circumscribed life of a college town. I began to associate anxious or harried feelings with New York, where anything could and would happen at any time—but in a bad way—as opposed to Providence, where nothing much seemed to ever happen at all.

I didn't miss New York. We had a child with medical issues, and treatments and driving him from doctor to doctor consumed a decade. When he was stable enough that I could travel, I could go into New York for the day on the train and be back in the early evening. One year, I judged a literary contest whose gala celebration was held at the Marriott Marquis in Times Square. The crowds were so thick, I got stuck in them like quicksand. Once I staggered into my room, there was still no peace: the crazy blinking NIKON CAMERA sign still invaded the space with its red neon light, even through the blackout curtains. This was all way too fast, annoying, unsustainable, right?

Actually, as with the addict who still dreams of the lingering taste of the forbidden, that upswelling feeling—of happiness, of unobserved observation, of the strangest kind of normalcy— came back with a rush, even staying in the tourist trap that is

Times Square. Yes, I had quit New York, but it hadn't quit me. I still carried around those feelings like a magnet that became reactivated every time I returned. But I had a child now, a teaching job, a house, and a community. New York was for the dreamers, the unattached, mobile types.

Act II: an opportunity for jobs in New York, for both my husband and me, came seemingly out of the blue. At first, we categorically dismissed it. It was going to be too hard on our son, now twelve. To prove it to ourselves, we brought him down for an interview at one of the specialized schools for the disabled and waited for the stress and endless tantrums. To our surprise, he didn't tantrum, not once. In his own unique way, he found the chaos oddly soothing. He lost his phobia of dogs in a day. He has severe cognitive impairments, so I know he didn't pine for New York or even know what it was. But he wasn't unhappy, and that's something because he often seems very, very unhappy. Could it be that New York might be a destination for him, the way it was for me?

Reader, we moved back.

MANHATTAN, ALWAYS OUT OF REACH

Ann Hood

"**Y**ou can go anywhere you want," my father told me, "except New York City."

It was 1973. I was sixteen years old and had my life savings—eight hundred dollars earned from modeling for our local department store—burning a hole in my bank account. Summer loomed. I'd ditched my boyfriend of two years, and now I was ready for an adventure.

When I approached my father with my cockeyed plan of taking my money and beginning what I hoped would be a lifetime of globe-trotting, New York City hadn't even occurred to me. I had palm trees on my mind. Sandy beaches. Sailboats and balmy nights. Boys. To me then, New York City existed in Doris

Day–Rock Hudson movies. Women wore pillbox hats, cute pajamas, bobbed hair. Everyone worked in a skyscraper. Men acted goofy; women whipped them into shape.

"Go to New York City, and you'll be grounded for life," my father continued. "People get murdered there. Or worse."

"Worse than murdered?" I said, unable to imagine what that might mean.

"That's right. And young girls are especially vulnerable."

I nodded, suddenly very interested in New York City.

"Do you understand me?" my father said with his *I mean business* glare.

I slid a brochure I'd picked up from the travel agency at the mall across the table to him.

"How about here?" I asked him.

The pink sand beaches of Bermuda glistened on the glossy cover.

My father smiled. "Perfect," he said.

For the next several years, I saved my money for those summer trips. Nassau? Okay with my father, who somehow missed that they'd just had a violent civil war. Rio? Sounded great to my father, who had no idea that crime there was higher than in New York City. Off I went, navigating pickpockets, street curfews, poverty. What, I wondered, could possibly be going on in New York City that was more dangerous, more threatening than all this? And, of course, like anyone who is told no often enough, I went to find out.

—

My first trip to New York City, when I was seven, was a whirlwind of Macy's, the Empire State Building, and club sandwiches at a diner. On a whim, my parents took us there for the day, and my strongest memory is of revolving doors. It seemed to me then that to enter anywhere in Manhattan, you had to step into one and spin. One night in college, my friends and I decided to drive to New York City. None of us had ever really been there, and so we drove into Times Square and, terrified by the porn shops and hooded drug dealers, turned around and drove home. Another college trip by bus took me to MOMA and then safely back to Rhode Island. That was it.

Until the November morning in 1982 when I boarded a flight in San Francisco and met the guy in 47F who was moving to New York that very day. I was a flight attendant, and even though I flew out of JFK, I lived in Boston, commuting by airplane to work. When I got stuck or had an early morning check-in, I crashed on my cousin's couch in his fifth-floor walk-up in Greenwich Village. Nothing I saw there enticed me to move to Manhattan. But that guy in 47F changed my mind. On our first date, we walked from his East Village apartment to the Riviera Café across town, the November wind making us cold enough to have to hold hands to stay warm.

I could see what my father didn't like. We had to sidestep homeless people who lined the sidewalks. The graffiti covered subways smelled like urine and unwashed bodies. Panhandlers, drug dealers, drug addicts, scam artists, and muggers crowded the streets. There was noise—traffic, shouting, horns, boom boxes. What surprised me was how my father had known that I would be seduced by the city and all it offered up to me.

On the walk back to 47F's apartment, I turned to him and, surprising both of us, announced: "I'm moving here."

"When?" he said, his brown eyes twinkling.

"Next week."

Always impulsive, always someone who leapt before she looked, the next week I found myself squatting in a half-empty apartment in my cousin's building on West Fourth Street. Some of my friends thought I'd moved for a guy. And they were partially right, I suppose. But what I realized that afternoon I spent walking in the cold, dirty city was that I had outgrown my life so far: the pretty seaside town where I'd lived with my springer spaniel, sailing and drinking oversized Cape Codders; the neat brownstone-lined streets of Boston, crowded with people in Izod shirts the colors of sherbet; the familiar roads of my hometown, with its sad empty mills and triple-decker houses.

But Manhattan seemed to open its filthy arms to me that day and beckon. I could not tell the Empire State Building from the Chrysler Building or uptown from downtown. I didn't know east from west or streets from avenues. I only knew that, despite my father's warnings and fears, I had finally found the place I belonged.

———

My first apartment was at 228 Sullivan Street, in a former convent painted pink, its Caribbean exterior a sharp contrast to all the grimy black around it. The day I moved in, I boldly left my 300-square-foot studio and walked the maze of Greenwich Village. The guy from 47F was going to show up that night, so the entire day stretched out before me without obligation or purpose. I wandered into Three Lives bookstore to browse, into Caffe Reggio for a cappuccino, into the Third Street Bazaar and the Grand Union and every tiny store that sold earrings or posters or fruit or magazines. At some point on that journey, it felt as if all my cells settled into place, as if my body had shifted, rearranged itself, and I became exactly who I was supposed to be.

I will never leave here, I thought that June afternoon. That thought repeated itself almost daily as my first summer moved along. It was a very hot summer, relentlessly so. I would go to the Grand Union supermarket on Bleecker Street and stand in the frozen food section to cool off. Or I would ride the Staten Island ferry for a nickel round-trip and stand at the front each way to catch a breeze thick with East River stench. On the Fourth of July, I joined the throngs on the closed FDR Drive to watch fireworks. *I will never leave here,* I thought as the neon colors exploded over the river.

That fall, I left Sullivan Street for another sublet at 320 West 23rd Street. I got a cat I named Daphne, and as I sat on my futon writing stories in a notebook, she perched on the windowsill and watched the pigeons through the iron grate there. One day she jumped down and landed with an odd thud. As soon as I glanced up, I saw what I should have noticed sooner: Daphne was pregnant, had come to me already pregnant. Within a week, she gave birth to a litter of six kittens in my only closet. That same week I bought a co-op at 77 Bleecker Street, and as soon as I could move them I took a taxi there with a box of kittens, Daphne, and my trash bag of clothes. A U-Haul met us there, filled with my belongings from my former life.

I had only lived in New York City for a little over a year, but it felt like a lifetime already. When I opened the boxes I had carefully packed and labeled, what I found inside seemed to belong to a stranger. The blue-flowered couch I'd saved for years earlier looked out of place now; the brass bed with its red-and-blue sheets and matching comforter made me cringe. How could I have changed so much so quickly? My clothes, bought at a vintage store called Cheap Jack's, hung only briefly beside the winter coat I'd worn in Boston and Polo sweaters I used to collect, before I packed up everything from my old life and put it all out on the sidewalk. That winter, I didn't have a coat. Instead, I bought a black motorcycle jacket and a scarf from a street vendor. My uniform. *Me*.

———

I WILL NEVER LEAVE HERE, I THOUGHT EVERY DAY.

Yet all I did was leave. Again and again, my heart breaking each time I watched Manhattan recede.

The first time I moved away, I decided to follow my heart to live with a man in Washington, DC. He rented us a house with a screened-in back porch in a nondescript neighborhood near Georgetown. From the minute I stepped inside, I knew I had made a mistake. But I'd given up everything to try this, so try I did. I got a car after years of subways and walking. I searched for the kinds of places I'd grown to love back in New York, the perfect bookstore and café and restaurant, the vintage stores and one-of-a-kind shops. Surely, they were out there. I was in a big city, wasn't I? But everything I found fell short. The entire city felt off somehow. *I* felt off. I would spend entire afternoons flopped on the bed, a pillow over my face, trying to figure out how I could find my way back to where I belonged. Finally, my father convinced me to just do it. Leave, he told me.

On a walk that night with the man I had followed there, I announced that I was going back to New York. "Well then," he said, "let's get married." Confused, I told him I was leaving, moving away. He nodded. "Okay," he said, "but let's get married." And just like that I found myself back in Manhattan, in a sublet apartment in the Ansonia on the Upper West Side, with a husband.

A husband who hated New York.

As soon as I'd happily settled in, he was looking for a way out. Every night he offered me a new city or town. Portland, Maine. Nyack, New York. Montclair, New Jersey. Boston. Or Boxborough, Massachusetts. Westport, Connecticut. No, I'd say. No, no, no. When the sublet fell through, we found ourselves homeless and at an impasse. I was touring lofts in Tribeca; he was house hunting in Westchester County. "Can't we just give someplace else a try?" he asked as we stood in front of a white house a few blocks from the main street in Katonah, a suburb just an hour's train ride from the city.

"If I hate it," I said, hating it already, "we move back to Manhattan."

The deal struck, I found myself lost again. I took that train into the city as often as I could, wandering the streets of the East Village, crying. Meeting friends for lunch and crying. Sitting on the train back to Katonah, crying. There, I'd drive the beautiful country roads wondering what was wrong with me. Why couldn't I love it out here? In no time, I was back on the bed with a pillow over my face, making an escape plan. "Just leave," my father said again.

"I'm moving back to the city," I announced over dinner. "I hate it here."

The man I'd married looked upset. But then he brightened and offered me yet another option. "How about Brooklyn?"

I took it.

BACK THEN, NO ONE REALLY WANTED TO LIVE IN BROOKLYN. Now, when I see twenty-somethings eagerly leaving Manhattan for Brooklyn, I can't help but remember how our Manhattan friends wouldn't even come out to Park Slope for dinner. We moved into the third floor of a brownstone on Montgomery Place, and although I wasn't completely happy with my latest compromise, I wasn't miserable either. Now that I was near enough to Manhattan to feel at home, now that my cells could settle into place again, I realized that although our geographic preferences differed, it was actually the marriage that wasn't making me happy.

I didn't need my father to tell me what to do this time. I was going to leave my marriage, and when I did, I was going back to Manhattan. We carefully divided everything in half, and with my half I moved into a skinny duplex on Leroy Street. Just as quickly as those other places felt wrong, this one felt right. I would lie in bed on Sunday mornings with my fat *New York Times* and NPR playing, my cats on my feet, and the sounds of the city outside my window, content.

I will never leave here, I'd think.

And then, yet again, I left.

———

"YOU ARE GOING TO MOVE TO PROVIDENCE AND MARRY ME AND have a baby," the handsome man told me.

I laughed. "You're crazy. I'm never leaving New York."

Six months later, his prophecy came true.

This time, with a baby on the way, I didn't have time to feel miserable. I was too busy being terrified, excited, confused. When that baby was born, my crying began. I didn't know anybody except my handsome husband, who went off to work every day. So I strapped Sam into his car seat and went to New York. All the time. We slept on friends' sofas. We ate at Benny's Burritos and the Cowgirl Hall of Fame. I agreed to teach writing workshops at NYU and lived a half-life in Manhattan and a half-life in Providence. Whenever my handsome husband and I fought, I reminded him how much I missed New York. But this time, there was no going back. Not really.

I had a baby and then another baby. Even spending half my time there became difficult. Eventually, I stopped teaching at NYU. I made friends in Providence. I built a life. A nice life. A happy one.

Until the day my five-year-old daughter died suddenly from a virulent form of strep, and in that instant, nothing was the same. The young woman who had moved to New York City and who had spent so much time trying to get back there seemed distant and foreign to me. My world became the walls of my bedroom. Beyond it lay too many painful memories. Sparkles from Grace's art projects still littered the floor. Her laundered clothes waited to be put away. The contents of her backpack—a perfectly filled-in *Weekly Reader*, a Ramona Quimby book, a paper on which she'd counted by tens all the way to five hundred—and her shoes tossed by the door and her ballet bag and her lunch box, all of it was out there. New York didn't matter. Nothing mattered.

I locked myself in my bedroom and thought, *I will never leave here.*

———

TIME PASSES. IT DOES. THE FOG OF GRIEF LIFTS, UNBELIEVABLY. And when it did, I found that I needed to redefine myself. Or at least, to try to remember who I had been and who I would be from now on.

When I was invited to teach in New York, I asked my husband and son what they thought. Maybe they knew me then better than I knew myself. Do it, they told me. I rented an apartment on Barrow Street, and two nights a week I stayed there. I did it partially for convenience but also to reclaim that piece of myself. It didn't feel like a half-life this time. Instead, New York reminded me who I was.

I was a woman who liked to walk the streets of New York City, fast and for hours.

I liked to eat Vietnamese sandwiches standing up or to walk across town to try a new dive restaurant. I liked to spend hours in the Strand Bookstore or in a museum or even waiting in line for half-price theater tickets. All those years ago, my cells had settled into place that first time I left my Sullivan Street apartment. Now I was getting in touch with that girl I was—optimistic, open to anything, wide-eyed and willing. Grief had taken that part of me. It had turned me fearful and sad. But that winter in New York, that fear began to crumble. I understood that it would never leave me entirely. Nor would the grief. But somehow, I could open my heart again.

Even though I've kept an apartment in the city ever since that sublet on Barrow Street, my heart still breaks a little every time I leave. And it lifts every time I go back. My New York, no longer filthy or crime ridden, still opens its arms to me and takes me in when I need it. Even though my father believed it was a dangerous place, what I know now is that to me it is a place of comfort. It is a place of discovery. It is the place where I found my own true self, again and again and again.

FONDLY, MARIE

Lisa Ko

At the San Francisco Office of Vital Records, I paid ten dollars for a copy of the death certificate of a woman I had never met.

It was September 2005. A few weeks before, I had broken up with my boyfriend of more than a year. My roommates and I had been hosting a party; we were moving out of our house the next day. My boyfriend had given me the silent treatment again because he saw me talking to a male friend. Exhausted, I had told him it was over. The following week he emailed me a rant, ending with a line that made me gasp: "I hope you get raped to death."

We had been planning to move in together in the fall. Although I had known for months that it was the wrong decision, I had been afraid of breaking up with him. I was afraid of him.

He had never physically harmed me, but he was quick to rage in a way that frightened me.

So I shipped my belongings to my parents' house in New Jersey, gave notice at my job at a film-production company, made arrangements for work in New York City, and bought a cross-country train ticket. After five years in San Francisco, I was ready to return to New York, where I hoped he would never find me.

The morning after the party, my roommate drove me to a studio apartment on a hilly side street that I was subletting for the next month. It was the first time I had lived alone in San Francisco, and I stayed up late watching movies and dreamily looking out a little window, the downtown lights just visible behind thick swirls of fog. I read books at breakfast, bought flowers for the kitchen table.

All my life I have loved being alone. An only child, I grew up reading and writing stories while my parents worked. As an adult, some of my happiest times have been days by myself in new cities, as I wandered the streets of Tokyo and Bangkok and Paris, deciding what to do on a whim.

When I had first moved to San Francisco and hadn't yet made many friends, I spent hours riding the bus from one end of the city to another, gazing out the window with my headphones on, studying neighborhoods. Unlike New York, the streets here had yet to be filled with associations: fighting with a boyfriend in low whispers on a park bench, drinking too much at a party and eating at a slice joint on the way home. One day, I thought, the map of San Francisco will mean more than just lines on a page. But five years later, when so many lines represented memories and it seemed impossible to go out without running into someone I knew, had worked with, lived with, or dated, I fantasized about anonymity again. I started going to far-flung neighborhoods where I knew no one, in hopes of being left alone.

I called my mother and told her I had broken up with my boyfriend and was moving back to New York.

She said I must have done something to anger him, maybe I should apologize. "He'll marry someone else, and you'll be alone," she said. "You're going to be thirty in two months."

Her anxiety irritated me, but I worried, too. My roommates and friends were moving in with their boyfriends and girlfriends. Some were getting engaged. I didn't want that, yet I feared something was wrong with me for not wanting what everyone else did. It made me uncomfortable, like I became when people expressed concern that I was traveling alone.

"Won't you be lonely?" they asked.

"No," I said, but I wondered if I was lying to myself.

It was a craving for anonymity that had brought me from New York to California in the first place. I was twenty-five and had never lived anywhere but in or near New York City. I loved the city, but I didn't want to always live there without ever having lived somewhere else—temporarily, because New York was home. The West Coast was another world, curious and distant. In the span of one summer, my job ended, a two-year relationship imploded, and my apartment's lease was up. New York became too attached to heartbreak.

I booked a one-way ticket to San Francisco, packed two bags, and found a three-month sublet. At first, I was suspicious of California's beauty, still too in thrall to New York cool, its sharpness and scale. Compared to New York, San Francisco was sleepy and toy-like. Everything shut down early. Lacking a comprehensive subway system, my friends and I rode our bicycles around town like a pack of overgrown kids. When my sublet ended, I found another one, then another. I got a lease and a full-time job. After two years, flying back to San Francisco after visiting New York felt like a homecoming, almost a relief, rather than a sense of loss. After another two years, I began missing New York so bad it felt like heartbreak. Instead of feeling as if I had escaped something by leaving, I felt I was missing out by staying in California.

I had barely spent any time in San Francisco before I moved there. I first knew of it through my childhood pen pal, Marie Sasselli, a woman more than seventy years my senior.

My father had met Marie when he was a college student from the Philippines, waiting tables in a San Francisco cafeteria on his summer break. Marie accidentally left a twenty-dollar bill on the table, far too large to be a tip back then. When she returned a few hours later, my father gave the money back to her. They became friends.

She was in her late fifties at the time and had never been married or had children. Perhaps she didn't want to get married. Perhaps she didn't want to marry men. She and her "gentleman friend" took my father to Ocean Beach and Berkeley on his days off. After he returned to Utah State University and, later, when he moved to Queens and then to New Jersey, he and Marie exchanged Christmas cards.

I was eight, obsessed with the mail and looking for any excuse to send a letter, when my mother said, "Why don't you write to Marie? She's alone."

For years Marie was my most loyal pen pal, sending typewritten letters on thick pastel stationery. She sent me postcards of the Golden Gate Bridge, detailing the weather and her room in a residency hotel. These images were my knowledge of San Francisco before I moved there: bridges, fog, cable cars, voluptuous hills.

As I got older, I took longer to respond, preferring pen pals my own age. When I came home hoping to find the latest issue of *Spin* and saw one of Marie's pink envelopes instead, I would feel disappointed.

We called her once at Christmastime. She was in her room, surprised to hear from us. "Have a wonderful holiday with your family," she told me, and I thought it was strange that she didn't have a family of her own.

In 1988, when I was twelve and Marie was eighty-four, a letter I sent to her came back, marked "Attempted: Not Known." My father called but there was no answer. My parents said she might have died. I hadn't even considered that she could. I wondered who had cleaned out her room and if they had found my letters.

Now, living in my sublet, I remembered where Marie had lived: on Post Street, not far from where I was. Could she still be alive? It was unlikely; she would be 101. I went out and walked around the street but couldn't remember her address.

Which led me to the Office of Vital Records. I paid a fee; an hour later, a clerk slid me a white envelope that contained Marie's death certificate. Born January 22, 1904, died June 20, 1988. (That same summer, I had been smearing neon zinc on my nose at the town pool.) Marital status: Single. Occupation: Secretary. Marie had died in the hospital, of a heart attack. Her address had been 628 Post Street.

The death certificate offered a finality I hadn't expected. After work, I went to Post Street but couldn't find 628. I went into a restaurant and asked if there had ever been a residential hotel at 628. Nobody knew.

Three nights later, I returned to my sublet after my goodbye party. In the morning I would board the train to New York; my bags were already packed and in the hallway.

I sat at the kitchen table, watching my reflection in the window. I loved to be alone, but what if I liked it too much? What if I ended up like Marie? I studied the paintings on the walls, the flowers in their glass vase.

I had hugged my friends goodbye and cried. I would miss them, but I was also excited. Since I had broken up with my ex, I no longer worried about him lashing out at me or storming from the house at some perceived slight. To have those hours of fighting and screaming replaced by a precarious quiet felt like a gift. To have my days returned to me, to be by myself again. I was sleeping well for the first time in years.

Maybe Marie would have liked that I came looking for her, that she was still remembered. My mother had thought Marie's life was lonely and sad. But living in a hotel in downtown San Francisco didn't sound bad to me. Staying in an unhappy relationship because you were afraid you weren't strong enough to be on your own—that was lonely and sad.

I thought about the decisions Marie had made. I would never know what she had settled for, what she had insisted upon, but I knew what I would refuse to compromise.

In the morning a friend dropped me off at the Amtrak station, and as the train pulled away, I felt a giddy joy. We rolled through the Sierras, then the Rockies, and I felt my old life receding, something new unspooling.

Days passed. I transferred in Chicago. When I heard New York accents again, I knew I was home.

I moved into an apartment near the Brooklyn waterfront, painted the rooms yellow, blue, and pink. By then it was winter and so cold, with the wind howling on the streets outside, but inside my home I was warm. I was alone, so alone, and I had never been happier.

RUSSIA, WITH LOVE

Emily Gould

During the first half of 2009, I left Brooklyn to spend three months in Moscow. The city was cold, smelly, and uncomfortable, and despite some effortful hours spent shouting into the headset provided with the Rosetta Stone software I impulse-bought on the day I applied for my visa, I didn't speak the language. I had no idea what I was supposed to be doing there. One of my most vivid memories from that first trip is of eating tainted Uzbek veal-tongue salad and, as a result, coming the closest I've ever come to shitting myself in public. I managed to make it to a squat toilet outside a train station that I had to pay—God, figuring out that transaction!—an elderly woman for the privilege of using. I had a lot of bougie Brooklyn-born expectations about how things should work and how things should smell and how people should act, and I felt guilty for feeling peeved when those expectations weren't met. I felt my foreignness emphatically all the time. I never really came around to the food. It was probably the happiest I've ever been in my life.

Of course, if you'd asked me how I was feeling at the time, I would have said that I was confused and scared, insecure and angry, worried about who I'd been and who I might become. I had come there to stay with a man I loved but still didn't know very well, and some of the time we got along and other times there was a heartbreakingly vast gulf between us, exacerbated by his being comfortable in Russia, and in Russian, and fundamentally unable to imagine how it might feel not to be comfortable there at all. I was working on a book at the time, my first real book, which I'd sold based on a very brief and frankly terrible proposal, and I had no idea whether I'd be able to actually write it. My Russian boyfriend was an established writer, and I compared myself with him a lot. It was not a flattering comparison.

So I felt like a phony who might be found out at any time. I wasn't the kind of person who jetted off to Moscow for no real reason besides that there was nothing preventing me from doing so. I'd never been anywhere before: my twenties up until that point had been spent working a series of all-consuming jobs in Manhattan; my longest vacation from the city since graduating from college there had been a week spent in Delaware. I wasn't on vacation in Moscow, exactly, but I wasn't exactly working, either. I was wandering around the city and procrastinating about my book for many hours every day. I was still coasting on the burst of editorial goodwill that had floated me into the book deal, and there were a couple of easy-peasy freelance assignments that had helped me to pay for my plane ticket. One was a roundup

of Hollywood types' favorite onscreen moments from the previous year, and it was easy to do the interviews because the time
difference worked in my favor: I could procrastinate until late
in the evening, and people would be just getting to work on the
West Coast. Other than this goofy assignment and my book, I
was supposed to be writing something about my impressions of
Moscow for an oligarch-funded English-language Russian magazine; my impressions of Moscow were so stupid that even that
fluffy publication politely declined to publish them.

Nearly four years later, my impressions are still a bit confused
and confusing. After much more experience of Russia and Russians, including the Russian who brought me there in the first
place, I almost feel as though I understand the culture even less.
It took me a long time to realize, for example, that Russian people aren't mean and cold; they're just not fake. They don't pretend
to love the strangers they encounter in shops and restaurants the
way Americans do. Russians save their warmth for friends and
family and dispense it mostly in the privacy of their own homes.
This meant that no one humored me when I tried to bluff and
joke and apologize through customer service interactions. When
I ordered tea in Russian, the person taking my order would dis-
passionately ask me, in English, what size I wanted: "Smol or
lahj?" "Small," I would say, feeling cheated of an opportunity to
say one of the twenty or so words I knew off the top of my head.
(I would have gotten the case ending wrong, anyway, though.)

I was mostly alone in these wanderings, which was terrifying
at first; navigating the metro with only vague hunches about how
the station names being announced corresponded to the Cyrillic
characters on the subway map made me constantly hypervigilant

lest I end up inadvertently traveling to the Moscow equivalent of the South Bronx. My arrival coincided with the closing of an issue of the literary magazine where my boyfriend worked, and he didn't have time to do anything but point me toward various attractions. I spent my first few days in a haze of jet lag, visiting tourist attractions because I felt I had to: the Tretyakov Gallery; the impressive, forbiddingly too-perfect mall near Red Square; onion-domed churches galore. I don't remember any of these places very well, only the palm-sweaty interactions I had with ticket takers at their entrances.

My first vivid memories are of grocery shopping, which really was too complicated for me to undertake on my own because, except in the fanciest Western-style overpriced supermarkets, the various foods were kept behind counters and you have to go around asking the meat guy, the canned goods lady, the egg person, the produce mistress, et cetera, to get you what you want. In one basement-level food market near the apartment where we were staying, there was a honey counter (Russian people love honey and take it very seriously) staffed by a man in a white lab coat whom we called "the honey doctor." I wanted very badly to cook for Keith's little grandmother, Baba Ruzya; I thought she would appreciate a night off from the laborious production of the borscht, fried meatballs, and mashed potatoes that constituted our unchanging diet. Of course, when I finally did undertake a meal, producing a salty chicken soup flavored with garlic and ginger that was a highlight of my repertoire at the time, she sweetly refused to eat it, as I should have known she would. She was charmed by my efforts, which I for some reason continued to make during the remainder of my stay, but she simply did not recognize what they produced as food. In retrospect, I understand why someone who has managed to become a nonagenarian by eating nothing but borscht and meatballs would be hesitant to change her diet. Well, that's an exaggeration: she also loved pastries, candy, and the extraordinarily unappealing Russian take on ham, which is a creepy pale pinkish gray. "No, thank you. I'm not very hungry," she would say in Russian when I offered her food I'd made, and then eat an impressive pile of gray ham.

When I imagine myself during this time, I see someone who spent a lot of time blithely trying to feed the world an unappealing experimental soup despite overwhelming evidence that no one found it quite as delicious as I did. In many ways this hiatus from my life in New York, with its many competing distractions, marked the end of my oblivious youthful obnoxiousness. No one was really buying my shtick there. No one was impressed when I took yoga classes in Russian and couldn't understand anything the teacher was saying. No one indulgently smiled when I sat on the wrong bench or bagged my own produce at the grocery store; they yelled at me loudly and I had no idea what they were saying and I just stood there with a stupid American expression on my bizarrely, aberrantly un-made-up face and then made my way back to the apartment and cried about it later on in the (low-pressure) shower. No one was sympathetic to my feelings of lostness and loneliness and homesickness and pointlessness and confusion, except my boyfriend, who assured me that feeling lonely was important; loneliness would help me to write my book.

Loneliness did help me to write my book, loneliness and having no internet access in Baba Ruzya's apartment. (Well, there was one corner of the window ledge that you could occasionally get a whiff of Wi-Fi in, especially if you stood on the ledge and held your laptop aloft to get the signal, which I often did.) After a few weeks of aimless wandering into internet cafés, I woke up one morning and, without knowing exactly how or why, became a slightly different person.

Something had shifted in my brain while I slept, breathing the acrid smell of Moscow that drifted in through the always cracked window of the overheated apartment: diesel exhaust, cigarette smoke, snow and garbage and perfume. Keith made us breakfast: instant coffee made tolerable with condensed milk, buckwheat kasha fried with eggs. I did a few yoga poses in the living room while Baba Ruzya peeked in occasionally to murmur something admiring; occasionally she would walk by and give me a friendly swat on the behind. And then I sat down at my laptop, facing the window with a view of the courtyard behind the building with its dingy old playground equipment and parking lot, and I wrote "World of Blues."

I realize this doesn't sound very important or impressive. More disciplined and productive writers probably have days like this several days a week, but sadly, that was the only time in my life that I've sat down in the morning, started writing, and then stood up seven hours later feeling confident about having finished something, something real. It was Moscow, or kasha, or new love, or loneliness, or not being in New York, or it was just something that happened. That essay isn't the "best" one in my book. It might not even be in the top three. But it's an important one to me because, though I didn't think about it in these terms during that perfect, trance-like day, writing that essay—which is about a brief stint spent serving cocktails in a very bad blues bar on Bleecker Street—was the first time I realized how important it is to illuminate the subjectivity of the character who's usually hanging out at the periphery of men's stories: the waitress, the girlfriend, the living prop that male narrators project their fantasies onto. I would tell her story, which happened to be my story. The course of the rest of my life was set.

MY CITY

Dani Shapiro

1. The city was what people from New Jersey called it. The city, as if there were no other. If you were a suburban Jewish girl in the late 1970s, aching to burst out of the tepid swamp of your adolescence (synagogue! field hockey! cigarettes!), the magnetic pull of the city from across the water was irresistible. Between you and the city were the smokestacks of Newark, the stench of oil refineries, the soaring Budweiser eagle, its lit-up wings flapping high above the manufacturing plant. That eagle— if you were a certain kind of girl, you wanted to leap on its neon back and be carried away. On weekend trips into the city, you'd watch from the back seat of your parents' car for the line in the Lincoln Tunnel that divided New Jersey from New York because you felt dead on one side and alive on the other.

2. At least once or twice a month when I was in high school, I'd slip out of third-period algebra. No one noticed. I'd walk a mile to the train station in Elizabeth and board the 11:33 to Penn Station. The windows were gray with the film of cigarette smoke. You could write your name on them. The train car, largely empty. The men who worked downtown had long since commuted, and the women tended to drive or stay home. Some of my friends' mothers had never even been to the city. It was the end of the 1970s. I was fifteen, and not a soul knew my whereabouts. I disembarked in Penn Station and made my way through its urine-stained halls in my corduroys and Fair Isle sweater, trudging along in my Wallabees. North up Eighth Avenue, past strip joints, neon XXX signs, bodegas. I stopped when I reached Lincoln Center and took a moment by the fountain in the plaza, looking at the Chagalls framed by the arched windows of the Metropolitan Opera. Hungry, I continued north to 72nd Street, where I spent my allowance on a turkey, tongue, and coleslaw sandwich and a Dr. Brown's Cel-Ray soda at the Fine & Schapiro delicatessen. I imagined that I was already a woman, that I had shed Jersey, my extreme youth, like a layer of baby fat. By the end of the school day, I'd be back home, delivering monosyllabic answers to the question, "How was your day?" But secretly, I was high on the knowledge that I had done it. I had been *there*.

3. In a popular TV commercial of that era for Charlie perfume, an actress named Shelley Hack strode across the screen in her pantsuit, blonde mane flying. She was the Charlie girl—tall, urban, glamorous, on her way to important places—someone who was "kinda young, kinda now, Charlie," as the jingle went. She had it all—and why not? With the hubris of the very young, I planted both feet in my fantasy. I was the Charlie girl. My life

in New York was going to involve some sort of career in which I could wear pantsuits like that.

4. I moved to New York at nineteen, into the West 75th Street walk-up apartment of a boyfriend. The boyfriend owned a small shop on Columbus that sold South American artifacts and the peasant clothes popular with a certain urban-bohemian crowd. My father—an Orthodox Jew—threatened to disown me if I shacked up (his words) with my boyfriend. So I married him. It seemed like a fine solution. We divorced a year later. But in between—as a college student—I threw dinner parties in that brownstone apartment, making the one dish I knew how: Chicken Marbella from *The Silver Palate Cookbook*, with olives, prunes, and cinnamon, flavors I haven't liked in combination since. In photos from that time I see a round-faced girl with feathered hair (hello, Farrah), dimples, and a ring that had no business being on her finger. Our block was home to several dancers from the New York City corps de ballet whom I'd see heading to rehearsal early in the mornings, their heads small and neat, their long necks wrapped in soft scarves. I made the mistake of thinking that we were alike, these dancers and I, because we were the same age. But in fact, they were moving toward life, and I—masquerading as a happy homemaker—was drifting away from it.

5. "Kinda free, kinda wow, Charlie." Another one of the Charlie girls was an actress named Shelly Hack, who went on to briefly become one of Charlie's Angels (no relation). And then there was a model, Shelley Smith, whom I would meet many years later—in another life, a future I couldn't possibly imagine—after she had opened an egg donation agency in Beverly Hills and I was trying to have a second child. But back then, to me, she was part

of a trifecta of blondes who epitomized life among skyscrapers—a burnished, free-floating glamour that seemed, in itself, a worthy goal.

6. Divorced and twenty. How many people can claim that? For years, I erased that marriage from my life story. It was just too hard to explain—to others, to myself. But now, thirty years later, I wish I could reach back through time and shake some sense into that lost little girl. I wish I could tell her to wait, to hold on. That becoming a grown-up is not something that happens overnight, or on paper. That rings and certificates and apartments and meals have nothing to do with it. That everything we do matters. *Wait*, I want to say—but she is impatient, racing ahead of me.

7. The city. It isn't possible for me to write about the city without writing about real estate and men. From the baby-marriage, I moved on to a full-blown affair with an older married man. From a walk-up on 75th, I graduated to a duplex in the West Village and finally to an apartment on the top floor of the Dakota. The Dakota apartment looked like a dollhouse, with a string of tiny rooms, slanted ceilings, walls papered with peach and lavender Laura Ashley flowers. I ate next to nothing and drank white wine and frozen margaritas. I drank champagne with my girlfriends at Petrossian, and we charged our drinks to our parents' credit cards. I had my nails done next to Madonna, my hair blown out next to the original uptown girl, Christie Brinkley. I took back-to-back aerobics classes at Bjorkman and Martin, a cultish studio run by a compact woman with powerful thighs named Lee who taught us intricate dance steps and yelled at those who couldn't follow. When the space shuttle *Challenger* exploded over Cape Canaveral, we—all of us drenched in perspiration at that studio—held hands and said a prayer.

8. There were other apartments, other men. Chance encoun-
ters, coincidence, desires, and invitations. Another brief, failed
marriage. All before I was thirty. I was trying, flailing, failing,
in an attempt to chisel myself into a woman who existed only as
a fantasy, airbrushed, photoshopped, as lost as that high school
sophomore who wandered in a fugue state past the strip joints of
Times Square. I was a girl who hadn't gotten the memo about not
taking candy from strangers—and New York was full of those
strangers. A girl who was playing a part she was wrong for, whose
own gifts were elusive and strange to her, contraband, brought
home from a foreign country and best stored out of reach.

9. But still, all the while, I was becoming a writer. How to
explain this—how, without conceiving myself as a split screen,
one part of me blurry and undefined and the other honing skills,
finding the words, becoming, in the invisibility, the solitude of
these rooms, these apartments, someone with something to say.
I wrote my first novel, then another. I began to teach. I interned
at a literary magazine on 17th, lugged home laundry bags full of
manuscripts, and sat cross-legged on my bed as if mining through
coals for gold. I went to book parties in clubs and smoky bars and
had them thrown for me. I lunched on vertical salads with my
terrifying agent at Michael's on West 55th Street, where table
position determined pecking order, and no one was ever quite
focused on their own dining companion. Wasn't that Barbara
Walters being shown to the window table? I posed for a portrait
in *Vanity Fair* in a tiny lemon-yellow suit, my hair big and fluffy,
a face covered in makeup, in a coffee shop on West 83rd Street.
Once, late at night, as I was in bed reading manuscripts, a giant
water bug flew across the bedroom and landed on my shoulder.
I screamed and called the doorman, a man who must have been

in his late seventies, who poked with a broom through the shoes and boots littering my closet floor until he found and disposed of it.

10. I could lecture on metaphor; I could teach graduate students; I could locate and deconstruct the animal imagery in *Madame Bovary*. But I could not squash a water bug by myself. The practicalities of life eluded me. The city—which I knew with the intimacy of a lover—made it very possible to continue like this, carried along on a stream of light, motion, energy, noise. The city was a bracing wind that never stopped blowing, and I was a lone leaf slapped up against the side of a building, a hydrant, a tree.

11. I am writing this from a small study in a house high on a hill in the Connecticut countryside, two hours north of the city. It is winter. The bare branches of wisteria that climb our roof are banging against the window. One of my dogs is curled up at my feet. I hear the sharp pitter-patter of the other as he forages through the house for crumbs left from a party we threw the other night. The walls of my study are hung with photographs: My son as a ring bearer at a friend's wedding, tiny in his first tuxedo. My husband, from his years as a war correspondent, lighting a cigarette in his flak jacket on a rooftop in Somalia—a reminder that he, too, had a life that he left behind when he met me. While I was drinking champagne on my parents' credit card, he was filing stories from the bloody streets of Mogadishu.

12. It has been ten years since we left the city. A decade—long enough for our friends to stop taking bets on how long it would take us to come to our senses and return to New York. *What do you do up there? Whom do you see? What's it like?* They drive up to visit us in their Zip cars or rental SUVs, bearing urban bounty: shopping bags from Citarella filled with pungent Epoisses and

chorizo tortellini; boxes of linzer cookies from Sarabeth's; delicate, pastel Ladurée macarons. In turn, we take our houseguests
on hikes or to lakeside beaches or to quaint village streets lined
with shops selling cashmere and tweed. But we aren't hearty
country folk. I don't own muck boots or a Barbour coat. We don't
ski or own horses or build bonfires in our backyard. I spend most
of my days alone in my writing study, with a midday yoga break
in the next room. My husband now writes and directs films, and
the closest he gets to an outdoor activity is when he takes his
chain saw out into our woods to clear brush. Our son, like us,
is an indoor dreamer. We are urban Jews, descended from the
shtetl, pale and neurasthenic. Living in our heads.

13. Deep within my recesses there is a turntable, its needle
skipping, skipping. My twenty-year-old self, straight from Jersey, watches me, hands on hips. *How could you?* she accuses me.
When we'd come so far? I want to tell her that we were refugees,
my husband, son, and I, fleeing north, heading away from a place
and time that we hoped would recede, like the view from our
rearview mirror, until it disappeared entirely, until it became
nothing more than a memory. I want to tell her that my baby had
been very sick. That my father was dead, my mother dying. That
we watched as one plane, then another, crashed into the towers, debris swirling in the sky above us like a storm of blackened
snow. That everything I thought I knew about living no longer
applied. That the champagne and the men and the real estate and
the book parties were like the fool's gold that my now-teenage,
healthy son unearths on his geology field trips. Look, I want to
say. This life you think you want is a shiny apparition. Those
restaurants and clubs, those bars bathed in a light pinker than
sunset? Those cafés where photographers from magazines took

your picture, and makeup artists dusted your pretty nose? They will be submerged, as in a shipwreck, the seas of time washing over them until something new has taken their place. The joint where you now drink those frozen margaritas will become an organic juice bar. The bistro with the best steak frites is now a T-Mobile store. The bookstore where you will eventually give your first reading sells boxes of hair dye and curling irons. It all changes—even institutions, even concrete towers, even, or perhaps most of all, our very selves—my foolish little sweetheart. That's how I could leave. Trust me. You'll thank me someday.

14. I am not yet old, but I am no longer young. My city—the one that beckoned just beyond the smokestacks and Budweiser plant—has vanished. Only glimpses of it remain, in the sandstone façade of a Fifth Avenue building, or Washington Square Park, when seen from a certain angle. My city broke its promise to me, and I to it. I fell out of love, and then I fell back in—with my small town, its winding country roads, and the ladies at the post office who know my name. I did my best to become the airbrushed girl on its billboards, but even airbrushed girls grow up. We soften over time, or maybe harden. One way or another, life will have its way with us.

15. I still drive into the city once a week or so. I see doctors, get my hair done, have lunch with my agent, have dinner with a girlfriend at a candlelit restaurant where we share a bottle of wine and order the cheese plate. I give readings from my books in crowded East Village bars. If I can, I squeeze in a yoga class near Union Square, in a loft filled with plants and statues of the Buddha. Mostly, I watch the young people—their new designs in facial hair, piercings, and tattoos—who are in the midst of their own love affair. They're from Ohio or Nebraska. Or New Jersey.

They've arrived, and they're here to stay, just as I once was. It's their city now. I have become invisible to them. I could be their mother. They laugh and whisper, lovely heads bent together. Sometimes, if it's going to be a late night—the theater, perhaps, or a boozy dinner party—my husband and I stay over at a hotel. We pull up to the entrance in our SUV with Connecticut plates, a middle-aged couple from out of town, just as my parents once were. "Can I help you folks get a taxi?" the doorman asks. "Do you need directions?" No, my husband tells him. That's okay. We're from here. We know our way around.

SOMEDAY, SOME MORNING, SOMETIME

Emma Straub

Most people get to move to New York, the city's gritty seductiveness pulling them out of their family's clutches, sometime in their early twenties. They get to arrive by car or airplane or bus and see the skyline and say "wow." They live in an apartment with four roommates somewhere in Bushwick or Murray Hill or Windsor Terrace, and six months later, they refer to themselves as New Yorkers. This is a story about how I want to smother those people in their sleep, but this is also a story about how I envy those yokels, not for their wide-eyed wonder but for the fact that they will be able to leave the city someday without having an existential crisis. The city isn't theirs, and they aren't its people—they're interlopers, long-form tourists, around long enough to be able to tell their children stories about when they lived in New York, lo those many years ago.

I grew up on the Upper West Side of Manhattan, half a block from Central Park, two and a half blocks from Broadway, a city girl from the start. My parents weren't native born, but they both loved New York unequivocally. The people were more interesting in the city, more open-minded, smarter, cooler—these were things I understood as facts. New York was the center of the world—not just my world, the entire world. My parents had friends from other countries and other cities, and they would all wind up in New York eventually, at our dining room table. This did not seem like a coincidence. All the time, every single day, people came to New York City because they couldn't get what it had to offer anywhere else.

I went to Saint Ann's for high school, all the way in Brooklyn Heights. The subway ride was forty-five minutes each way, but it could have been twice as long and I wouldn't have minded. The school was not what it sounded like—not a prim Catholic school but a progressive one started by lunatic visionaries in the basement of a church, with no knee-length kilts unless they were ironic. No grades were offered. The school had a reputation for producing brilliant drug addicts, though it was only true of one section of the population—the other half were brilliant mathematicians, brilliant painters, brilliant actors, brilliant talkers, plus a handful of dummies with very rich parents. There was poetry hanging in the stairwells, the students looked like fashion models, and I was in heaven. My friends and I ran wild all over Manhattan and Brooklyn, our drunken little bodies falling in and out of taxicabs and each other's houses, each of us mad with love for the Brooklyn Bridge, for the way the pavement glittered in the moonlight, for our own youth, which by its very existence seemed made of pixie dust and dreams. Until then, New York City had only mattered to me because the Macy's Thanksgiving Day Parade lined up on my corner, and I could eat H&H bagels warm out of the bin, but once I was able to traverse the city without my parents in tow, New York became my jungle gym and playmate all at once.

This is the trait I have come to loathe in others, this rhapsodic reverence, though I'm much better at controlling myself than I used to be. When I came home from college in Ohio (because where else would I go but home), I was horrified to discover that my entire graduating class seemed to be following me back. Worse yet, they were excited about it! They all moved to Williamsburg and rented practice spaces for their bands. I would get email invitations to their shows, their house parties, and their art openings and feel sick to my stomach. It was like watching someone—an entire fleet of someones—fall in love simultaneously, all the goofy grins and public declarations of affection.

I don't like to talk about this in public because I know it paints me in a very specific light—overly precious about my youth, selfish, spoiled. These things are all true. But still, even at thirty-two years old, I refuse to admit that I'm in the wrong. It might be uncharitable or close-minded, but there aren't very many places in the country that people revere the way they do New York. I do have friends who grew up in Los Angeles who feel this way, and maybe this is the way everyone feels about their hometown. *This is my place. I was here first. You don't get to say what's good or cool because it's mine.* But because my hometown is New York City, everyone else thinks it belongs to them, too.

Don't get the wrong impression—I want everyone I know to love New York, just as I want everyone I know to love my parents, because they're as much a part of me as my limbs. I want strangers to love New York, as long as they're not walking slowly in front of me, their faces turned skyward in amazement. I love giving directions to tourists and scribbling down embarrassingly long lists of recommendations for recent transplants: Sahadi's for hummus, labne, and dried fruit; BookCourt, Word, and Three Lives for books; Mary's Fish Camp for lobster rolls; the Shake Shack for hamburgers; the Film Forum for both the movies and the popcorn. I cover the backs of envelopes with illegible penmanship, imploring the visitor to eat six meals a day, if they have to, to absorb as much as possible.

———

When I went to college in Ohio, I saw the whole thing as temporary, like boarding school or prison—you don't move there, you just sleep there for a little while. Most of my college friends were from New York, if not from my high school then from another one nearby. We'd gone to one another's parties and had all the same reference points. It was like making cake from a box—all the ingredients were already inside. I was miserable and lonely there, in a town with only a handful of traffic lights and a smaller handful of restaurants. By my senior year, I'd made some progress, but not much. I was a horse with blinders on, thinking the whole world was one long, narrow street.

When I was twenty-four, I moved in with my boyfriend. We lived in Carroll Gardens, Brooklyn, in an apartment directly over an Italian restaurant—we had to walk through the restaurant to get to the stairs to our door, and the hallways always smelled like tomato sauce. None of my high school or elementary school or summer camp friends left the city, and then all of my college friends arrived. I saw my parents once a week and had jobs through which I made additional friends, and suddenly, there was never enough time. I began to imagine life outside New York City—life outside one's hometown—as empty calendar days, where someone canceling plans disappointed you rather than cheered you up, where you could take a walk and not run into every single person you'd ever known. That might seem backward to those who grew up in small towns and found them stiflingly small, but one of the greatest gifts New York City has to offer to newcomers is anonymity, and that wasn't on the table for me.

Two years later, I applied to graduate school and was accepted at the University of Wisconsin–Madison. My boyfriend and I went to visit and took long walks by the two lakes at the center of town. (Madison's capitol building is on an isthmus, the rarest and most delightful of land formations.) We sat in a park and were nuzzled by a roaming pussycat, clearly someone's pet. To think! You could live somewhere and let your pets run free with nothing more than a collar, secure in thinking that they wouldn't get run over by a car, or stolen by some pet poacher, or eaten by a pit bull, or infected by sewer rats! When we finally moved that summer, we took everything—our own two cats, our heaviest furniture, things to hang on the walls, and the tools with which to hang them. Even so, the program was only two years long, and that was exactly as long as I thought we'd stay. In the end, we stayed for three years, but in all that time, I didn't swap my New York driver's license for a Wisconsin one.

Life in Wisconsin was quiet—our house was quiet, our street was quiet, our neighborhood was quiet. At first, I was frightened by the calm, sure that it meant an axe murderer was going to climb into my window. (That didn't happen, but for the record my house in Madison *was* robbed, something that has never happened to me in New York City.) A few months in, a sense of calm arrived, along with the cold and the snow. I knew so few people in town that I invited every single one of them to every party I had. This meant that my relationships were strong—stronger, probably, than many of the friendships I'd left behind, built as they were on long-ago memories and shared experiences we'd outgrown. In Madison, my friendships were forged out of proximity and time, as in, suddenly, I had the time! I had time to take a walk with a friend because she only lived three blocks away, and we had nothing to do otherwise. It was like living on the stage of an absurdist play, where the characters sit on a darkened set until they have another scene, or like *Sleeping with the Enemy*, the Julia Roberts movie in which she swims away from her abusive husband to start a new life. I was Julia Roberts, and New York City was my husband.

Things became clearer with distance—the way I had always deferred to my friends, the way my friends had always been kind of mean, the way New York City looked from the middle of the country, like some haughty socialite obsessed with her own reflection. When I went home to visit, I was instantly exhausted by the city's pace and by my own insistence on seeing as many people as possible, even if it meant having a date for breakfast, a date for lunch, a date for dinner, and a date for after-dinner drinks. My boyfriend and I fought like rabid dogs on those trips, stressed from the overstimulation. One miserable trip, we met a friend and his wife and his parents at a department store the day before Christmas for a quick chat in the handbag section because that's all we could spare, tourists with shopping bags shouldering past us.

In contrast, Madison seemed like paradise. Everything that had ever bothered me about New York—the cranky postal employees, the trash-strewn sidewalks, those shopping-bag-laden tourists—was gone. My boyfriend and I walked for miles every day, only occasionally crossing paths with other people. We were hermits who weren't afraid to leave the house. The movie theater was never crowded; neither were the restaurants. Nothing was expensive. No one was trying to seem cool. We joined the food co-op and cooked our own meals. We could even find decent pizza and bagels. If it weren't for the winters, we might have stayed. If it weren't for the lack of a literary community, we might have stayed. If it weren't for the lack of family and friends, we might have stayed. If it weren't for not being New York, we might have stayed.

Why didn't we stay?

Part of our deal going into Madison was that my boyfriend would be able to choose where we went next. When it came time to leave, he wanted to move west, all the way to California. Married now, we loved to visit Los Angeles, to tool around in a rented car and suddenly find ourselves at the beach. It was lovely to be outside even in the dead of winter, a perfect contrast to Wisconsin, where we wore mittens as large as boxing gloves. Our rent would be more than it was in Madison, but less than it would be in New York. I could wear dresses without tights most of the year and bury my snow boots in the back of my closet. We had some friends there, but not too many—a proposition that seemed like a continuation of our social life in Wisconsin, where we could easily keep up with all the demands on our time.

Despite our deal, I said no. I had never thought for a second that he'd choose anywhere other than New York. My father had been having some serious health problems, and the thought of moving even farther away scared me. It was hard enough to be in Madison, which was less than a two-hour flight. I wanted to go home.

And so we moved back to New York, into a beautiful house in a neighborhood far enough away from everyone else we knew that it felt like a retreat. But even if the streets are clear of people we know (not counting our neighbors), they are still crowded with people, and the frustrations of living in the city have come back. Not a week passes that we don't talk about Madison, or Los Angeles, or that perfect fantasy place in between, cosmopolitan enough to keep us from getting bored and feeling deprived but quiet and low key enough to maintain our normal blood pressure. Is it Chapel Hill? Rhinebeck? Montauk? Is it Albuquerque? I like the way my husband looks in a sweater and a jacket—if we moved to California, would it be all T-shirts, all the time? Would we learn to surf?

In the three years we'd been gone, things had changed. Once I was back, I met new friends, this time out of shared interest instead of just proximity, and that added a whole roster of people into the rotation for dinner dates. My schedule is worse now than it has ever been, but the busy-ness has helped ensure that the people I see are the people I love—the older I get, the less time I waste on the one-sided friendships of my youth. My father's health is better than it has been but still goes up and down. My parents will be seventy this year, and I'm six months pregnant with our first child. I can't imagine our lives getting any simpler from now on.

WHEN MY HUSBAND AND I FIRST TRAVELED ABROAD TO-
gether, years before we moved to Madison, he guffawed at the
sight of my passport, which clearly states that I was born in Nor-
walk, Connecticut. His says "New York, New York," though he
was born in White Plains and lived in Mamaroneck until he
was twelve, when his parents moved the family south to Jupiter,
Florida. You can tell by my need to qualify the place of his birth
that I remain somewhat salty about these bare, clean facts. I was
born in Connecticut, forty-five miles from the house I grew up
in on the Upper West Side. When I entered preschool in Manhattan, shortly after our move, no one seemed to think anything
of it, but by the time I hit elementary school, several of my classmates refused to think of me as a genuine New Yorker. I'd already missed so much in those first years of life—how would I
ever catch up? How many years does it take for the city to become home?

My parents, now married for almost fifty years, have lived in
New York City for thirty years. Still, if you walked up to them
on the sidewalk in front of their house and asked them where
they were from, they would say Milwaukee and begin to check
you for physical resemblances to people they knew there, friends
from their childhoods. If they were somewhere else, though,
traveling in this country or another, they would say, "We are
from New York." And, of course, they are. Most of my friends
who grew up outside the city always knew they would leave their
hometowns—if they were ambitious, leaving was a given. In New
York, the opposite is true. The ambitious stay, forever elbowing
back the newcomers. The ones who don't like the hustle get the
hell out of town, and fast.

Would it be easier for me to leave my parents behind if they
lived somewhere else? Maybe. Which came first, my devotion to

my family or my devotion to my city? I know several people who have moved out of the city, their former lover, to be closer to their families. These people almost always have small children, which might mean that families win out over cultural advantages, especially if the babysitting is free. I wonder how their Brooklyn Bridge tattoos fare out there in the world—what can they say? "For a few years, I lived sort of near this"? As for me, I'm forever on the fence, searching for my own Shangri-La, though I assume no such place exists. I spend a little time every day looking at real estate listings on the internet, telling myself, *It would only be for a little while. I wouldn't stay away for the long run. How could I? Could I?*

BROOKLYN SUMMER

Danielle A. Jackson

The summer I was seventeen, my sister was thirty-one and six months pregnant with her first and only child. We were both fresh from breakups. Hers had been a slow-burning catastrophe with my new niece's father that had messy emotional residue and a long half-life. Mine was an extended quarrel with the boy I first met in seventh grade and had been dating since giggling on the phone past 11:30 PM with the hum of a TV screen in the background. The geeky, anxious temperaments we shared meant that in between classes and extracurriculars, we were often hurting each other's feelings. I was a serious, competitive student then, working late nights at the dining room table in the tiny brick house I lived in with my mother. My summers were a respite, and often I got to let the stress of the school year melt away on a trip to my big sister's.

Kim was a corporate manager and lived just outside Charlotte, North Carolina, in a two-story house on a woodsy cul-de-sac. I loved that house—the pale blue carpet, the circular stairwell, the spaciousness and calm. The summer before, we'd driven together sixteen hours from our hometown on the western tip of Tennessee to her house, stopping in mountain towns and diners along the way. But the summer I was seventeen was the year before I was to leave for college, and there were schools in places I'd never before seen that I hoped to visit.

New York City was most urgent. I think it started when I joined an acting troupe in the sixth grade, or maybe it was the spoken-word scenes I found myself drawn to, or the way the music I listened to made the city sound like it teemed with a vibrant bohemianism. I knew Erykah Badu lived in the city, and Lauryn Hill was across the river in South Orange. At a reading at Sidewalk University in Midtown Memphis, the poet Jessica Care Moore said she and Saul Williams lived in the same Brooklyn neighborhood, like their heroes, Sonia Sanchez and Haki Madhubuti, once did.

As the summer sweltered, my mother and Auntie scrambled up money for a single plane ticket to fly me to New York, where Kim was to meet me. They lectured me about pickpockets and subway muggings and not wearing a purse. The two of us stayed in a hotel in Midtown East and mostly walked everywhere, Kim by my side with a pregnant waddle. At NYU I saw Tricia Rose give a talk in an auditorium so crowded it overwhelmed me, and two girls kissed each other on the yard at Barnard, which had a student club called Labia. I was a Southern Baptist who'd taken a purity vow during sex ed. It was the summer "Doo Wop (That Thing)," from Lauryn Hill's debut album *The Miseducation of*

Lauryn Hill, topped the charts. Twenty years on, the lyrics about *pretty-faced men, sneaky silent men,* and *Jezebel's sin* sound labored and judgmental. It was the peak of bling-bling and the early days of the video vixen's reign, when music videos were flashy and glamorously attired Black women were often accoutrements— curvy bodies the Moët got poured over. In the split-screen treatment for Hill's video, she plays a singer at a block party in two different eras, rapping the verses, singing the hooks, backing up herself. In other words: she could do it all. I know now that Hill suffered greatly for the high-wire act; there is a way to wholeness without self-laceration.

It made me sweat to hold on to my cross-body bag when we walked in Times Square because I was holding on so tight. When we took the subway downtown I stood, not because it was crowded but because I could. We ate jerk chicken by candlelight at Justin's, Puff Daddy's restaurant in the Meat Packing District that would be closed by 2007. The meal made Kim nauseous; now I'm struck by the commitment she'd made to me. Though heavily pregnant, she'd come out on the town, in Manhattan, no less, because I needed her. I remember feeling something between irritability and sadness. I was anxious for my life to start, but also, the depth of my need was a frightening thing to stare down.

Kim moved home with my mother and me to give birth. My brother, a recent dropout from a PhD program, had also been living at home. Kim had been afraid to tell him she was pregnant and unmarried. I didn't see it then, but we all share a perfectionism born of surviving great odds and an intense fear of mistakes. When she went into labor, the four of us squeezed into our mother's Corolla and drove the slow and winding way around

I-40 to Baptist East. Kai was born after hours of painful contractions my sister bore in a way I knew I never could.

———

ONCE MY MOTHER TOLD ME SHE DREAMED OF MOVING TO COL-orado, Vermont, or Arizona, places I associate with an airy spaciousness and bohemianism our hometown isn't known for. She'd stayed in Memphis while raising us, working for decades at the large public hospital without much advancement. It wasn't a terrible place to grow up. Mama had her friends, did well at school, sang in a trio. Her mother had moved from a Delta town in rural Mississippi and made a go of things in Detroit and Chicago before settling down, ultimately, in Memphis, then the biggest city in Tennessee. A Firestone plant had opened in 1936 off Manassas Street, three miles northwest of the Mississippi River. My grandmother's husband worked there as a machinist; by the fifties, when Mama was a young girl, North Memphis was a bustling business district and manufacturing hub with facilities owned by Kraftco and International Harvester in addition to Firestone. The family bought a small bungalow with three rooms and a front and back porch; my grandmother opened a café at Hollywood and Vandale. It was a raucous place where they played the electric blues out of Chicago and endured police raids and loud fights between lovers. There was a blue room toward the back, where couples would go for quiet time, and a grill my grandmother built herself. Now this part of North Memphis is beset by blight and has the city's highest rate of unemployment.

My mother was the youngest of nine. Because I was also the baby of the family, by a wide margin, she was different for me than she was for my siblings. When we lived alone, we didn't talk much, and I ached for her company. I'm lucky; she was there in a way my father wasn't. Still, it was my sister who got us settled in a new house when Mama's marriage to a new man crumbled. And it was Auntie who paid the security deposit for my first apartment.

When I was deciding between schools in five states, including dream schools in New York and DC, I felt as though I was alone before an abyss. There was the careful calculus of merit scholarships and financial aid. And beyond a vague notion of wanting to write and travel, I couldn't verbalize exactly what I wanted to *do* with my life. With my new niece, my sister had moved to a Jersey suburb for a new job, which started to cool me on the city. I wanted to help my sister with the new baby, who I immediately adored, but I was also afraid of being swallowed up by family duty. It shamed me to feel this way. There was always so much to do, and all I had then was my own bundle of wants to offer into what felt like a yawning void.

The summer before I was set to leave, I volleyed between NYU, a women's college outside Boston, and a school in DC so incessantly my friends couldn't keep up. "What is it that you want?" they'd ask. My fears and all the pressure—so much rested on that one choice, it seemed—calcified into indecision. Finally, I picked the private school in DC because they'd increased their scholarship over the summer, and I was excited by the class on third world fiction on my schedule for the first semester. In college, I met Black people from all over the world, which I'd known about in theory, but the lesson bloomed to life in reggae clubs in Adams Morgan, go-gos in the Northeast, and bowls of joloff rice and pepper soup I ate with friends in Silver Spring. Soon, it was the early 2000s, and top 40 radio, which every college kid lives or eats or parties in some proximity to, became more hip-hop-centric. And hip-hop was simultaneously becoming southern. I started to see myself, refracted as I was: a Black southern woman a thousand miles from home. And I found words for who I wanted to be: "I want to write, to be an editor of something"—says a journal entry from shortly after graduation.

The summer of 2004, I was fresh from another breakup, this time with my college boyfriend. He'd wanted to get married, and it had been difficult to leave him. I wasn't playful with my sexuality when youth beckoned it; I thought if I was dating a boy, he should be my boyfriend, and that we would wait to talk about sex when we'd fallen in love. Somehow along the way, I'd learned how marriage was the ultimate goal, the ideal container for the body's unwieldiness. Even though I'd fallen out of love a few months after we'd started having sex, I still didn't think I should leave him. He was kind to me, a solid person who'd lived all his life in the DMV and wanted to enjoy finally having arrived at a middle-class life. He hated how much I wanted to leave town and didn't get excited when I tried to talk to him about what I was hoping for. It was only beginning to make sense to me.

I took an Amtrak into Penn Station from the DC apartment I'd shared with him with two large suitcases and little else. I hailed a cab and rode up the West Side Highway to Harlem, where I'd found a room in a sunny apartment on the edge of Central Park. Though I'd arrived at dusk, it was sticky hot and rank from the piles of garbage bags left outside.

—

WHAT DOES IT MEAN TO FEEL SOUTHERN IF IT IS NOT WRAPPED up, somehow, in longing? I had to leave the South to feel any connection to it. My uncle Pluto was the first artist I knew—a hairdresser, fashion stylist, and dancer who'd left to make a life in San Francisco before dying at home with us in his early forties. He'd been my mother's closest confidant growing up, her protector, and when she was in labor with me, he was the person who drove her to the hospital. He was tall and charismatic with manicured brows and a big laugh. Kim said he was the first person to tell her she was a "beautiful Black woman." As a child, he'd been bullied for being gay; leaving was a question of survival. It is a fundamental yearning to see what you become when you are away from what you know best. Leaving is the subject of many blues songs. "My baby caught the train, left me all alone," sings Howlin' Wolf in "Who's Been Talking?" before admitting that he was the reason she'd had to go.

At a grand a month, the rent on my Harlem room was a tough squeeze on my entry-level salary. Little by little, I furnished the place and learned to feed myself. The tightrope gave me great anxiety. I had a panic attack at a Gristedes on 72nd and a recurring dream that blood was being drained from my body. My first poetry workshop was in a cramped apartment on the Upper East Side, led by a bespectacled white lady with a short gray cut who'd performed at the Nuyorican Poets Cafe. By the time I'd gotten to the city, the vital spontaneity of scenes like that was already slipping away. I wrote short stories and terrible poems, all without discipline or any thought of publishing. Surviving seemed most important; that was the bargain I accepted to stay in the city. I landed a day job at a publisher of books on visual art. Then I left for a corporate job with a $50,000 salary. Around that time, I published a book review in an independent magazine based in the Bronx. I made $50, and I was proud to get it. No one

alive in my family made a living from making art. It didn't occur
to me that I could.

When I got tired of roommates in 2012, I moved to Brooklyn and found a spacious one-bedroom on a cypress-lined block
in Bed-Stuy. It had shiny hardwood floors, a nook that could be
an office or a large closet, its own dining room. There were still
dope boys on the corner then, and only one coffee shop within
a few blocks radius. Then the neighborhood began to change,
one shiny new bar, one renovated brownstone at a time. I found
a writers' group that met on Saturday mornings at the Brooklyn
Historical Society. There was a soul singer from Saint Louis, a
social worker, an academic, a retired teacher. We read Wendy
Walters's *Multiply/Divide* and work by one another. The winters grew colder, more cantankerous. A year turned into ten, and
then fifteen.

—

ONE NIGHT, I WALKED THREE BLOCKS EAST, TOWARD MARCUS
Garvey Boulevard, to meet a new man at a bar with a house band.
They had two trumpets, congas, a saxophone player, a white
Latin male vocalist. The night was wet and overcast, the kind of
evening where the bounty of a Brooklyn summer had yet to fully
bloom. Still, you knew it was coming. Cars sped by a hair slower
than usual, pedestrians dropped by wine shops or a neighbor's
house on their way home.

R had dark eyes, a bald head. A creative entrepreneur type, he
worked all the time, mostly from his own apartment. By then,
I worked at a publishing company and as a freelance writer and
editor. It was also the first time in four years I hadn't gone back
to the boyfriend who'd lied to me about his wife—my longest

stretch of time alone since the disappointing serial monogamy of most of my New York years to date.

Early on, R and I had a fun and easy way with each other. One night, we sat up past dawn on my purple velvet sofa, looking out the window onto my fire escape, smoking Parliament Lights. There was music, music I played, music I chose: Eddie Kendricks, Lil Wayne, the Manhattans. I liked R's willingness to enter a world of my creation, to sink into a couch made warm by the imprint of my body. So, for a while, I overlooked what he described as a polyamorous lifestyle, which I later learned to be an erudite, fashionable way of reasoning away deception.

On that Friday night in late June, I walked toward him without thinking of the obstructions or obfuscations. We met under a streetlight. A woman who recognized us both stopped at a corner—how quaint, how compact New York City can feel! After polite greetings, we prattled on, and somehow the subject of '90s R&B arose. *Lauryn Hill was the greatest; Groove Theory's album was still unmatched; artists today don't make music with that much feeling.* Most of what we said I'd heard, or even said before myself. R told us we should listen to Ari Lennox, specifically the album *Shea Butter Baby*, which had just debuted a few weeks before.

"It's like music of that time, like *Miseducation*, but it still feels new," he said, speaking to our mutual friend then turning to look down at me.

I may have nodded, or possibly I didn't.

"Especially her song 'New Apartment.' She's really good at really bringing you into the feeling of moving into a brand-new place. And she's really very soulful."

Days later, when I looked her up and found photos, I saw a beautiful brown young woman endorsed and flanked by men in the business, like J. Cole. I was in my late thirties by then. And here was R, a man who let me know from the beginning that he wouldn't ever be "mine" in any traditional sense. He'd just gotten out of a decade-long romance with a woman he'd lived with, to whom he'd been perennially unfaithful. He told me he never wanted to marry or have children on our first date. Still, that night, I kissed him. Then I let more dates happen, which spilled from bars and restaurants onto my stoop and living room and further, still, into my space.

Still, I knew. Even when I sat beside him on my fire escape under a waning moon. Even when we showered together and then went to bed. So that night in June, when I had the tortured kind of conversation I always had in New York with loose acquaintances, when he told me about Ari Lennox, for a split second, it felt as though he spoke her name with a reverence and intimacy I knew we would never have.

On her album, *Shea Butter Baby*, DC native Ari Lennox sounds much more like an everywoman than I thought she would, much more companionable and vulnerable, even wounded. There's an earthy sense of humor to her lyrics and her interludes, about garbanzo beans and tense friendships and trips to Target. Most of all, Ari wants things, like all the blues women before her. She wants good sex, even when it begets regret. She wants to spend less money. She wants to forget her ex, she wants a good job, she wants a love that doesn't cost her dignity.

I settled into a grind of revolving deadlines, and an exhaustion settled into me. I had also developed a sense of feeling unheard at work: imitated and uncredited, unrecognized, underpaid and underappreciated. My landlord refused to exterminate the building when mice moved in. I saw a rat burrow into a hole on our stoop. I had a job but no health insurance. I had given the city my youth. Nearly everyone I knew was cobbling together a way of life out of freelance and permalancer gigs, which, as I hurtled toward the end of my thirties, became less and less appealing.

Eventually, something in me softened. I felt my body relax; I knew it would need to, to prepare myself for what was to come.

That autumn, I went to a wedding in Miami and stayed on the secluded north end of the beach, where I could hear the shore from my rented apartment. The morning I arrived, I put on a red bikini and waded into the Atlantic. In Miami, the southernmost city of Florida, I felt a summoning I couldn't yet name.

For years, I'd had pangs of envy every time I read about an artist or politician who'd left the South and returned to create and to lead. I followed elections in Jackson and Montgomery and new co-ops in East Atlanta. When I heard of a job in between Memphis and my mother's new home in Saint Louis, I applied for it. And so I left R behind, and then also New York City. I do not know if it is forever. The ability to leave and start again, both an inheritance and a cultivated skill, is what I treasure most. It will be useful when I long, again, for something new.

LOSING NEW YORK

Lauren Elkin

People move to New York from all over the world, drawn to what it stands for: work, success, freedom, acceptance, glamour; give me your tired, your poor, your ambitious, your determined. But they are always approaching the city from somewhere else, which amplifies its power. There are so many viewpoints on the city that "New York"—the idea—is magnified in the imagination through thousands of tiny windowpanes.

But it's hard to get any perspective on it when you grow up next door. My parents are from the city, and as soon as they married they bought a house in the suburbs, where they raised me and my sister. (We, in turn, moved back to the city as adults.) That decision created my particular attitude toward New York, my particular windowpane. To those of us who grew up not *in* it but *next* to it, in its shadow, a short train ride away on the Long Island

Rail Road or the PATH or Metro North, New York is the city. As if there are no others. And for the rest of our lives, our relationships to cities will be defined by New York.

Unlike Joan Didion's Sacramento, the suburbs of New York derive their very identity from the city. Elizabeth Bishop describes the city's "long long legs" stretching out into the countryside, begging it to "subside." The suburbs take shape under the weight of that pressure. They are New York but not "New York," the city. They are New York but not "New York," the state. They are somewhere in between. "Where are you from?" people ask me. "New York," I say. "The city?" they ask. Well—and then the answer depends on my mood, on whom I'm talking to, on how well they know New York. Can they be trusted not to say "Oh, Long Island. You're not from New York, then."

Am I? Am I not? When you're from New York but not from "New York," you're on shaky ground. I spent seven years in Manhattan, first for university, then for work, and then for graduate school, before I moved abroad in 2004. If I had moved to the city from somewhere else in 2004, by now I might be saying I'm from there and no one would question me. New York is one of those cities that welcomes you, takes you in, lends you its name. Instead, I moved from New York to Paris, where I'll never be able to say, "I'm from Paris," no matter how long I live there.

———

In Amor Towles's recent novel *Rules of Civility*, the heroine, born and bred in Brighton Beach but trying to make her way in the upper echelons of New York society, pretends not to know someone from her past when he recognizes her at a newsstand. Observing their exchange, the newsman pronounces:

"That's the problem with being born in New York . . . You've got no New York to run away to." When people ask me why I moved to Paris, I sometimes say it's because I was tired of New York, and when New Yorkers are tired of New York, there's nowhere else for them to go but Paris. But that doesn't explain why I left. I'm not sure I have an answer to that question.

I had a certain kind of clichéd, magical New York childhood, full of Broadway shows and the Met and FAO Schwarz and Tribeca restaurants. New York in adulthood is less magical. Everything costs more than it should. It takes forever to get anywhere. Life moves so fast things are half over before you notice they've begun. It's dirty, cramped, and smells bad. Adoptive New Yorkers will brook no criticism of it; it represents everything to which they have aspired. The smell and the grit are part of the dream. But why would you stay there when there are so many more pleasant places to live?

Of course, Parisians think I'm out of my mind. They feel exactly—*exactly*—the same way about their city as I do about mine. The French have two fantasies about the United States: a West Coast fantasy and an East Coast one. The West Coast Parisians dream of giant trees and the sun setting over the Pacific. The East Coast Parisians want to eat cupcakes in the West Village or drink with hipsters in Brooklyn. They're the ones who spend the most time asking me questions. How could I, why would I, give up my city for theirs? New York is not a city you leave. But it's a hard city to start from.

When I left New York, it was well before the 2008 economic crisis, a time when you could find headlines in *New York* magazine like "Filthy Stinking Rich," "Growing Up Trump," "The Best Beauty Docs," "Where to Buy [small parentheses: "or rent"]

Now," and anxiously in 2003, "Will the Bubble Burst?" The cult of wealth in New York was too much for me: I couldn't ever see myself getting a foothold in it. I was working in publishing but envisioned a transition to academe and to writing. But how would I ever support myself? I would never have been able to do it on my own; I would have needed a partner with money. I found one, and he was very good to me, but I couldn't shake the sense that I was some kind of dirty mistress to him, living a life he paid for that I could never have afforded.

Although, as Didion writes, "it is often said that New York is a city for only the very rich and the very poor," it could also be said that "New York is also, at least for those of us who came from somewhere else, a city only for the very young." And yet all around me, friends were careening toward a New York adulthood. They were being hired at corporate jobs at ridiculous salaries and living in doorman buildings with gyms and private cinemas. They were moving in with their boyfriends and talking about what cut of diamond they preferred. The New York I knew then was for the very rich and young who wanted quite badly to be no longer young. My own live-in boyfriend bought a car and used it to drive out to see his parents on Long Island every weekend. He talked about buying an apartment and eventually a house in Nassau County. It made me uncomfortable, all the getting and spending and the courting of maturity. One night I was out for dinner on Long Island with him, his parents, and my parents, and I had a panic attack right there at the table. There were electric currents of energy shooting down my spine and into my legs, and I had to jump up from the table and go stand outside the restaurant. It wasn't only that I couldn't afford those things.

It was that I didn't want those things, or not yet, or not the way they wanted them.

In leaving New York there's an element of failure. Why couldn't I make a go of it? "If I can make it there, I'll make it anywhere" you hear after every Yankees game, but there's a strange kind of pressure behind those lyrics, an implicit challenge for a native New Yorker. *What if I can't make it here?* you have to ask yourself. *What then?* Moving to Paris seemed like a way to make it on my own terms.

Which begs the question. Why couldn't I just rewrite my life in New York? Start over with new friends with priorities more in line with my own? I think I can't live in New York for the same reason I can't cook in my mother's kitchen. She's set it up so that it works for her, and she has her ways of doing things within that space that I feel I can't deviate from without, somehow, rejecting her. I love my family's New York, but I can't succeed by its rules, and I can't live within its limitations. The New York that I would inhabit, if I moved back there—hail, literary Brooklyn—is difficult to reach from Long Island and is as foreign a place to me as Moscow. It was easier to move to a different country and start my whole life over from scratch than it was to continue on their path. I sensed that I could make my own choices in Paris, that I could make a life for myself on my own terms, in a context that was mine alone. I didn't know anybody when I first arrived, so there was no one looking over my shoulder, no one to attempt to enforce continuity on my life. I could reinvent myself. For the first time, I met people who were like me: writers, thinkers, adventurers. I knew writers and thinkers in New York, of course, but in the circle of friends I formed in Paris, we all had that in common: at a given moment, we had all chosen not to stay where we were from but to leave home and move to Paris. We were all high on that, though what we felt there was different for each of us.

When it comes to place, there are two kinds of writers: those who more or less stay where they're put and look around themselves, and those who need to go somewhere else to look around themselves there.

I've never been a writer content to look at the world I come from. Unlike John Cheever or A. M. Homes, I don't find the suburbs flint the creative spark. I'm more interested in what happens when people go other places, in the profound exchange that can occur between person and place when the two are foreign to each other. Maybe this, too, is my legacy as a New Yorker. My grandparents and great-grandparents came to New York from Italy, Latvia, Lithuania, Ireland, Germany, and the Deep South. That makes at least six places to which I am connected by blood, six places of origin, six places that have a claim on me. Perhaps lacking any kind of local personal history, I'm bound to need to go digging elsewhere.

In Paris, I have all I need to write. History, atmosphere, and the physical remnants of the modern city that so inspired the writers whose vision of the world has so shaped mine: the Surrealists, the Situationists, Benjamin, Beauvoir, Barthes. The slight differences in everyday life make even the crushing drone of popular culture more interesting: the crap songs on the radio, the gushing commercials on the television. Whatever inspiration needs to thrive, Paris has it in spades; whatever conditions facilitate discipline and hard work, Paris supplies as well.

CITIES ARE MANY DIFFERENT PEOPLE TO US. I NEVER FELT THE
way Didion felt about New York, didn't love it "the way you love
the first person who ever touches you and never love anyone
quite that way again." Maybe you have to meet it as a stranger
to love it that way. New York was always destined for me, as if
I were betrothed to it when I was a baby. Paris was the *coup de
foudre* who stole me away from my betrothed. I wanted to move
to Paris after I graduated, but then I got involved with another
Long Islander, and we eventually moved in together, living first
in Gramercy and then on the Upper East Side. I told myself that
I belonged in New York, even though I was unhappy. "Has anyone ever been so young?" Didion wonders at her twenty-three-
year-old self, unable to call and ask for the air-conditioning to
be turned down because she didn't know how much to tip the
person they would send. I was twenty-five and I thought, with
the moral resolution (or perhaps the affected maturity) of the
very young, that because we lived together I had to stay. Finally,
I couldn't take it anymore; it felt like my choices were narrowing
more and more every day. I moved to Paris like I was coming up
for air.

Not that Paris is so terribly different from New York. The
Cartesian rationality that prevails in France has always priori-
tized the straight logic of the mathematically predictable. Look
at a French garden: order and geometry imposed on nature. The
Lettrist International (the precursors of the Situationists) complained of the authoritarian control these values exerted over
the population, citing a sign in Paris's Jardin des Plantes (my
neighborhood park) as an example: "One can discover at a single glance the Cartesian organization of the so-called 'labyrinth'
of the Jardin des Plantes and the inscription that announces it:

GAMES ARE FORBIDDEN IN THE LABYRINTH. One could not seek a clearer summary of the spirit of a whole civilization."

The same holds true in French life. For the wellborn French child, the road from *crèche* to *prépa* to *grande école* is well traced, and beyond that to marriage, country homes, *vacances scolaires*, and the repetition of the process with the next generation of wellborn French children. This is the status quo for the French 1 percent, and they will fight to maintain it. As Will Hutton commented in 2006 in the *Guardian*, the French are the only people on the planet who will take to the barricades to defend the status quo. In principle, it's similar to the narrative of success in America that I was raised with, but the difference is that you are set on your track much earlier in France, and if you deviate, you'll be off the track for the rest of your life. You might claw your way onto certain aspects of the track—you might get a good job, you might get a country home—but you'll always feel like an impostor. As a naïve young academic, I thought I could slip into my corresponding rung on the social and professional ladder. But it's clear—they have made it clear—that I'll always be on the outside here.

I think of that scene in Sofia Coppola's *Marie Antoinette*, the one in which the young archduchess Maria Antonia crosses the border from Austria to France by shedding every vestige of her old life—her clothes, her jewelry, even her little dog—to become Marie Antoinette. *It is the custom that the bride bring nothing belonging to a foreign court*, she is told. The French demand total assimilation, even as they remind you of your essential, immutable difference.

Yet I still feel more comfortable there than anywhere else. Probably because the French assume I'll never do anything their way, so they'll tolerate me—unlike Marie Antoinette—doing it my own way.

Revisiting New York in the first years after I left felt a bit like catching up with an ex: comfortable at first, familiar, but then you remember why it didn't work out and all the things that drove you crazy. Why are the sirens so loud? Why does the subway smell like piss? Why is it so exhausting to transfer from the 1/9 subway line to the N/R? Oh wait. They got rid of the 9. Is there still an R? You lose track of things. You no longer know where to eat. Is that Tuscan place on Park and 22nd still open? You lose track of people. Where are you working now? Where are you living now? You try to keep up, but it's impossible. If you lose your facility with New York, like a language once deciphered, it covers itself over again, becomes incomprehensible through disuse.

As I have built a life in Paris, I have moved ever further away from where I started. When I visit New York now, I feel at once like a native and a visitor. My home is no longer my home, but then again—yes, it is.

———

I HAVEN'T COME TO TERMS WITH LEAVING NEW YORK. IT IS hard to leave New York. Every time.

My parents drop me at Kennedy. They get on the Van Wyck Expressway. My mother's still crying, though she's trying not to. My father's wondering why I don't just come home. And I'm sitting on the tarmac, wondering the same thing.

The airfield at night, in the dark, is so beautiful, and it's like New York has the potential to transform itself into the kind of haunted place I'd need it to be to stay. Layers of yellow, red, and blue lights, and the horizon looks rimmed with fire, and there is the blue-lighted bridge beyond. The planes hang in the sky as they approach, flashing their lights to signal their arrival. A subway train runs alongside us, miles away, a string of lights on a track. And then we're 45 degrees from the earth, and the yellow lights of home arrange themselves geometrically and become a grid, until they disappear behind the fog and clouds.

But there is Paris on the other side.

———

WHEN I LOOK AT A MAP AT THE WHALE SHAPE OF LONG ISland, I could cry. My territory. My lost home. Perhaps if Long Island had a stronger identity all its own, or if it had another connotation than vulgarity and new wealth, I would be less reticent to claim it as my place of birth. But then why does the place you happen accidentally to be born in come to define you for the rest of your life?

Leaving home does something to your sense of identity. Either you become more of that place than you ever were while you lived there, or your identity calcifies around the rejection of this place. It is challenging to inhabit the space between these two positions.

All of these perspectives on the same place. It's dizzying.

———

NOT LONG AGO, WHEN HURRICANE SANDY WAS RAGING AND I couldn't get my parents on the phone, I passed a sleepless night checking the *New York Times'* live feed every half hour. I felt gutted not to be there. I haven't lived in New York for nearly a decade, but it's my home, and these were my people rowing themselves out of their flooded houses in Queens. The day after the storm,

I went on a short trip to Champagne with my partner. This trip had been planned for weeks, and there seemed no reason to cancel it, but I felt uncomfortable the whole time. What was I doing drinking champagne while New York was underwater?

But this is normal. Since I left New York to live in Paris in 2004, guilt is more a part of my life than it ever was when I lived there—and I come from a Jewish-Catholic background. Living abroad, I miss weddings, funerals, hurricanes, and everyday life, maintaining a lifeline through my parents, sister, friends, through Skype, Facebook, Twitter. I see New York, now, through the open windows of my computer screen. I see it, like the rest of the world, from someplace else.

CURRENCY

Elisa Albert

1.

Maybe you'll be an actress. Maybe you'll do stand-up. Maybe you'll suck dick for money. Maybe you'll wear intense glasses and make dramatic proclamations into a swank office telephone. Maybe you'll meet your married lover for a drink on a rainy night somewhere dark wearing nothing but lingerie under a coat. Maybe you'll make art in an airy loft in a deserted part of town. Surely there'll be long ruminative walks through the park. The voice-over will be witty as hell.

You can be weird in New York; you can be strange and melancholy and buxom and tall and dark and discerning and behave generally like the exuberant dyke you believe yourself to be. Apparently, they value that sort of thing there!

Ape the hell out of Didion's prose in conversing with Dear Diary and get into a decent college despite your hilariously low GPA. Damn, her sentences are cool. Mr. Bellon's English class is the only thing about which you can muster a shit to give.

"Let's go down to the East River and throw something in," Ani DiFranco growls over and over again, louder and louder over the din of your mother's tirades outside the locked bedroom door. "Something we can't live without and then let's start again." Mutter this phrase tunelessly to yourself while you ride out panic attacks in the shower. Soon you'll be there and here won't matter anymore.

It won't be Didion's New York, though. Not Ani DiFranco's. Not Nicole Holofcener's, Nora Ephron's, Fran Lebowitz's, Jonathan Lethem's, Susan Sontag's, Andy Warhol's, or Patti Smith's either. Silly, though tempting, to pretend otherwise.

You're neither spoiled nor truly reckless enough to fully inhabit the extremes of the experience, but do what you can. Get regularly shit-faced with a gaggle of girls more or less exactly like you. Give spike heels a try. Take strangers home from bars. (Fucking dork: keep a list of their first names, the names of every man with whom you ever so much as make out.) Rarely turn down an invitation or a narcotic. Wind up in strange/desperate/squalid/exorbitant apartments, clubs, bars, restaurants. Forget how you got there. Guzzle Jack-and-Cokes until everyone seems like a dear friend you'll meet again in another lifetime. Bring the house down at Marie's Crisis with your off-key "Adelaide's Lament."

The Second Avenue Deli, Veniero's, Tompkins Square on the verge of sanity. Grey Dog Coffee, where your first husband gets himself banned for general orneriness. City Bakery. The community garden on Avenue D. St. Mark's Bookshop. Flatiron office job, Midtown office job, Gramercy office job, Chelsea freelance job. Forever late to work. One boss gives you an embroidered robe from ABC made of wool and silk, which almost a decade and a half later turns out to still be one of the nicer things you own. LifeThyme Natural Foods, Cobble Hill Theater, Yoga Lab, the Victory, Flying Saucer, Blue Sky Bakery. Read the *New York Post* and the *New York Daily News* cover to cover over lunch.

There are so many people, other people, always more people. Don't bother to remember the bars; bars are interchangeable.

Dress in costume. The weirder the better. Going to the laundromat is a treat. Anytime you can walk the streets. Not as in LA, where life unfolded in the car or at home or in the car or at school or in the car or in the locked bedroom or in the car or at the mall or in the car. Barf, LA, where girls competed to see who could stand out the *least*, who could literally almost disappear. Your whole childhood boiled down to eating a surreptitious ice cream cone slumped behind a book in the back seat of a car driven by a raving lunatic. Ice cream and books got you through. The books all pointed in the general direction of New York.

Orthodox girls in doorman rental on West 96th. Railroad shit-hole with appalling broker's fee on East 11th. Nesting pigeons cooing in the air shaft day and night. Boyfriend's squat on Carmine. Transient girlfriend in a garret down on the Hudson. A garret! Amazing below-market brownstone floor-through on Washington Place. Your favorite college professor comes to crash. You host parties. Neighbors complain about noise.

Warren Street sublet. State Street gem. Fifth-floor walk-up with super in VFW cap forever smoking on the stoop. F train, A train, 2 train, 6 train. Bodega, bodega, bodega. Amazing consignment on Atlantic. Brooklyn promenade.

At Lil' Frankie's Friday nights, Matt the hot waiter picks up the tab and shares the last bottle with you and your bestie. She thinks he wants her, but you are pretty sure he wants you. It's a flirt-off! He wants you both, obviously, but you have zero desire for her, which is probably why you've been friends for so long. Some other girl eventually sleeps with him and years later informs you gleefully, as if she won something.

On a rooftop in Brooklyn at one in the morning, PJ Harvey sings about being on a rooftop in Brooklyn at one in the morning, and someone says something you've never forgotten. Your story's not seldom told, sweetheart.

Spend a summer stoned, Dean Wareham flooding the headphones. Cry constantly. Become a student of yoga. Lose friends. Write your way out. Write your way in. Filthy cliché. Fall in love and out and back in. Let a love or two pass you by, so you have something to think about wistfully in old age. Stop drinking, mostly. Have a baby in the bathtub of a condo on the fourth floor of the old Board of Education building on Livingston. Gather up your fledgling family and flee.

2.

The question is: Where do you belong?

"Where do you feel taller?" asks a tarot queen in the Berkshires on a perfect October afternoon. Excellent question. Up here, you guess.

"There's your answer," she says.

Growing up, you loathed being tall. Girls were not supposed to be tall. Girls were supposed to be as small as possible in every way.

What happened was a wildly great guy. No idea where Albany was, but you were game. Then the baby, and the living-in-two-places thing got old immediately. You could've fought to stay in the city. But you didn't have a whole lot of fight in you just then, and it was easy to say fuck the city. Felt pretty good, actually. Fuck Brooklyn. Fuck the scene and all who flock to it.

But then the harsh reality of Albany. There was some idea that it'd be a friendly place, an insta-community kind of place because people have to stick together, even more so in a postindustrial wasteland kind of place, right? No.

A town designed (rather, corrupted; see William Kennedy's "Everything Everybody Ever Wanted" in the definitive *O Albany!*) to discourage human contact, communal life, organic gathering places. Your basic urban-planning nightmare American state capital. Pathetic monument to the personal automobile. The highway blocks direct human access to the river. To reinvent Sinatra: if you can love it here, you can love it anywhere.

At first you get off on going to the mall. After a decade in the Center of the Universe, a cheeseball exurban mall seems the height of exoticism and delight. Classic beige sterile trying-too-hard fifteen plants in an atrium under a skylight of which some third-rate architect was very proud. State-of-the-art-twenty-years-ago multiplex with arcade. Escalators, Muzak, teenagers up to no good. Israelis accost you with samples of Dead Sea shit from a cart. The hideous seasonal store: Halloween crap, Christmas crap, Valentine's crap, St. Patrick's Day crap, Easter crap, Fourth of July crap, back-to-school crap, around again.

People in the city cock their heads and say, "How *is* it up there? Is it, like, really, really *cold* up there?" Don't blame them; you couldn't find it on a map two years ago, either.

A film buff tells you lots of early noir films were set in Albany, which adds a nice new dimension. We live on an Olmsted-inspired park in a grand, creaky house built around the time your great-great-grandmother was keeping house in some muddy shtetl. Fireplaces, oak moldings, 1950s tile, original tub. A stoop with pale pink columns. Wild, mature perennial garden. When people visit from the city, their jaws hang open. "Albany consolation prize," you explain.

Once, you and the kid get caught in a surprise summer downpour on your way home from the park, and a lady on her stoop sees you from across the street and calls you into her house, where she makes you tea and gives the kid toys and insists you stay for dinner. The struggling local businesses on bedraggled yet faintly charming Lark Street, forever On the Verge. At Lark Fest, drunk dudes urinate and puke on everyone's stoop and neighbors commiserate and it's almost cute. *Metroland*, the highly lovable alternative news weekly. Perpetual fryer smell from Bombers, where you eat once and vow never to eat again. Pristine haven of Crisan Bakery, treats made from scratch by Iggy and Claudia. Dove and Hudson: walk in and breathe books and something you've been thinking about—say, Mircea Eliade, or Paula Fox, or a guide to Ayurveda—appears on a shelf at eye level. They keep your honey's book in the window, next to the Robert Caro doorstop about Robert Moses, proud of the neighborhood guy who done good. Ben & Jerry's on the corner, across from the enormously fat cats at the bodega.

"Hi, kitty cats," waves your boy as he strollers then trikes then scooters on by.

A spring then summer then fall then winter.

"Little guy's growing too fast," says the pockmarked guy who stands out front smoking and keeping watch. A couple open an organic café and bakery on Delaware, down from the Spectrum and New World Bistro. She was crying once when you went in, and you understand that their undertaking is unimaginably difficult; traveling to Phish shows in the yellow VW van used to be way more fun than convincing this struggling shit-balls community to rally around its local organic café.

Takes time, but you find wonderful people. No worries about where the kid will "get in" to preschool. A shaggy collection of earthy midwifery-supportive fellow families. No one gives a flying fucking shit what you're wearing. There's always room for you and your laptop at the okay coffee roaster.

From your kitchen window, watch the sun rise on Empire State Plaza, Rockefeller's misguided monument to his prick, with its impressive collection of modern art, reflecting pool, neofascist concrete expanse, bizarre underground city, wintertime skating rink. The way those four capitol buildings stand sentinel on the horizon. The aptly named Egg, where Rickie Lee Jones opens with "Satellites" in the hundred-seat theater.

The drive on I-90 to preschool, past Nipper the dog, the hills and the river and the skies you would not believe. The river walk, the pedestrian walkway. Miles and miles of bike path. The U-Haul truck rotating slowly on top of a storage facility on the river.

At the Shitty Bagel Chain surrounded by Real People (meaning: not living metalives on top of actual lives, not trained in matters of ultimate coolness, not wealthy, not angling for notoriety), notice how it's a bit less noisy in the superego sense. You can relax. You have nothing to prove.

A Manhattan-reared artist who now lives in western Massachusetts shakes her head in disgust at the thought that anyone still wants to live there. "Take your art where it matters," she says. Think about an inward-focused life. Where can you best lead one? Do your thing, stand tall. Life's a turning inward, you're convinced lately, a getting quiet, learning to observe and be still. Some call it meditation, but you get scared off when it has a name.

Within a forty-five-minute radius: Troy and its vibrant art community, too many kick-ass farmers' markets to name, Saratoga, Hudson, Berkshires, Catskills, Ghent, Chatham, Great Barrington, Saugerties, MassMoca, Tanglewood, Kripalu. You actually love it here, turns out. Look closely: it's a promising place. There's work to be done. There's potential here. Put your money and effort and energy *here*, where it's possible to make a dent.

And God, how about those creepy birdcalls in the train station garage? They sound like rhesus monkeys. What the fuck are they? No one seems to know. Detailed conversations between those animals, day and night. It's so weird and uncool here that it turns out to be pretty cool. But the question remains, only partially because of the mindfuck of having recently become someone's mother: Who the hell are you and what are you doing here?

"Where upstate do you live?" wonders a cool girl behind the counter of a cool north Brooklyn café.

"Hudson," you say, because you can't deal with this chick writing you off as some irrelevant bumblefuck mom. Hudson has name recognition, artists and art and currency. You need this random chick to understand that You Are Culturally Relevant. Shame, rage. You're ridiculous. Why this need? Are you *twelve*?

"Oh my God, I love it up there!" she says. "Sooooo cool."

You nod. You matter. You are an arbiter, goddamn it! AN ARBITER.

3.

To TALK ABOUT NEW YORK—LIVING THERE, ASPIRING TO LIVE
there, having lived there—is to talk about currency. Not privilege
and not money, mind you; money is simple. Money is straightforward. Money can give you choices, options. Privilege skews
how you see yourself and others, fucks with your head. Currency
is something else. Currency is terrifically complex. Money and
privilege can make you comfortable, but only currency gives you
real power. You can't buy currency; it eludes plenty of rich, entitled people. Beauty, originality, fearlessness: these are some of
the currencies of New York.

Papa Irwin, small-time shyster genius youngest son of an alcoholic Montreal policeman, bought a parcel of land in Los Angeles
on the corner of what is now Sunset and La Brea in 1950 and
moved his family west. Rumor has it he and his uncle, traveling
salesmen, sold condoms to whorehouses. Papa called New York
City "that cesspool," aghast at your living there. Alone, no less.

Your parents got married at the hotel from *Pretty Woman*. Big
Brentwood Spanish-style homes, Bullocks Wilshire, I. Magnin,
Sweet Sixteen at Louise's. Birds-of-paradise, magnolias, palms.
The flats of Beverly Hills before the Persians. Bat mitzvah a few
blocks from Santa Monica beach. Fancy private school. At sixteen Maggie Gyllenhaal had sumptuously hairy armpits, a most
incredible vintage wardrobe, the confidence of a legend. (Currency, friends.)

It's not until you're long gone that you begin to understand: it's
unusual to be "from" a place that comprises a lot of fantasy lives.
But from there you are, and what an education you got, man.
The culture of name-dropping and status anxiety, the whiff of

desperation inherent in any attempt to assert oneself that way: it was in your microwaved baby formula.

"You don't seem like you're from LA," people always say.

"Thank you," you reply.

New York was your escape from that bullshit, all the *yeah so we were having brunch at Balthazar when I blew this marginally famous person in the bathroom of that bar on Ludlow the night of the Williamsburg heroin orgy wearing the dress I bought at the Barney's warehouse sale to the best show ever at the venue no one's heard of yet.* Puff out your chest and prove just how connected and pre-scient and rooted you are. When the real currency lies in who lives in the shittiest neighborhood and cares the least? Who gets in free? Whose art is so essential it cannot be ignored?

Love letters to New York are invariably designed to make the reader feel like a loser, no? You might feel powerless in New York, but you can always make some poor schmuck who's never lived there, or, better yet, *only recently just moved there,* feel even more powerless. Fine: so maybe you remember when Alphabet City was scary and Brooklyn was cheap. Maybe you went to Elaine's, KGB, Mars Bar. Maybe you got mugged. Congratulations. If you remember its previous incarnation, or the incarnation prior to that, you own New York. You came, you saw, you conquered. Here's your I HEART NYC T-shirt. You're legit. You're rooted. Now shush. An ultimately boring-ass economics, and honestly the whole marketplace can pretty much suck it.

Your identity isn't reliant on that place, on any place; it's just a construction. Magical thinking. It's as if you have Stockholm syndrome: the city took you captive, stole your heart, ran off with your imagination, left you broke and battered. Sure, sing it a freakin' love song. But make no mistake: the city owns you.

Still, you really miss that goddamned place, something about its weird, destructive pull. Plenty of good reasons to hop a train down: gigs, friends, family, marvelous headshrinker. Kiss your family, get on the southbound, read a silly rag, watch the river whiz by. Usually a whole row to yourself. The conductors smile. Mustachioed flattop guy and buxom grandma type are your favorites. Once in a while, the vibe's a little on the scary side. Once there were bomb-sniffing dogs and TSA agents. And compared to the train situation in, say, Western Europe, Amtrak is an overpriced disgrace.

But it's a lovely liminal space, the train. Put on headphones. More often than not a little stoned. (Only backfires when you miss your train. Once you had to drive to Poughkeepsie to catch Metro North absolutely baked, and your friend stayed on the phone with you the whole way, and you said out loud to her and to yourself and to the empty highway, "Okay, this is really not okay. I'm being an asshole and I gotta cool it with the pot.")

At Penn Station, gather up your stuff. Deep breath. Sentimental souls need rituals. Go up a few escalators and emerge across from the grand steps of the post office on Eighth Avenue, where the camera would pan up in a dizzy spiral, if there were a camera.

"Paying respects to lost youth," you text people. "Drink?" You hate making plans too far in advance. You also hate alcohol but want that looseness you used to enjoy, that who-knows-where-the-night-might-take-us, lately in such short supply.

Needless to say, you love your family. You are awash in love and gratitude for your beautiful life up the river. But you cherish these field trips. Time is not linear. The old you is a fossil trapped in amber here, perfectly preserved. Stay at a friend's tiny studio.

Read a good book over breakfast at the perfect tiny brasserie down the street.

Sit on your old stoop for a while. A couple of hours before the train home. The girls are all in costume. An old lady shuffles past, looking at you, amused. You're in costume, too: city drag. Way more "interesting" a look than is worth wasting on preschool pickup in Albany. Scribbling in a notebook, to boot. Two women walk by. One is pushing an infant in a stroller; the other's hugely pregnant. The pregnant one says she feels "a lot of pressure." The other one says something-something "heavy." If you're not immersed in such things, they can seem repetitive and boring. But if you are immersed in them, they comprise your life, so what are you supposed to do? You too waddled these streets with friends, talking about bodies and birth and pressure and heaviness. It now seems an almost unbearably special time, but it was just life unfolding.

This lovely film guy and his actress girlfriend moved in when you left. What if they find you sitting here on their stoop? That would be kind of sad. You once ran into the actress around the corner, and it was embarrassing, as if she knew you were casing her apartment. You're upset they live here, kind of. This magic gem of an apartment that used to be yours. They still get mail for you occasionally. The super died last year. Never saw him smile, but he was a good guy. The way he sat there, smoking, vacant stare. They way he said "yeahhhhhh" in his sandpaper voice.

You fell in love here a bunch, wrote a couple books, gave birth. How could that time not hold you in thrall? "Change is seen as something evil only by those who have lost their youth or sense of humor." That was Cookie Mueller on the East Village, 1985. The city's not the same and you're not the same and you'll never get that time back because time is a spiral, girl: a spiral. Life is elsewhere now. Live it.

All accountable, reasonably happy grown-ups are the same, but unhappy immature drama-queen wretches are all unhappy in their own way. There's something terrifically sad about growing up, which is why sometimes people refuse to do it. (Some of your very favorite people.) I mean, Jesus, it's only a place. It isn't responsible for who you've become; it could have been Tel Aviv or Berlin or San Francisco or London. Could've been rural Idaho, Sebastopol, Ireland, Texas. Anyway, how many people are lucky enough to *choose where they live* in the first place?

It's just you miss the reckless girl who lived here. Petulant funny stubborn blind unforgiving little wench, beholden to no one, blindly enacting her will on everything, everyone. She was nobody's mother. It was your youth! Now you're older and wiser and better in about a thousand ways. A halfway decent sense of self on a good day, for starters. Now you know a thing or two about where to put your energy, what it means to build up instead of tear down, what it's like to nurture valuable things so that they grow. You wouldn't trade anything for anything. All of this is true. And yet, let us not skirt the issue that something was lost. Something has been lost.

A WAR ZONE FOR ANYONE LOOKING FOR LOVE

Liza Monroy

Bear Stearns, August 23, 2001

I stood by the pay phone outside my former fiancé's office, fresh off a red-eye from LA and jet-lagged in the muggy afternoon. After barely speaking to him during the nine months since we had broken off our engagement, showing up unannounced to tell him I wanted him back and was moving to New York City to prove it was the kind of thing only stalkers, *Sex and the City* characters, or early twenty-somethings would do. I was at least one of those things.

My former fiancé, the boy from high school in spray-painted jeans and earrings who would go on to become one of Wall Street's youngest managing directors, proposed the year I turned twenty-one, while I was in LA for a three-month internship. I would move to New York to become an (Extremely) Young Wall Street Wife: find a job in publishing, go out on the town with investment bankers, and work toward my dream of becoming a writer. I just needed to figure out how. Judging by my idols (Joan Didion, Jack Kerouac), New York was the place to do that, too. Since it was the height of the *Sex and the City* era, though, my contemporary model was Carrie Bradshaw. That was how young I was, young enough to venerate Carrie Bradshaw and to think myself ready for marriage at twenty-one.

Since my former fiancé was a tall, offbeat, enigmatic, problematic, charming businessman, and since our relationship could ultimately best be described as a wetland deposit of dead organic material, I'll call him Mr. Bog.

Mr. Bog came downstairs to the lobby and informed me that I was crazy, and he was leaving on a business trip to Colombia in the morning.

"Inspecting a pipeline," he said, "in a jungle with gorillas. Could be dangerous."

"Gorillas?"

"*Guerrillas.*"

We met later near his apartment on 86th and York. He was walking an orange cat on a leash. We ascended to his studio—all pizza boxes, analyst reports, and overflowing trash cans—and dropped off the cat. At the bar downstairs, he listened to my reasons why breaking things off was a mistake.

"If you move here," he said, "we can see."

East Village, August 28, 2001

FROM A FRIEND'S ROOFTOP, THE TWIN TOWERS LOOMED ABOVE. I stared, almost praying, as if they were representations of deities at an altar: *Make my life in New York as sparkling and magical as you.*

Los Angeles, Fourteen Days Later

I ONLY BECAME MORE DETERMINED.

"Don't do it," my mother said. "There's anthrax there. The whole city's a mess."

Nothing would stop me. Not anthrax, orange-level terrorism alerts, or my mother.

Chelsea, April 2002

MY ROOMMATE AND BEST FRIEND, EMIR, MOVED WITH ME. WE stayed with my great-uncle in Chelsea for a few days, sleeping on couches in his theater space. He co-owned a theater company. Framed playbills and photographs from past performances lined the walls, and the place was cluttered with antiques.

When my mother and I visited when I was little, we stayed there and went to the theater, the Empire State Building, and the Central Park Zoo. She was in the Foreign Service, so I didn't have a home in the traditional sense. Constant change was home, or wherever I put down my suitcase. Maybe that was why, Mr. Bog aside, I felt connected to New York. It was both a constant and a place where every misfit fit in.

Mr. Bog emailed. He'd been in a surfing accident in Mexico, shattered his ankle against rocks. A blood clot from the ankle broke loose and lodged in his lung. While he was in the hospital, certain he was about to die, he thought of me, making him realize he did want to try again.

Lower East Side, April 2002

IN OUR NEW CLOSET-SIZED FIFTH-FLOOR WALK-UP, EMIR AND I assembled furniture from Ikea in New Jersey. Mr. Bog and I walked around Chinatown, and he came over to my little room where clothes hung on a wardrobe rack procured from my great-uncle's theater. We slept together for the first time since the broken engagement, but the following week, he said he "couldn't do this." Bog left me, but at least he left me with New York.

Midtown and Lower East Side, 2002–2003

MY FIRST JOB WAS IN THE NOTORIOUS AGENT-TRAINEE PRO-gram at the William Morris Agency, pushing a mail cart around the Midtown skyscraper in a suit. Between mail runs, we sat in the basement reading the trades and the *Times*. I earned four hundred dollars a week—enough to make my share of rent, then splurge on happy hour and the teriyaki-pineapple veggie dogs from Crif Dogs on St. Mark's.

In my tiny room with its distant view of the Manhattan Bridge, I wrote bad short stories featuring Mr. Bog. On weekends, I sought adventure in the city.

One of my mailroom colleagues used to work at *Saturday Night Live* and still got invited to the weekly after-parties thrown by cast members. "Tracy Morgan's party is tomorrow night," he mentioned nonchalantly one Friday afternoon.

The party was in an empty loft in a high-rise way downtown. I looked out the floor-to-ceiling glass at traffic rushing by on West Street twenty-something stories below. Naked women—high-class call girls, I presumed—wandered the party, men helping themselves as if they were appetizer trays, leading them over to only partially concealed couches in corners. Everyone was on something, and we stayed until the sun came up.

Welcome to New York.

I wrote in East Village cafés and wandered through Tompkins Square Park to meet Emir for gay-barhopping. I spent hours at the Met and in Williamsburg dive bars. I stood in line at three in the morning for the best pizza, Rosario's on the Lower East Side. In some small way, New York was mine, even though Mr. Bog was not. Sometimes he reappeared to help me do things like make decisions about my first 401(k) over cocktails at the Gramercy Hotel. I wondered whether we'd somehow become friends.

Chelsea, February–November 2004

AT TWENTY-FOUR, I WAS OUT OF THE MAILROOM AND WORKing for a literary agent. I had a small one-bedroom on 15th Street and Eighth Avenue and a boyfriend. An email from Mr. Bog arrived in my work inbox one snowy February morning, asking how I was doing. "Good," I replied, "but freezing." His response: an email confirmation for two first-class tickets to Puerto Rico. For that weekend. I broke up with my boyfriend.

Four years after ending our first engagement, I married Mr. Bog at city hall. I published some writing and left the agency to freelance for magazines. I could say I was a writer in Manhattan married to an investment banker, so New York dreams came true if you stayed long enough.

East Village, September 2007

IF YOU STAYED LONG ENOUGH, THEY ALSO UNRAVELED.

When I interviewed author Anthony Swofford for an article and the topic of love in New York came up, he said, "New York

City is a war zone for anyone looking for love. It's a city con-
structed for the ease of bad behavior and outright deceit. I loved
it for that reason for many years."

So did Mr. Bog. One clue was naked pictures from another
woman in his email, left open on our computer. She wanted
to know when he would return to Argentina, where Bog had
emerging-markets business. She was only a symptom of the larger
problem: Mr. Bog and I were not actually compatible. He loved
house music and bottle service on the expense account. I preferred
plays and literary readings. I convinced him to see Joan Didion's
The Year of Magical Thinking with Vanessa Redgrave (about, ironically, Didion losing her husband). Mr. Bog said, "Never again
will I spend two hours listening to some old lady in an Adiron-
dack chair." He gave me jewelry and tried to give away my books.

In the early morning hours after a night of clubbing for his
thirty-second birthday, Mr. Bog, drunk, grabbed my laptop off a
table and tried to throw it across the room. I knew he had problems with anger, but I hadn't seen its propensity to turn violent
until that night. It took that much to push me to end it. I couldn't
be with someone who crossed that line, no matter how much
history we had. We went through a Wall Street divorce, replete
with Manhattan lawyers on five-figure retainers. It was difficult
and sad as divorces are, and I longed to go back to a simpler time
in my New York life. I moved back to the Lower East Side. Simultaneously defeated and triumphant, I still had the city.

I'd become one of those people who said things like, "When I
moved here, Orchard Street was nothing but leather shops and
Williamsburg was where you went for cheaper rent."

I never considered going elsewhere to start over. That's the
thing about New York: no one ever wants to leave. Throngs of

hopeful protagonists arrive with their dreams and diminutive bank accounts. It's only in disaster movies that you see anyone wanting to get out, and it's because a meteor is coming or aliens are attacking. Divorce didn't mean failure. Leaving New York certainly would.

Prospect Heights, Brooklyn, 2008–2012

OVER FOURTEEN-DOLLAR COCKTAILS AT A FAUX SPEAKEASY, A friend complained that she was tired of high rent and a job that left her with no writing time. Many friends were writers without time to write; in New York, being there sometimes defeated the purpose of being there. She confessed she was thinking of moving to Pittsburgh or the South.

"That's a terrible idea," I began.

This scenario repeated itself with a small parade of disillusioned friends, starring me as stalwart for staying even when what they wanted most was to get out. In "Goodbye to All That," Didion says it never occurred to her that she was living a real life in New York. I thought living anywhere else meant you'd given up. Stay "too long at the Fair"? Preposterous. What was not true of my Bog marriage was true of the city: the successful people were simply the ones who stuck around. I was determined to become one of them.

This version barely resembled my twenty-two-year-old self: early thirties divorcée trampling around the city in six-inch-heeled boots giving directions in the West Village without pause. I had a faculty appointment teaching composition at Columbia, a Brooklyn one-bedroom, a sketchily procured Park Slope Food Coop membership, a literary agent, a Jungian psychoanalyst, and a by-referral-only tarot reader. That's New York: you wake up realizing this is what you dreamed of when you were younger, this is what it looks like, and yet there's still a long way to go, much more to do and accomplish. That is why I told the would-be deserters not to leave. Stay longer, see what happens. Ultimately, my friend who wanted to move to Pittsburgh or the South renewed her lease.

I had a couple of postdivorce boyfriends, but none lasted. One involved the guy taking revenge for my breaking up with him by shredding my clothes, trashing the apartment, and drowning my two laptops in the bathtub—the one Mr. Bog had tried to throw and one I'd acquired since. I don't know if such relationship failures had to do with trying to find love in New York City (see Swofford), being young, being me (impulsive), or some combination of any or all of the above. I settled into singlehood, for the first time thinking that would be all right. I thought I'd be lonely if I wasn't married in my thirties, but I wasn't lonely, even in a crowded city with so much room for isolation and so little for intimacy. I did hope I would meet someone. Specifically, at the Park Slope Food Coop, while I, and possibly he, were sweeping floors or slicing cheese. But I didn't.

———

THAT I—WHO CONVINCED PEOPLE NOT TO VENTURE INTO THE abyss of elsewhere—suddenly walked out on New York shocked me even more than the friends I talked out of doing this very thing. Emir, still my best friend (some things, even in the ever-changing landscape of New York, remain constant), quoted something he heard somewhere: "Good things happen gradually and over time. Great things happen all at once."

New York will invite you to pick up a quirky hobby. Mine was the Brazilian martial art capoeira. I trained almost nightly. The capoeira group had locations in other cities, too. At the end of my tenth September in New York, visitors arrived for a performance. One of them, from Santa Cruz, California, was an elementary school teacher and the capoeira equivalent of a black belt. "He's a special guy," a mutual friend mentioned in passing, "charismatic and smart." She was right. I was instantly at ease around him. He was funny, interesting, easy to be with. I was glad to have made this nice new friend from California.

The nice new friend from California wanted to see the High Line, the former elevated train line on Manhattan's West Side that's been converted to a park. I told him I could take him and anyone else who wanted to go. We turned out to be the only ones.

He was at Starbucks when I arrived, eating a bagel. I would have told him to throw that Starbucks bagel away, that I could take him to get a real one, but bagels fell from my mind when he looked up at me and I never mentioned them. During that High Line walk, I had a better time in his company than I ever had on any date, and we weren't even on a date. He kept joking that I put up with him all day.

Two nights later, we kissed on the subway. When he went back to California, I didn't know if I would see him again, but also unlike my New York lovers, he didn't play games. I planned to visit for three weeks in November. Instead I got engaged and stayed. It seems that when something is meant to happen, nothing can stop it, which sounds like something a by-referral-only tarot reader or someone who lives in Santa Cruz would say.

Santa Cruz, Today

I WEAR FLIP-FLOPS IN JANUARY AND LIVE IN A HOUSE A MILE from the beach. In August, my fiancé and I are getting married in a redwood grove. Friends and my mother have asked how I could move across the country and get engaged to someone I'd only known for a few months. The only answer I can give is that it felt right in a way that nothing did before, not even being in New York. That's true but not the whole story: he did offer to move to Brooklyn, if that was what I wanted. But what I wanted was to join him. In this zephyrean beachside paradise, sea lion barks under the pier replaced subway rumblings beneath sidewalk grates. Drivers stop if they see a pedestrian so much as eyeball a crosswalk.

Maybe I was wrong to convince those would-be southerners and Pittsburghers not to leave. I wonder, if you come from somewhere else and stay long enough, whether New York is a place you inevitably outgrow, whether you take from it what you can, then go. If that was the case, I didn't realize it until I had a reason to leave—not because I failed, but because I found something worth leaving for, the kind of love I thought I was only imagining existed. Turns out I was only imagining it existed, for me, in New York.

REAL ESTATE

Sari Botton

"**I**'m hearing the words *'Don't give up the apartment.'*"

It was my first of what would eventually add up to ten yearly appointments with Sophie, a psychic who was popular among media types—a ritual I'd later refer to as my "annual checkup."

We were seated in the run-down, rent-controlled sixth-floor walk-up Sophie herself had held on to for twenty-odd years at the corner of Mott and Prince Streets. In the fall of 1993 that neighborhood was still considered Little Italy. It would be another few years before realtors would rebrand it as Nolita.

Petite and tomboyish in her forties, Sophie sat across from me at a table strewn with tarot cards, alternately flipping them and pushing back her little-girl bangs with the heel of her hand.

"Yes, that's definitely the message," she said after closing her eyes for a moment. *"Don't give up the apartment."*

Well, no shit, I thought. I had a lease on a marginally decrepit but livable rent-stabilized one-bedroom in a tenement on East 13th Street, for which I paid about $600 a month. I didn't need a clairvoyant to caution me against relinquishing it.

Besides, real estate advice was hardly what I wanted for my $150. No, I wanted Sophie to tell me what most people go to psychics to hear: that there was love on the horizon.

———

I WAS TWENTY-EIGHT, TWO YEARS OUT OF AN ILL-CONSIDERED marriage I'd entered at twenty-three. Add to the usual difficulties associated with finding love in New York that I was a bit of an odd bird, difficult to match. All my life I'd been a strange mix of loner, social butterfly, and musical theater geek, sometimes painfully shy and awkward around people, at other times charming and entertaining. I felt like some kind of alien, out of step with the kids I grew up with (even fellow theater geeks thought I was weird), my classmates in college, and my coworkers at the assorted publications where I worked over the years. I didn't like the same clothes, hairstyles, movies, music, and food that most of my peers did, and I had this insistent need to do most things my own peculiar way, even if it made no sense.

Not only would a man in my life have all that to contend with, but he'd also have stiff competition for my attention from the city itself. My idea of a good time—pretty much *the best time*—was walking leisurely around Manhattan and Brooklyn from neighborhood to neighborhood by myself, with no particular destination or goal. I preferred it to doing just about anything with anyone—other than singing, which I also did mostly by myself.

Walking the city aimlessly alone had been my favorite activity since I was fourteen. I got the idea after some older camp friends brought me along for an afternoon of simply kicking around, mostly in the Village. That day, New York City transformed for me. It stopped being some kind of Oz, the fancy place where you went to see Broadway shows, the Little Orchestra Society at Lincoln Center, my singer dad's operatic concerts, and all manner of culture with a capital C. This New York, the one my friends showed me, was a different kind of exotic. It was gritty and real; a place to take your time and people-watch; a place where what was happening outside, in the streets, on the sidewalks, in the parks, was the main attraction.

Soon after that day, for the first of many times, I lied to my mother the way other girls lied about hanging out with boys, telling her I was taking the Long Island Rail Road only four stops to see a friend in Lynbrook, but instead riding all the way to Penn Station so I could wander the city for hours, as far as my babysitting money would take me. I would sip hot chocolate as I observed the skaters at Rockefeller Center. I'd eat soup in Chinatown and observe the other bridge-and-tunnel diners in from the suburbs as they greedily inhaled their spare ribs and chow mein. I'd browse vintage clothing stores in the West Village and hang around Washington Square Park so I could observe the buskers around the fountain and the colorful, loud tourists cheering them on. I liked to observe non-loner-alien people, and New York City was the best place to do that.

The bonus: I could do it all without having to ask my mother to drive me from place to place as I had to on Long Island. Here, on foot, I was free. Wherever my feet took me, I was happy to have the city as my sole companion. I loved the feeling of being alone but among people.

The preference for my own company naturally made it difficult to couple up too comfortably as an adult. I was horribly lonely and wanted to find that one other outsider who was put on this strange planet just for me—one who would, of course, give me plenty of space for my loner activities. So far, I only knew how to get that from guys who were difficult to pin down, emotionally withholding, and typically addicted to at least one substance, which is to say even less available than I was. Say what you will about unavailable guys, but you don't run the risk of making them feel neglected when you want to do your own thing. Dating them so I wouldn't feel hemmed in turned out to be a faulty strategy, though, because they drained me of my psychic energy—when they were around and when they weren't—so I never really got to be *alone* when I was alone, and when we were together, I was never fulfilled.

As for nice, available guys, I seemed to be utterly allergic to them as mates but great at being friends with them. And so I introduced all my male friends to female friends. When the second of five couples married, they dubbed me the "East Village Yenta."

The matchmaker had no talent for setting herself up, though. This job I'd have to outsource. That's where Sophie came in.

———

"I SEE THE LETTER B," SHE SAID IN HER FLAT WESTERN NEW York accent. "Hmm. Who could that be? Pick nine cards."

When I was done choosing, she shifted the cards around into different formations. "Okay. So, this person whose name begins with B. He's got a goatee, maybe? I see him in a room with sharp angles and a buffet with really mediocre food."

For years afterward, I would scrutinize intently the "angles" of one mediocre-buffet-filled room and then another to determine whether they might in fact be "sharp."

Just then Sophie's cat jumped onto the table. "Oh, Edie," she said, stroking her. "You know what this means?" No, I didn't. "When she climbs on the table during a reading, it's usually a sign of true love. This guy with the letter B—this could be something! Yeah, look at that: the nine of cups," she said, pointing. "That card can mean marriage. You might have a marriage to a guy whose name starts with B."

Oh great. I'd just divorced a guy whose name started with B. There went $150.

It's a wonder I went back a second time, a year later. At that first appointment with Sophie, I didn't yet know about the strange, random accuracy of at least some of her predictions—like the suggestion I keep my eye out for a good job offer from "someone named Horace—no, Horst" three years before I'd receive an assignment to ghostwrite a book for a guy with the unusual name of . . . Horst.

Incidentally, a three-year gap between a prediction and its coming to fruition was relatively short in Sophie-time. As she explained, "What I see here could happen in ten minutes or ten years from now. It's all very Agatha Christie. I'll hear a name, or I'll see an article of clothing, and ten years from now you'll go, 'Oh my God—there's that guy with the red shoes Sophie was telling me about!' And he might not actually *be* your guy. But you can bet he will have *something to do with* your guy."

Ten minutes or *ten years?* Couldn't she pinpoint the timing of her predictions just a little more accurately?

"But time isn't linear, dear." Whatever that meant.

I WAS ALSO EAGER TO HEAR FROM SOPHIE WHETHER THERE was a career break in my near future—some high-profile writing job or assignment that would both pay out and put an end to my six years languishing in the humdrum world of trade magazines. I'd wanted to be a writer living in New York City since I was a teen, after my grandparents took me to dinner at a restaurant in the East 60s and I spotted a woman eating by herself, with a notebook and pen as her only companions. I'd already been writing since I was in grade school. (I won the school-wide essay contest two years in a row.) But that woman writing and eating by herself put images in my head of a writing life located specifically in the city.

Not included in those images, to the best of my recollection, was one of me toiling endlessly at trade magazines with names like *Body Fashions/Intimate Apparel, Fashion Jewelry Plus!,* and *Home Furnishings News,* at the last of which I grudgingly covered the most bizarre assortment of beats: luxury linens, decorative pillows, air purifiers, and car alarms. I was always flying out from LaGuardia to housewares trade shows in Vegas and Chicago, where I'd moderate panel discussions on such exciting topics as whether HEPA air filtration was more or less effective than ionic particulation. I put in long hours at my desk, lunching and sometimes dinnering on salty soups and flavorless packaged salads from the nearest Smiler's deli in the bland, sprawling corporate park that is much of Midtown. That particular New York seemed galaxies away from the one I wanted to inhabit. I wanted Sophie to tell me I'd soon get to put that all behind me and move on to more glorified and satisfying assignments. And, more importantly, success with my own creative writing.

"Well, I *am* seeing something," she said. "I'm seeing book-shelves . . ."

Oh my God, *bookshelves.* I cut her off. "Do you think that means it's time for me to write my book?"

I was referring to *Adventures in Divorce,* the memoir I'd been planning to write on the cheerful topic of my family's legacy of failed marriages, including my own at twenty-six. (Even my step-parents have stepparents.) If Sophie didn't envision the book being published soon and to critical acclaim, I didn't want to put myself through the slow torture of sitting quietly at my desk after my day job, enduring loneliness and boredom, recalling painful and embarrassing experiences, and wrestling unwieldy sentences into submission. I wasn't going to take any chances if the time wasn't right and if I didn't already *know* it was going to be well received.

"Well, let's ask the cards," Sophie said. "Pick seven . . ."

And the answer was . . .

"The cards are saying that any time from now on is a good time." That certainly narrowed things down.

Of course, it was the right answer. It's always the right time to get started writing. Duh. And it's always difficult, and there will never be any guarantees. And it's a process, a slow one. *Blah, blah, blah.* I'd resisted that wisdom when it was imparted by instructors at the two MFA programs I'd dabbled in before quitting, plus every self-help book on writing I'd ever read, and I was less than thrilled when the distilled essence of it was delivered again by a high-priced psychic.

———

IF I WASN'T PRODUCING MUCH WRITING, IT WASN'T FOR LACK of space. My East 13th Street apartment had an extra little room for me to write in, and I did, some—mostly freelance articles and essays and a lame proposal for *Adventures in Divorce*. But I never pushed far enough through the difficulty of writing any one piece of the book for it to really go anywhere.

I had any number of ways to distract myself from that difficulty. There were countless hours of mental gymnastics trying to figure out one intermittently interested guy after another. There were longer and longer runs around the East River Park. There was singing, at the top of my lungs, in my apartment (my upstairs neighbor once popped down to ask, "Can we move the Joni Mitchell hour to a time when I'm not home?") and at the weekly jazz open mics at Cleopatra's Needle on the Upper West Side, and Rue B in my neighborhood. I took to the task of organizing casual dinners among the group of friends I considered my East Village family as if I were a professional event planner.

I had a place I could afford to write and live in alone in New York City, and I was squandering my time there. I tried not to think about that, and so I stopped noticing. But the years ticked by, quite linearly I might add, and somehow one day I was twenty-eight, and the next I was thirty-eight. I assumed I'd have that rent-stabilized apartment forever, which at twenty-eight seemed like a great thing for a struggling writer. But at thirty-eight, still lonely and with few details of my life changed, I started to imagine that I'd grow old and die alone in that run-down shoe-box, and it scared me.

———

LET ME CUT TO THE CHASE HERE. TEN YEARS ALMOST TO THE day after my first reading from Sophie, in the fall of 2003, I met a (goateed) guy named Brian.

Brian. *Whose named starts with* B.

An hour after our first date, brunch at Life Café, I attended a wedding reception—*in a room with sharp angles and a buffet with really mediocre food*. Well, the closest any room's angles had come to being "sharp" in the decade since Sophie had predicted that detail. (The wedding was at the industrial-chic, poured-concrete-walled Tenth Street Lounge, where there were no soft edges. Whatever. Work with me.)

Brian was a really nice guy, and fortunately, thanks to roughly $20,000 worth of psychotherapy, I no longer had a strong aversion to that. He was cute, smart, funny, creative, and, I would later learn, totally cool with me being a weird loner when I needed to be. He'd also soon come to encourage me to stop making my singing a private affair and accompany me on pretty much every instrument on recordings we'd make together.

But let's get to the important stuff: he had *real estate*, specifically a rambling below-market-value loft in a Gothic Victorian former yeshiva on Avenue B, across from Tompkins Square Park. After our third date, he invited me up. As I stepped in behind him, I couldn't believe my eyes—1,800 square feet on two levels, three bedrooms, high ceilings, exposed brick, big windows, an arched entryway, and other interesting architectural details. It was run-down with chipping paint, which gave it a bohemian feel similar to that in my apartment. Brian and I shared the same threadbare flea market style, with mismatched furniture, some of it picked up right off the curb—the same place I'd found my writing desk.

Only a few months after we started dating, I moved, unofficially, into that incredible, gaping loft and began renting out my place on 13th Street—by the weekend, by the week, by the month via a company called New York Habitat, a precursor to Airbnb—as a way to keep it, just in case things with Brian didn't work out. Eventually, though, toward the end of 2004, my super warned me that I was in danger of getting busted. "The landlord's been asking me if you really live here," he said. Brian and I had gotten engaged. There was no question we'd ultimately choose his 1,800 square feet over my 350. Maybe it was time to hand over my keys.

My last day in the apartment, after all my stuff had been moved out, I sat for a while on the scraped-up hardwood floor. I couldn't decide whether, now that it was empty, the place looked like a spare art gallery or a seedy slum. New York City real estate is like that. How you perceive it is relative, mostly to time and to what other conditions you've lived in. The $600 dump I'd moved into with lumpy plaster walls, lopsided floors, and peeling paint hadn't changed much over the years. Even with new windows, it was probably still a dump by many people's standards. Although the next tenant would pay $2,150. *Tenants*, plural, that is. When I stopped by a few months later, the super told me there were four young women, NYU students, sharing the space. (In 2020, I saw it listed for $3,500.)

Without my furniture, clothes, books, the memory-steeped markers of my time there, the place had a peacefulness to it that

I wanted to inhabit for one moment longer. It struck me that the sunlight streaming in was the same golden hue it had been when I moved in. I swear it could have been the same day. Had any of the things I remembered actually even happened here? The many lonely, gloomy days interspersed with relatively brighter ones? The all-nighters to meet freelance deadlines? *Twelve* birthdays? The parade of bad boyfriends, first nights together, tearful last nights, promises made and broken? Was this the moment before or the moment after? Maybe time *isn't* linear.

———

BRIAN AND I WERE OFFICIALLY COHABITING ON TOMPKINS Square Park for one measly month when we got the news: we were getting kicked out. The building had been awarded landmark status, and we were allowed to stay just one more year, with our $1,350 rent nearly tripled. The week after we eloped, at thirty-nine and forty-two, we welcomed two roommates to help us afford the place. Yes—we got married *and then we got roommates.*

The building would undergo major renovations, and the rents would skyrocket to $6,500 and higher. Michel Gondry, followed by Matt Dillon, would each spend a couple of years living in our space.

First, though, we'd spend a bitter year in housing court trying to fight it. Toward the end of the expensive, infuriating legal process, when it became clear that we were probably going to lose the place, one of our lawyers asked each member of the tenants' association, "Have you got some other place to go?"

And that's when I heard it—Sophie's voice. *"Don't give up the apartment."*

Shit! I gave up the apartment! *How could I have given up the apartment?!* I was suddenly sure those words Sophie had uttered so many years before pertained specifically to our current situation. I couldn't believe it. I began to kick myself.

But also at some point during that struggle, Brian and I both found ourselves feeling soured on the East Village and the city as a whole. Never mind that we were getting priced out. The city wasn't the same anymore. Of course, New York is never the same, from one day to the next. But now it seemed there was a more extreme, rapid level of gentrification. Every neighborhood was starting to appear and feel the same. Each one lost its individual character as nearly every deli, pizza place, shoemaker, or thrift shop was replaced by a Chase or a Duane Reade or a Chipotle or a pricey, twee mini-cupcake shop. One by one, our favorite restaurants and shops went out of business. A three-dollar umbrella was now five. The Second Avenue Deli was now on Third Avenue. All this made it mercifully easy to leave the island we were getting kicked off anyway.

We moved upstate to Rosendale, a depressed, funky little river town that's become an outpost of what I've labeled the Downtown Diaspora. Nearly all our friends there moved up from either Lower Manhattan or Brooklyn—not realizing at the time that now *we* were the gentrifiers, upstate.

———

THE FIRST FEW YEARS UPSTATE, WE DIDN'T REALLY MISS THE city. We'd take the Trailways down as needed. One summer weekend, when we stayed at a friend's West Village apartment, we went to breakfast at La Bonbonniere, a long-standing greasy spoon on Eighth Avenue near Horatio Street. (I'm obsessed with patronizing old, authentic, non-corporately-owned establish-ments before they perish.)

Seated next to us was a heavily made-up woman in her eight-ies who wasted no time striking up a conversation with us. She seemed to be one of those New York lonely people who spend so much time by themselves that as soon as they come into contact with other humans, they start babbling, almost involuntarily. I'd once been terrified of becoming one of them.

The woman, a onetime musical theater actress, asked us where we were from, and we somehow wound up on the topic of the apartment I'd let go. "I still sometimes kick myself," I said.

"Listen to me," she insisted. "A rent-controlled apartment can be a life sentence! I've been in my place for over sixty years, and it has kept me from the other things in life." She said she'd for-gone yearlong US and European tours with shows for fear of los-ing her studio now $150 if she'd sublet it. The place wasn't big enough for two, and anytime living with someone or getting married was on the table, she felt too shackled to her low rent to take a chance and move out. There had been two broken engage-ments. She was filled with regret. "You made the right choice," she said. It turned out New York City fell short as a life partner.

For a while afterward, that encounter helped me make peace with having forgotten Sophie's first words to me when I finally needed them. But now, fifteen years after having left, I am back to kicking myself—sometimes. After nine years, Rosendale got very small on us and we moved a few miles north to slightly big-ger, more urban Kingston, trading a town of 6,000 for a city of 24,000. But in Kingston's nine square miles, there's still just a tiny fraction of the restaurants, shops, movie theaters, and other estab-lishments that were in my neighborhood within the East Village.

I love my life upstate. But I also miss New York. I yearn for it something awful, the way you'd yearn for a lost lover. So what if the Lower East Side is now littered with gleaming glass buildings? So what if the familiar is steadily replaced by the unfamiliar? So what else is new? I miss the crowds. I miss the variety—of *everything*. I miss having perfect knowledge of where to eat and the latest rerouting of the B, D, Q line. I keep a MetroCard in my wallet at all times to ward off the feeling of being bridge-and-tunnel again.

I miss my cute little apartment. I miss having a home base, a place to drop my bags or even just to pee. Most of all, I miss the serendipity of simply walking out of my building and seeing where I land.

Every now and then, even without an appointment of any kind, I'll hop on the Trailways to Port Authority the way I'd once hopped on the Long Island Rail Road, and I'll walk for hours. I don't make any plans. I don't call any friends. I want it to once again be just the city and me.

MAYBE I LOVED YOU

Marcy Dermansky

I left New York City about a year and a half ago for Germany. I still can't entirely believe it. I mean, what the fuck did I do? I lived in New York for ten years. Maybe ten years is not a long time. Sometimes, a day can take forever.

I grew up in Englewood, New Jersey, and went to the city all my life. In the eighth grade, I invited three of the popular girls in my class to go shopping at Canal Jeans. My mother drove us in. We bought clothes and then went to Washington Square Park. This venture, however, did not make me popular. As a child, I used to go with my family into the city for museums, dinners in Little Italy, shows on Broadway. I went to my first concert in Central Park: James Taylor in the Sheep Meadow.

But I was always a little bit scared of New York, too. When I got older, I would go in on my own. I didn't like the trip: the porn shops that used to line 42nd Street, the grime, the homeless people. That part of New York seems strangely gone, wiped clean, though I don't particularly like the shiny lights either. All the shopping, stores you could just as easily go to in just about any mall. The tourists. The crowds. And where are the homeless people? Where have they gone?

I didn't move to New York after graduating from college; I went to San Francisco because a friend told me I would like it there. And I did. I loved San Francisco, but I left after five years, quitting a high-paying administrative job to go to graduate school in Hattiesburg, Mississippi. People thought I was crazy. Even the UPS man delivering boxes to my new apartment thought I was crazy. I still miss San Francisco but have never made it back for more than a brief visit.

I didn't make it to New York City until I was thirty years old. When I rented my first apartment, it wasn't in Manhattan and it wasn't in Brooklyn, either. I moved to Astoria, Queens. The neighborhood had been on the cover of *Time Out* the week we started looking for an apartment. I had been married for all of two weeks, marrying my German boyfriend from graduate school at city hall. We found an apartment we could afford, seven blocks from the N train, much too close to the Grand Central Parkway. We didn't know any better.

Astoria, famous for its Greek restaurants. I never fell in love with the Greek restaurants. Honestly, I never fell in love with Astoria. Some people do. I understand why. There were a great many things about the place that I liked. I have not been completely happy anywhere. At least not yet.

In the ten years I lived in Astoria, I wrote and I published two novels. I had the same job for nine years, a content editor for a start-up, Screaming Media, a hip company with free M&Ms and granola in the kitchen, a company that got bought and sold, and then bought and sold again and again. Every time, I was rehired. At some point, I swung benefits, vacation days. Wow, that job—it was like an NEA grant. Mornings, I worked. Afternoons and evenings, I wrote. Which was all that I ever really wanted to do.

Every day, I took the subway into Manhattan. In our one-bedroom apartment, I did not have a proper desk. At the Writers Room, where I was a member for almost a decade, there were more than forty desks, but I could write at maybe six of them. The desk had to be near a window. I couldn't sit next to a loud typer, a heavy breather. If a good desk wasn't open, I would wander the streets. Which was okay because the space was in the East Village, and I liked that. I'd go to Union Square, buy produce at the farmers' market, and later, when Trader Joe's opened, I would go there, too, buy bags of groceries and wine, and carry the heavy bags home on the subway.

I'd wander into the St. Mark's Bookshop and gaze at the shelves of new paperbacks on the front wall. I always wanted to write a book; I always wanted my book to be there, on *that* wall. Later, when my books were published, they never quite made it there. St. Mark's carried my novels but shelved them in the stacks.

Sometimes, I worked at the Writers Room late into the night, when all the good desks were open. I would take breaks, walk the empty aisles, stand in front of the big picture window, and gaze at the lights of the Empire State Building.

—

THE MAGIC OF NEW YORK WAS NOT LOST ON ME. DO NOT THINK that I didn't eat my share of Thai food. Or Indian. Or Japanese.

Often, I long for the crispy squid served at a Vietnamese restaurant downtown, not far from city hall, where I got married, across the street from a prison called the Tombs. Don't think that I didn't go out for bagels or eat pizza or, on indulgent days, have sushi delivered for lunch. Do not think that I didn't go to movies, readings, gallery openings, and free concerts in the park.

———

MY OLDER BROTHER LIVES ON THE UPPER WEST SIDE. HIS apartment is only blocks from Columbia University, close to Riverside Park. Going to his apartment felt like entering another world.

Michael would visit me in Queens. He called it "the land of junk." He had a point, of course. My brother reveled in the dollar stores. He bought Elmo T-shirts for his daughters, random plastic toys. I took him out for huevos rancheros. He was polite, picked at the refried beans, but did not like them. His wife once told me she loved Queens because of the US Open, but the tennis tournament was not part of my life in Queens, even though I used to go to the Open with my brother when I was a teenager.

We would have fun, my brother and I, watching matches in the outer courts. There's a picture of me taken with him and a woman who was in the tournament that year. She was a tall, beautiful, Black tennis player named Camille Benjamin. My mother framed this picture. It was the year I was fifteen, the year I had short hair.

———

I WAS ALSO A FILM CRITIC AT ABOUT.COM DURING MY YEARS IN New York. I loved to see movies in screening rooms, to sit on the plush leather couches in the Sony building, so comfortable that sometimes I would fall asleep, regardless of the movie. I used to attend film parties and drink free drinks. I went to press junkets, and I loved that, too. To wander into fancy New York hotels, sit at a crowded table full of overeager online film critics—nobodies, all of us—across from genuine famous people: Woody Allen, Scarlett Johansson, Sean Penn, Maggie Gyllenhaal, Sofia Coppola, Gael García Bernal, Cate Blanchett, Parker Posey. I interviewed French actress Isild Le Besco in a café. I once stood next to Daniel Day-Lewis at a premiere. He was surprisingly tall. I would go to the morning press screenings at the New York Film Festival and Rendez-Vous with French Cinema at Lincoln Center, and then out for the lunch special at Ollie's, the Chinese restaurant down the block.

I think about that, those days of movies, riding the subway into Manhattan. I miss it. Wonder how I gave it up. So what that About.com, like Screaming Media, also got bought and sold, bought and sold again? That my pay there was cut in half. That I felt a little bit dirty, sitting at those press junkets, watching stars cringe as they were asked questions they clearly did not want to answer. I still want to go back. Back to the movies. Back in time.

But honestly, for the last two years that I lived in New York, I went to very few movies. I had a baby. I was laid off. I could not afford childcare to go to the movies. Irrationally, I did not want childcare. I wanted to take care of my daughter.

I was in love with her, Nina, a burning crazy passionate love. My life in New York City pretty much fell apart after she was born.

———

I DID NOT KNOW WHEN I MOVED TO ASTORIA THAT I WOULD BE there for ten years. Once, when the lease ended on our first apartment, my husband and I looked at apartments in Brooklyn. We were discouraged by the higher rents, the smaller spaces. We gave up, perhaps too easily, found another apartment, a better apartment, not aware that the auto repair shop next door, so quiet in the winter, would make us feel crazy on beautiful spring days, when we would open our windows to the sound of its industrial noise.

The truth is, of course, that I have always envied what money buys in New York City. I envy the Brooklyn writers. I wished then, as I wish now, that I could be better at making money.

I wrote and I published those two novels. *Twins. Bad Marie.* I hired a publicist, bought dresses, had book parties, was reviewed and later profiled in the *New York Times*, and was written about in glossy magazines. I got to feel a little bit fancy, a little bit proud of myself. A lot of people go to New York City to be artists, to write books, and end up doing something else. I published two books, and somehow, it wasn't enough. I sound like a petulant child. Often, I feel like a petulant child.

I made money from my books, but really, I made rent and health insurance through my job. It was the job—not reviewing films, not writing fiction, but editing headlines for corporate websites—that paid. I knew not to take it for granted. New York is an expensive place to live. Nina was two months old when I was laid off.

Nina is three and a half now. I no longer live in New York City. I have been gone for a year and a half, but it feels like forever.

I moved to Wiesbaden, Germany.

I actually did that.

We left New York for Germany to get affordable health insurance, something I lost with my job after COBRA ran out. My husband promised to find a job in Germany, where social media was only just beginning to take off. I could almost picture it. Monthly *kindergeld*. European vacation time, six weeks a year. Free babysitting. My husband's parents are much younger than mine. They promised to help with Nina. I would have time to write. *I would have time to write.*

I think that, alone, was what sold me.

I had left San Francisco, after all, for graduate school in Hattiesburg, Mississippi, and the chance to write.

Many people think it's cool to live in Europe, raise a bilingual child. Leave America, which was steadily going downhill. That is what they told me, before I left. What do they know?

I am homesick.

I am waiting to hear from my agent about the new book I am writing. I am waiting for emails from my friends back in New York. There is a six-hour time difference, and I am often waiting for my friends to wake up. I am in a constant state of waiting.

―

I LOST MY JOB THE YEAR *BAD MARIE* CAME OUT. IT DIDN'T SEEM like such a terrible thing. I would be able to get another job. I received severance pay. I was able to go on unemployment, stay home with my child.

The day my novel was written about in *Time* magazine, I went for my first appointment at the unemployment office out in Flushing. It felt surreal to me, sitting in a crowded room full of newly jobless people, a room full of immigrants and white, middle-class me. I felt like I had a secret: I didn't belong there. Of course, I did belong there. I had lost my job and my benefits. The advance I received from *Bad Marie* would not pay my rent. I had a five-minute session with an employment counselor who, befuddled by my résumé, told me about a new racetrack opening up on the edge of Queens that was looking for cashiers.

Then I went out for lunch. I loved that lunch, how decadent it felt, to sit alone in a restaurant by myself, eating Chinese broccoli, drinking tea, out without the baby. I had been to Flushing only once before, for dim sum.

Months later, I would have to go back to that unemployment office to prove that I was still looking for work. I was, but I also wasn't. I was promoting my novel. I was taking care of Nina. I was getting by. The appointment was early in the morning. My Romanian babysitter couldn't make it. My husband, sick in bed, couldn't watch Nina. And so I put her in the stroller, packed the diaper bag, and went on my own, all of it so much harder with a baby: taking the subway, transferring trains, finding the elevators in Roosevelt Station. I remember missing my second train, the door closing in my face. Almost panicking when I couldn't find the elevator at the Flushing station, taking the escalator up instead, and then racing through the crowded streets of Flushing, only to get there late, fifteen minutes late, more than twenty minutes by the time I made it to the front of the line.

That was me: writer, new mother, beyond exhausted, in a shirt covered with spit-up and milk, sweaty and flushed because it was summer and I had been racing to get there, pushing a stroller. Nervous. Wildly nervous. I had missed my appointment.

"Too late," the Asian woman behind the counter told me, not coldly, just indifferent.

There was, of course, a line of people behind me. I started to cry. I think now: *Why didn't I tell my mother?* She didn't know then that I was on unemployment. Why didn't I tell her? At

the very least, she would have told me to take a taxi. She would
have paid for the taxi. All those years in New York, I never took
enough taxis.

My parents had helped us with the hospital bill after Nina's
birth. Nina spent the first four days of her life in the neonatal
intensive care unit at NYU Hospital. We had good health insurance then and still could not afford that hospital bill. This is
the same NICU where sick babies were carried down nine flights
of stairs by nurses when the backup generator failed after Hurricane Sandy. I remember those stairs. Those four long days, I
was a floor below, being treated for complications from the birth.
The doctors had told me to take the elevator when going from my
room on the eighth floor to the NICU on the ninth, but often, I
couldn't wait, and I walked.

I stood there and cried at the unemployment office in Flushing,
and the woman behind the desk looked up at me, reconsidered.
She decided to accept my updated résumé and the piece of paper
on which I had diligently written the jobs I had applied for, the
jobs I would apply for. The woman processed a form for me; she
told me that I was fine, until the next time.

And this is what I think of when I remember my life in New
York. Not the plush couches at the Sony screening room or the
hip bars in Nolita or the book parties. I think of the unemployment office in Flushing. And my Romanian babysitter Mary and
her overweight teenage daughter whose name I can't remember,
who had recently been released from the psych ward. They would
pick up Nina at my apartment and take her around the neighborhood, while I tried to work. I am surprised by how often I think
about Mary, wondering how she is now, what happened to her
daughter.

I think about how scared I felt, how out of control.

———

THOSE TEN YEARS I LIVED IN NEW YORK, WHY DID I NEVER fall in love with the city? I had the screening rooms. The takeout sushi. A place to write. I had my friends. I had my family.

But I always had something to complain about. The subway. The cost of brunch. The lines for brunch. How crowded it would get at the bagel shop. Sometimes, I couldn't even get a table. The noise. The crowded streets. The tiny aisles in the supermarket. My neighborhood and how ugly it was.

I don't fall in love easily. My husband had to work to woo me, and I mean hard. It was months and months before I would kiss him. I had to get over my life in San Francisco first and a former boyfriend. Sometimes, it takes me a while.

Like now. Writing this essay, sitting on a couch in a café in Wiesbaden, irrationally angry at the Germans not far from me, angry at them for speaking German, for being German, I think that I might have actually loved New York. That I could have figured it out, found Nina regular childcare back home. Not crossed an ocean to get steady writing time. Here, I take the bus almost every day, and I miss the subway.

Only now, living in Germany, where I don't speak the language and the people seem impossibly cold and distant, do I think: *Maybe I loved New York.*

And maybe I didn't.

Maybe I don't.

Maybe I just don't like where I am now.

I am not sure how, but I want to go back.

LONG TRAINS LEAVING

Emily St. John Mandel

1.

I came to New York City by train on a cold evening in February. I'd been living in Toronto for some years, ever since I crossed 2,800 miles of Canada to attend the School of Toronto Dance Theatre at eighteen. Now I was twenty-two, and it turned out my ties to Toronto were so light and so few that it was possible to decide to move to New York City and then leave ten days later.

My friends' reactions to this decision varied. "She's moving to a foreign country to live with a man old enough to be her father," someone close to me said. This was factually correct, although the man in question—let's call him Owen—would've been a young father. But the point wasn't really Owen, although I did love him at the time, or his age, which was inconsequential to me.

The point was the word "foreign." The point was that I longed for change.

I'd come to Toronto to dance, but now that I'd graduated, I wasn't dancing. I was working twelve hours a day as an assistant to a designer, and I was aware that I was drawn not to the work, exactly, but to losing myself in it. All I'd ever wanted was to be a dancer, but now I wasn't sure I wanted that anymore and there was nothing in that moment to replace it.

I had slept very little the night before I boarded the train, and sleep deprivation lent the passing landscape a hallucinatory glaze. I read *Pale Fire* and gazed out at southern Ontario. I'd never been to New York and didn't even have an especially clear mental image of the place. When I thought of New York I thought of *Law and Order* and *Seinfeld*, of towers collapsing six months earlier on the morning news, of the piles of flowers outside the US consulate.

Somewhere near the US border the train tracks curved close to Lake Ontario, and I saw Toronto for a moment across the brilliant water, a collection of towers and spires rendered ghostly by enormous distance, pale against a milky sky. The city flashed out of view and receded into memory. Can you isolate the instant when a place ceases to be home?

"I'm visiting my boyfriend in Manhattan for a few weeks," I told an agent at the border.

"Are you planning on working while you're down there?" the agent asked.

"No," I lied. He stamped my passport and handed it back to me. As the hours passed, rural New York State faded into twilight, my reflection appearing on the darkening train window like a Polaroid coming into focus. Even before I arrived, the story was beginning to seem improbable: I slipped like magic across a guarded border and arrived in Manhattan with sixty-five dollars, two suitcases, and no Social Security number. I don't mean to imply that it was an especially hard landing. Owen met me at Penn Station with a rose.

But the only one of those details that remains truly relevant, all these years later, is that when I disembarked at Penn Station I found home.

2.

I FOUND A JOB SELLING EXPENSIVE OBJECTS IN A STORE IN Soho. Every two weeks they gave me an envelope of cash, because a year would pass before I realized that the fact of my father having been born in California made me a US citizen by default. Once freed from the sales floor, I went for long walks through the streets of Lower Manhattan. I watched old men feed pigeons in Father Demo Square and listened to musicians on the street. I stumbled upon Ground Zero—machines grinding down through the basement levels of the towers, a sense of disaster still hanging in the air—and had dreams about towers falling. I wrote in cafés. I'd been writing all my life, but in New York this habit acquired a new force. Perhaps, I thought, writing was what would come next. Spring arrived, flowers on trees. In Toronto I had walked the streets for hours, looking for something I couldn't name. In my first days in New York City, I realized that I'd found it. This was the city I'd been looking for.

But neither of us was really making enough money for New York City. We were behind on the rent. The thought of leaving the city was wrenching to me, but in May we decided to move to Montreal because it was a new adventure and because the rent's cheap there. In July we packed our belongings into a bright yellow truck and drove north. I was aware of New York City receding behind us.

"Welcome home," the Canadian customs agent said at the border, but I couldn't shake the uneasy thought that home was behind me.

3.

WE HAD A BLUE APARTMENT ON RUE DE LA VISITATION, WHICH I had a difficult time pronouncing because I'd never studied French. French is, of course, one of the two official languages of Canada and a core subject in English Canadian schools, but I was homeschooled as a child and French had never quite made an appearance in my parents' improvised curriculum. In fairness to them, it can't have seemed very relevant. I was born and raised in British Columbia, three thousand miles to the west of Montreal. Before I came to Quebec, I'd heard French spoken in passing perhaps a dozen times, and it had the inscrutability of any other perfectly unfamiliar tongue. It slipped past me in a blur of sound. I couldn't differentiate individual words. I'd been under the impression, based on one or two brief visits, that I'd be able to get by in Montreal speaking one out of two official languages, but it was immediately obvious that I'd been horribly naïve. Not long after we arrived, a man approached me when I was walking alone, and I understood that he was asking for directions. "Je ne parle pas français," I said, the one phrase I pronounced with confidence in those days. "Je suis désolé."

Is it fair to say he spat at me then? I'm never entirely sure how to describe the moment that followed. He made a spitting gesture at my feet—I jumped back, realizing what was coming—but it was all sound and motion and contempt, no actual spit.

"He was just expressing an opinion," Owen said. Owen loved Montreal. He spoke French.

The week we arrived, I set out walking with a stack of résumés. I was beginning very tentatively to describe myself as a writer, and writing, I'd realized, would require the same split life I'd become accustomed to as a dancer. Almost every dancer I knew had a job or two on the side, and in the years since I'd started supporting myself at eighteen, I'd built up the sort of aimless work history that only happens when one's interests lie emphatically elsewhere: I'd made sandwiches, martinis, and lattes; I'd sold everything from sofas to ballet shoes; I'd been a janitor and a designer's assistant. Now that I'd arrived in Quebec, I knew my inability to speak French would make finding work difficult, but I thought perhaps someone might hire me to move boxes in a retail stockroom, far from customers. I'd held such jobs in the past.

"Est-ce que vous parlez français?" a long sequence of retail managers asked.

"No," I said. "I'm trying to learn. I was hoping it wouldn't matter so much in a stockroom position."

"Well," one told me helpfully, "not being able to speak French is really not an asset."

"I've noticed that," I said. I felt a slight vertigo sometimes—how had I landed in Montreal when I'd set out so recently for a new life in New York?—but I was determined to adapt. I learned that Quebec offers free French lessons to new arrivals in the province, which was exciting, but it turned out these lessons were available to everyone except English Canadians. ("It's policy, madame. You'll have to go to a private school.") I didn't think there could possibly be any lessons that I could afford, so I studied in cafés with a French-English dictionary, translating the newspaper, trying to memorize words. There were wonderful surprises. I was delighted to learn that *trombone* could refer to either a trombone or a paper clip. I spent hours walking, stopping with my dictionary to translate the signs. I was trying very hard to fall in love with the city, but the trouble was that New York was at the edge of every thought.

"How are you liking Montreal?" my boyfriend's friends would occasionally ask. Owen had lived here before and had friends in the city. I didn't know anyone in the city but him.

"It's actually been a bit difficult," I would say, understating wildly. "I don't speak the right language. A guy sort of spat on me on the street." There were things I liked about the city, but I was having a hard time getting that episode out of my mind. It was only the most blatant expression of a low-level hostility that I sensed all around me.

"Montreal's just a *great city*," they would say, as though I'd said something entirely different. Their willful deafness was eerie, but it occurred to me later that they weren't necessarily wrong. Edmund Wilson once wrote that no two people ever read the same book, and I've come to believe that no two people ever live in the same city. I've met people who find New York to be desperate and gray.

4.

I FOUND A JOB WHERE IT DIDN'T MATTER THAT I COULDN'T speak the right language. Every morning at 7 AM, I met a delivery truck in front of the Caban store on Rue Ste.-Catherine and helped shift boxes into an underground stockroom. I spent the next seven hours putting price stickers on martini glasses, bubble-wrapping mirrors, unpacking scented soaps, and stacking objects and boxes on metal shelves. The pay was $8.50 an hour.

My coworkers were a mildly burnt-out anglophone musician and an Iranian film student. We listened to English-language radio all day.

I didn't mind the work. It covered my rent, and there was time to write in the afternoons. The problem was that occasionally I'd have to walk across the sales floor, and customers would invariably approach me in French. I wasn't progressing very rapidly with the newspaper-and-dictionary method, but I did know how to say, "Pardon me, I don't speak French," and then I'd offer to find a French-speaking sales associate. Sometimes the customer would smile and switch to English without skipping a beat, and I was secretly so grateful that I could've kissed them, every time. Sometimes they would gaze coldly at me and say, "I see." On two occasions a customer glared at me, turned, and stormed out of the building rather than be contaminated for one more second by my Englishness.

"It's no big deal," my manager told me. "People are crazy."

But I was shot through with dread, because while people throw phrases like "language police" around all the time, Quebec actually has them. There are laws in Quebec to protect the French language. Businesses over a certain size must conduct their operations in French. There are complicated regulations involving signage: if English appears on a sign, it must appear after the French and in smaller letters.

These laws are enforced by means of a tip line for citizen informants. If you spot a business sign in which English appears before the French, for instance, or if you walk into a store and the sales associate greets you in English, or if, as in one particular instance I remember reading about, a bartender gives you a coaster for your drink and you realize—*quelle horreur!*—that all the words on said coaster are in English, you can call a 1-800 number and report the infraction to the French language commission. Penalties can include fines and revoked business licenses.

Every time a customer looked at me, I feared offending them by speaking the wrong language, and then what if they called the tip line and reported the store? If the store were fined by the language authorities, would I lose my job? I worried that if I lost this job, I might not be able to find another one. None of the recipients of the other twenty-five or thirty résumés I'd distributed had called back. My résumé was in English.

The weight of speaking the wrong language followed me everywhere. There was a graffiti message that I walked by on my way to work every day: MONTREAL EN FRANÇAIS: 101 OU 401. Bill 101 is a Quebec law that restricts the use of the English language. The 401 is the highway out of the city. This, then, is the translation: MONTREAL IN FRENCH: SPEAK FRENCH OR GET OUT.

5.

AT THE END OF THE SUMMER, OWEN ANNOUNCED THAT HE'D prefer to be single. He broke up with me, then changed his mind and took me back, then broke up with me again, and after that I was dazzlingly alone.

There are times when life goes dark and still. I moved into a cheap apartment share in the Latin Quarter. I drifted through the hours of my workday. I'd worked for the Caban store in Toronto until six months before I'd left for New York, and in the winter boxes arrived with my handwriting already on them, surplus inventory I'd boxed up in another city the year before. Now they were surfacing out of far-off warehouses, like bottles rising out of the sea. I went alone to the English-language movie theater on St. Catherine Street and watched whatever was playing—anything, it didn't matter. I just wanted the hours to pass. I saw *Chicago* twice.

"A quiet room in Brooklyn," I wrote in my notebook. The idea was a fixation. *If I could only find a way to return to New York*, I thought, *then perhaps I would be less sad.*

By the end of November it was so cold that when my eyes watered, my eyelashes would freeze. I wrapped a scarf around my face, but then the condensation from my breath froze too, a thin layer of ice between the scarf and my skin. I didn't own a watch, so I carried a tiny travel alarm clock around in my coat pocket. It got me to work on time, but usually it was six hours behind by nightfall because batteries fail as the temperature approaches minus 18 degrees Celsius, 0 degrees Fahrenheit. I felt a curious compassion for my alarm clock; I wasn't holding up very well either. Every sound was too loud. Every light was too bright. I stepped outside and felt translucent, the cold passing through me. I'd stopped trying to learn French.

"Marooned in a hostile city," I wrote in my notebook, but there were moments even in the dead of winter when the city of Montreal was beautiful to me. These streets of gray stone and ice, spiral staircases with their burdens of snow. Moments of friendship and grace. I adored my roommates, a brother and sister from Ontario who spoke English at home.

We couldn't afford to turn the heat up very high in the apartment. I would sometimes go to bed at 6 or 7 PM because it was warmer under the covers. I would wake at midnight or one in the morning, rise in the freezing darkness, and go out to write. A ritual: I dressed in my best clothes, sometimes put on a tie. I gathered my papers and my laptop computer, bundled up as best

I could, and stepped out into the breathtaking cold. It felt like embarking on a profound adventure.

At the open-all-night Café Dépôt on St. Lawrence Boulevard, two blocks away, I took a table near the window and wrote through the night. A memory of a ballet class when I was a teenager, a teacher glancing at me as I struggled through a difficult adagio, nodding approvingly at how hard I was working in that moment: "That's the work," she'd said, and the line stayed with me. *This is the work*, I thought, writing by the hour in the café. This is the discipline. This is what writing will take. I worked for hours at a time, trying to distill my wild fragments and false starts into a novel, drinking cup after cup of tea. I watched the night progress in stages. The freezing club kids ferried away by a fleet of taxis at 1:30 or 2 AM, the last few stragglers stumbling homeward with greasy pizza slices at 3 and 3:30. By 4 AM the street was quiet, scoured by salt and ice. A line from my first novel: "Outside the café the cold deepened until the streets froze white."

By 4:30, the first movements toward daylight. More cars on the street, a few tired workers coming in for coffee. By 5 AM, I saw the bread trucks, and by the time the bread trucks came, I was too tired to write anymore. I had been reading Jeanette Winterson's *Art and Lies*, with its fractured plot and half-grammatical incantations: "My City, and long trains leaving."

In the early mornings I walked back to my apartment and lay shivering under the blankets until I could fall asleep. Writing held me together, but it wasn't enough. I was desperate for the moment when I might look back on this place from the window of a long train leaving, anguished and exultant and perfectly free.

6.

I DON'T COME FROM A FAMILY WITH MONEY. WE WERE NEVER even middle-class. My education was made possible by student loans. But the year I was in Montreal my grandmother died and left my father some money, and he sent me a money order for a thousand dollars. I remember opening the envelope in the living room in Montreal, staring at the unfathomable sum on the scrap of paper, and thinking of train tickets.

A few weeks later, in late January, I received an unexpected phone call from Owen: someone he knew in Manhattan was leaving town for two weeks, and would I like to sublet her apartment while she was away? He knew I wanted to return to New York, and it would be a cheap place to stay while I looked for an apartment and a job.

Six days later I took a taxi to Station Bonaventure in the freezing morning and stepped aboard a southbound train. It was the second day of February, a year minus three weeks from the day I'd first set out for New York. I took photograph after photograph of Montreal as the train departed, trying to freeze the moment of escape. I crossed the US border without incident and continued south through the afternoon.

This is the future: In a few hours the train will arrive in Penn Station, and I'll set out walking into the winter night. In twenty-four hours I will meet my future husband, and in eighteen months he'll propose in Central Park, fireflies rising from the grass around us. We will marry a year later and walk home up Fifth Avenue after the reception, me in my wedding dress in the cold spring night; we'll stop for eggs in a diner at two in the morning where the waiter will take our order without comment, deadpan, as though women in wedding dresses order eggs in his diner every day, and perhaps they do. It's New York.

There will be years of quiet rooms in Brooklyn, years of books and cats. In 2012 my French publisher will bring me to Paris, and we'll wander the streets, my beloved husband and I, in love with the city, the country, the language, trying out our terrible French on waitresses. I'll have been studying French for six months by then. "Mais c'est fasciste!" a Parisian journalist will exclaim when I tell her about the Quebec language laws, which feature in the book, and we'll agree that Montreal and Paris are very different.

But first there was a year of long trains leaving, of traveling between countries and cities and lives. On the train from Montreal to New York, I stared out the window and wondered what would become of me. I was twenty-three and felt very old. Night fell and there were only occasional lights and deep shadows, the small stations of upstate New York. The manuscript pages that would eventually become my first novel were bundled together with old shoelaces in a bag by my feet. I tried to write, or to read, but my impatience and my longing to see New York City again grew with each passing hour. I eventually gave up and just watched the landscape, the movement, the passing stations and lights.

SO LONG, SUCKERS

Rebecca Wolff

first said goodbye to all that—though I don't hold New York to be *all that*, a monolith precluding the *all thatness* of other places—a long time ago, in 1985, at seventeen. I had been the sort of manor-born Manhattanite to whom that famous *New Yorker* cartoon, the one that shows everything west of the Hudson River as a perspectival plain of diminishing signification, didn't seem funny at all. *What's funny about that? It's totally true,* and everybody knows it.

Yeah, arrogance. New York is full of it; I was full of it: the kind of arrogance that's extra numbing, mind-stuffing, because it's backed up by what I've come to know as "seeming inevitability," that anyone who's anyone will at some point move to New York. Or die in obscurity with failed dreams. Yeah, all the brilliant people are here. Yeah, here's where it's really at, and you know it's true, and anyone who says anything else is just not up to the challenge.

In the diffused sparkle of refraction of Joan Didion's adorable and probably accurate portrayal of what it's like to be from somewhere else and move to New York and get what you can from it and stay a little bit too long and then leave, I proudly and grouchily represent the bright lights of the native. For visitors—you can stay a lifetime and be a visitor—what is at stake, according to Didion, is the dream of New York, the abstracted coordinates of its glamour and legendariness. You want to be there because it is like living on a Monopoly board. It is like living in Oz. Natives get that, are fed it along with their mother's milk, plus they get the extra added glamour of secret knowledge and self-exile and hardwired urbanity. Didions bring a knowingness to their efforts at urbanity: *rubanity*, I'll call it. Natives just bring it.

In high school I went out a lot, to nightclubs and bars. Danceteria, the Mudd Club, Limelight, Save the Robots, Pyramid, Area, Beirut, bars in the East Village, which at that time ended at Avenue A. Beyond, purportedly lay a river. I snorted lots of cocaine and made out with bouncers in exchange for free entry to clubs. Bouncers—Nigerian bouncers, bouncers from Berlin, underage bouncers I had known in grade school—waved my friends and me out of the crowd, to the front of the line, ushered us inside where we would shed our coats and get free drinks and dance dance dance until five in the morning. That's what I did in high school. By the time I left for college, I had renounced a bunch of things, including the high life, and was leading with latent bookishness and vegetarianism and a closet full of attitudinal old clothes I had amassed at the Salvation Army on my corner next to the gay bar, long before old clothes were called "vintage."

Goodbye to all that, hello end-of-the-world rural pinhead Vermont for college, dropping out to live in Boston "You-Call-This-a-City" Massachusetts for a couple of years, and then back for more college in the Happy Valley of Western Mass, where I had my first sweet taste of real small-town, albeit college-town, life.

I moved to a very small city, really a town, in Iowa for graduate school. There at the outskirts where true rurality abruptly swelled, I witnessed organic vegetable farming, cooperative living, and the fulsomeness of rubes and radicals and serious artists doing their business in generative ease, relative privacy, and cheap comfort. Lots of bands and visuals and ideas. I did not miss the compression of the city; I did not miss my parents, who I felt in their high-mannerist urbanity had taught me nothing of worth. I spent summers on screened-in porches and went back home about once a year, and when I walked the streets in the late 1980s to early 1990s, it made me cry. This is before the homeless people were stored wherever they are currently being stored: then they were living, eating, shitting, sleeping all over the streets, and one had to step over them at every corner, doorway, subway grate, and step over them everyone did, as though it was an acceptable situation. Seemingly inevitable: oh, it's just so fabulous in New York, you can really just learn to step over people's suffering bodies. Cities are so cool, and this is the coolest, so hard core, and you can learn to live with this. No one spoke of it. I would come home from my night out and ask my parents how they could live like this. They honestly had no idea what I was talking about: this was their fabulous city. I was inured to the fabulousness by the dirty, hungry people lying around on the street; they were inured to the dirty, hungry people lying around on the street by the imprint of fabulousness, the fabulousness impressed upon them when they arrived in the West Village in the 1950s from their respective outposts.

———

AT THE AGE OF THIRTY I CAME BACK TO NEW YORK TO BE LIT-erary, and it worked. Return of the native in the clothing of the naïf. Wolf in sheep's clothing. I had abruptly tired of outposts, of decentralized living—the city still an epicenter—and I had something very specific I wanted to do within the specific culture of the literary. And I had noticed that every time I came back to visit, I had a marvelous time, suddenly, in that specific cul-ture, at parties and drinky lunches and magical, hidden offices. So I came back, and said hello again to all that, and it genuflected back at me. I sucked up the transitional, transactional energy like a newborn mosquito. That's where language is. I get my total buzz on when the buzz is there to beget. It turns out I am su-premely familiar, you could say "comfortable," with cityscape—noise, bustle, crowds, action; stimuli such as the very poor, the very rich, the very beautiful, and the degraded; lights and smells of food on the street; shouts of people selling things for lots of money or begging for money or scamming with infants in their laps. Bumping into people I know in parks and bookstores and art houses. For six or seven inexhaustible years I was one of those culture workers who expend themselves beautifully, for whom the city is working, and what I did there I probably could not have done anywhere else. Once I had accomplished that, I was just as abruptly done with New York.

New York is a place for being public, for *wanting* to be famous. I achieved a degree of recognition in my field and became a pub-lic figure and found I didn't like it. I didn't like being public, the attendant flush and two-facedness and gaze. It served me well in launching my Literary Project—*Fence*, a journal of poetry, fiction, and criticism, and later Fence Books, a press—but did not serve my soul well, my soul, which had been forged in that very vault.

When I left the city, I was surprised at how complete I made the break. I did not invite friends to visit me; I did not come back often. I made new friends and found new ways to keep my Project visible and sustainable. *Fence* eventually required less and less of my long-distance personal spiritual life force—my precious ectoplasm—and just as though it were an infant, I have been able to cut its cord. The labor of love does result in independent life.

I didn't move far away—up the river to the tiny, quixotic city of Hudson—but I will never move back, and I still don't visit as often as you might think, and when I do I am happy to leave again, often on the same day. SOHO GIVES ME HIVES: that's a T-shirt meme I brainstormed in the late 1990s, as the transformation of that deathly quiet neighborhood from artists' cheap housing and site of freewheeling conceptualism to Mall of Outrageous Crap was completed. There are lots of neighborhoods and enclaves and scenes and nodes of NYC behavior that give me hives—too many to give shout-outs to. There are wonderful brainy sexy people I see only in the city, who stubbornly refuse to get on the train of diminishing signification and whom I sadly bid farewell after each brief encounter.

I go down about once a month, two hours on the train with the other suckers, usually to attend or present or facilitate a potentially dazzling literary event. In New York City, in the dusk-filled streets or in the cold wintry streets, in streets when the light is pretty or streets when everything looks crappy and grimy, I see a tremendous amount of samey-ness, the kind that didn't used to be there. Poseurs and wannabes and money-hounds EVERY-WHERE, when in my youth they were restricted to the bridge-and-tunnel funnels of Eighth Street and Midtown, Lexington Avenue and Central Park and, eventually, Soho. You could spot these chumps a mile away, and they were different from tourists, who came to gawk and then went back home; they were tour-ists who overstayed, put down roots for no good reason, who could lay no legitimate claim to the greatness of the city's historic convergent energies, who could simply make money anywhere and could therefore make it here. New York City manifests it-self now shamefacedly as a chump-factory, a chumphouse. It's Chumptown. Artists who live there are living dangerously, close to extinction, dangerously close to the source of their art's di-minishment, an ouroboros of economic exigency. It's well doc-umented: chumps need artists and artists need chumps, but they're supposed to stay out of one another's sight in order to maintain the necessary illusions! There have always been chumps in New York, but they used to be bashful chumps who bought the brilliant ones their drinks.

There's this thing that happens, where I speak to a twenty-something or thirty-something sweetheart, a Joan Didion who's moved to New York recently, and I realize at a certain point that their expectations of it are actually very low, compared to my own, because they cannot possibly imagine what it used to be like, the New York of the recent past, of the late 1970s, 1980s, 1990s. They have no idea how far any of it has fallen, how sterile Chelsea, how horror-show Soho, how lame-ass the Lower East Side. All by comparison. I'm not even going to mention Brooklyn because Brooklyn is nothing but a brand name. Forget Queens.

Visual culture does not often represent what's past; I'm sure a slew of movies soon will, but right now with the exception of *Chico and the Man* and early, secret, legendary Madonna as incarnated in Lady Gaga, I don't know what is widely culturally understood of what was cool in those times. Whit Stillman? The 1980s art world via Basquiat? Graffiti? Michael Douglas in *Wall Street*? I'm afraid this latter giant face has eclipsed the faces I knew, the faces of the brazen, the bold, the class- and culture- and gender-vultures, nonrich aspirants to splendor, gamy artist-class fast-talkers, children of choreographers, children of sculptors, excitable children of alcoholic midwesterners, those for whom there was no money involved in the transaction.

There is the fallacy of nostalgia, and there is the fallacy of the fallacy of nostalgia. You're not supposed to ever say that something used to be better, because then you are vainly trying to hold that something in stasis, cold in the frame of reference in which you knew it, and this is narcissistic and regressive and cranky and blindered. It is ungenerous to those whose references are framed more recently, to those whom we must make way for and learn from: to the young. Those who are making their way in the world and making the world. Those who could, at this point, be our children, if we had given birth to the children we aborted in high school and college and graduate school.

But we have already said goodbye to all that dualistic relativism, in this new world. It's a "both/and" world we live in: every cranky, aging generation feels that things used to be cooler or more imaginative or riskier; many things actually *did* use to be cooler, riskier, et cetera, and this argument against the insistence that something could actually have been qualitatively so— probably quantifiably if you had the time—serves most those for whom the status quo is best maintained: chumps. For if it's never true that things have degraded, deteriorated, absolutely—and, of course, the same is true of improvement—then there's never any impetus to halt the degradation. Or to look for something better elsewhere. You'll keep paying rent until you can't.

So yes, it's true. New York City used to be cool, and now it's not. It's not at all. It is boring and dismaying and stymied; everything potentially cool in it is overwhelmed and inflated and parodied and sold. You can't even love the absurdity of it because it's too painful, and we cannot be allowed any more to callously love, for their absurdity, systems that oppress and impoverish. New York City is mediated by money so visibly. Everywhere everything is mediated by money, so perhaps you could make a brutalist argument for how fabulous it is to live with that so in your face, but my face hurts. New York is a giant sinking pile of crap compared to what it used to be. Literally sinking, now that the waters rise so much more quickly, the winds blow so much harder than even scientists predicted. Lately I like to imagine that I will have the privilege of seeing in my lifetime real estate values in the city plunge wildly, in free fall, as Climate Events force Permanent Visitors to admit that they pay Top Dollar to perch on Coastal Landfill. But I hope that my parents sell off their holdings before this happens. I still love to visit them in the apartment I grew up in, on the tree-lined residential block I grew up on; love the first ten exhilarating hours of each overnight stay at the beginning of which I swing down Seventh Avenue like Georgy Girl, join an audience of haters or buyers or tourists to see some pasteurized, predigested art or film or poetry; hate the twin mattress perched on top of a desk in my father's office; hate the last six hours in which nothing has been as brilliant as I thought it would be and

I am left hungover, teeth-grindingly claustrophobic, chock-full of morbidity.

In New York City these days I see loads and loads of formerly brilliant people—gender champions, visual whizzes, start-up ho's, crackerjack dancers, actors, journalists, and chefs—who have "stayed too long at the Fair," to use Joan's wistful archaic turn of phrase, who are baffled and internally conflicted as to why they can't admit that New York sucks so hard. Why they can't draw the proper conclusion. That if they are to work all the time to pay superhigh rents that make it impossible for them to do their art, if they never have a chance to see the people they came here to see, who are also less brilliant now that they are muffled by the smog of wrongness that hangs over New York (thicker than the smog of smog that hangs over Los Angeles, another city that's not even half as cool as everyone who's moving there says it is), if they are living somewhere that is giving them less than they are giving to it, then they should leave. (What goes on in Queens is hysterical. Why do you need to displace natives of Queens from their apartments to be a member of a community of artists who do not want to go to Manhattan, ever? Or who never get to be at home in Queens because they can't afford to waste the time going back there? Why not populate Detroit? Or Albany? Or Pittsburgh? Or some other charming small city with a low profile and vacant properties you can buy from the city for a dollar? From there you can FTP your PDFs for a fraction of the cost of living, and when it's time to have babies you can stay where you are because your apartment is big enough! Or you live in a house. You live in a house with a door that opens onto a yard. Maybe you share the house with friends.) They should find somewhere to live, perhaps collectively, perhaps not individually; perhaps they should try to make sense of this whole living-somewhere thing in a way that doesn't pretend, as New York City does, that we are all ruthless rock stars with amnesia and aphasia and lifetime amniotic sacs.

The brilliance of Didion's essay: She makes no claims for New York City but that it is what it is to those who regard it. She claims only that for various ineffable reasons having mostly to do with aspirations and the qualities of light at different times of day, people come to New York bringing with them their youth and they apply their youth, and they ought to leave before their youth is exhausted and it no longer applies to New York. This seems to happen just as their prime breeding years clock in. As a native of New York, I grapple herein with a different set of coordinates for departure: I must leave behind my love, my home, my turf, my territory, my breeding ground. I must punish New York for its lameness by my desertion. Reprove and improve. How can *you* help New York City to rise to some of its former coolness? Leave it before you yourself are a chump, and perhaps by attrition it will float up.

CRASH AND BURN

Eva Tenuto

It was the summer of 1991, and at eighteen, I was finally getting the chance I'd daydreamed about for years: I was packing my bags and moving from the sleepy Hudson Valley to New York City to become A Professional Actress.

I grew up only ninety miles from New York City, but worlds away from it in rural New Paltz, on five wooded acres along a silent, dead-end road. Having spent very little time in the city as a kid, I could only imagine it was like my favorite television show, *Fame*. I wanted to "learn how to fly"! I wanted people to "remember my name"!

Then, in my senior year of high school, I cut school a few times to hop on the Metro North train from Poughkeepsie to Grand Central Station. From my first hit of New York City, I was hooked. I got high off the energy and craved it when I returned to my quiet, boring country home. I found comfort in knowing there were freaks in abundance in the Village, discovered how easy it was to buy pot in Washington Square Park, and quickly learned no one cared about the legal drinking age in this city.

My next moves became perfectly clear: move to New York City and go to acting school. I auditioned and got into the American Academy of Dramatic Arts. It seemed my acting dreams were about to come true.

I was fiercely dedicated to "the craft" not only because I wanted to be famous, but because when I was eleven, acting saved my life. I was the eldest of three girls. We lived in a small two-bedroom apartment temporarily while my father, with his own two hands, was building our family's dream home. But in the short six months when he was building from the ground up, my world came crashing down.

In the space of just a few weeks, first I overheard my mother talking on the phone to a friend about a son she'd given away when she was much younger and whom she was looking to find. Then I stumbled upon her journal, in which she wrote about an affair she was having and how she was contemplating divorce.

I have a brother? My mother is having an affair while my dad is building a new house for our family? My parents might get a divorce? *No one must ever know*, I told myself. *My sisters and father must never find out. It's my responsibility to keep this to myself, or my family will fall apart.* And so, in an effort to make sure nothing ever slipped, at eleven, I stopped talking and started eating.

Since my parents didn't know what I knew, they also didn't know what came over me. I became a mystery. My sudden outbursts and crying fits. My mysterious weight gain from sneaking downstairs in the middle of the night and stuffing the secrets down with food. By the time the house was finished and we moved in, I had shut down and blown up. I gained weight and lost friends. I was teased ferociously. Practically overnight, I'd gone from being a happy child to a damaged reject.

That's when my mother decided to enroll me in an acting class. There, miraculously, I was reborn. I found my voice again. Well, not *my* voice—I found I was able to channel the voices of others through me, which felt so much safer. I could be emotional and open and free, and not have to worry about leaking any of my own material. It was true love.

In my freshman year at the academy, I discovered my second love: booze. With alcohol, I no longer needed food at all. After my first sip of beer, I felt all the discomfort I had been carrying around, all the self-consciousness and fear, slip away. I started limiting my food as obsessively as I'd previously consumed it and lost a lot of weight in a very short period of time.

The first place I lived was a residency hall on Gramercy Park run by the Salvation Army. It housed elderly women, mentally retarded women, and actresses. For $650 per month, two meals a day were included—meals like beef cubes and gravy, canned peas and potatoes with meatloaf—not the diet of an aspiring actress in New York with a mild eating disorder, that's for sure.

But I didn't really mind starving myself. There was so much to do and see. We got free tickets to everything. I got to see Al Pacino in *Salomé* and Glenn Close, Richard Dreyfuss, and Gene Hackman in the preview of *Death and the Maiden*. I saw Laurence Fishburne in *Two Trains Running* and bumped into Tony Randall in the audience. I fell in love with the Off-Broadway production of *From the Mississippi Delta* because it was a powerful story told simply, with three actresses playing multiple characters and no set—just a few boxes onstage. I couldn't wait to be done with school and join the actors onstage.

I loved New York City. I welcomed its grit. I felt relieved to be in an environment where the secrets lived so much closer to the surface. There was no wondering what lay beneath when homeless men masturbated in Midtown delis and junkies shot up drugs on the street. Although when a dead prostitute lay on display on the steps leading up to the building of my second apartment in Hell's Kitchen, my roommates and I decided we should probably move. We relocated to the East Village. There, I felt I had found home.

In the beginning, New York City seemed to love me too. When I started acting school, I was a teachers' favorite. I was asked repeatedly how I was able to exhibit such a mature range of emotions at such a young age. But as the year progressed, I became less and less confident. The critiques and competition with my colleagues made me feel pressured and extremely self-conscious. I found myself reaching for what had previously come so naturally. By the end of the year, I was fully aware that I was not nearly as good as when I'd begun.

Still, I was invited back to the second-year program—a highly coveted invitation, as only a quarter of the students were invited back. I looked around at the others who were invited. They were not the most talented of the lot. They were *marketable*. They were thin and blond and would look great in the school's brochure. Others, much stronger in skill but a little less easy on the eyes, were rejected. The stench of the business was seeping through the selection process. I could feel some of my love for acting being compromised by a growing disgust. I declined the invitation. I claimed feminist objection, but mainly I was terrified of getting worse and being rejected the next time around.

I changed course and went to Hunter College, where I became a women's studies major. I moved to, and immediately hated, Murray Hill. There were no artists living in this Midtown span of mediocrity. I shared an overpriced, roach-infested apartment at the top of a steep six-floor walk-up with a Bulgarian woman who inhaled canisters of Whip-Its for breakfast. This was not the New York City experience I'd dreamed of.

While at school, I started a women's theater group. I decided I would rather spend my time creating the work that I believed in than auditioning for someone else's work. *Who wants to stand in line to land a commercial and end up playing an anal polyp, or some poor woman who needs relief from vaginal itching?* I asked myself. Not me. I was going to be in control of my destiny.

Unfortunately, my coping mechanism for living in the city derailed me from that destiny. I became exactly what I did not want to be: a drunk waitress dreaming of becoming an actress. The club scene, a major escape for me, started to matter way more than the theater scene. The once-ostracized child in me got high on being part of a group that didn't have to wait in line at all the clubs in the East Village and the Lower East Side. I was a regular at Bob and Sapphire Lounge and went to Lucky Cheng's when it was still called Stella's. I started to explore my sexuality. I bedded the hottest men and women I could find. I chose men who could have had careers in modeling but in reality were bouncers, drug dealers, or guys who eventually admitted to being unemployed and still living with their mothers. The women I chose were beautiful too, tall and thin—they had the bodies I dreamed of having. I found the ultimate validation in sleeping with them all because it meant I was wanted, and hopefully hot by association. Despite my better judgment, I was now using people to silence the echoes of the teasing from grade school, the shame I carried for my mother, the endless critiques of the acting business—all of which boiled down to a constant inner critic that said, "You are not good enough." What I wasn't expecting was to fall in love with the women I got involved with. But I did. And then I had something else to hide.

For years, my work life mostly consisted of waiting tables at a chain of greasy spoons, but eventually, after eight years of waitressing, in 1999 I moved up the ladder to a fine Italian restaurant in Tribeca, Rose Marie's. It's there that I found myself waiting on Robert De Niro. I was so nervous but tried to appear casual. He ordered a Cosmopolitan—my favorite drink at the time. We had something in common! But when I returned to take his dinner order, he sent the drink back because it had a bug in it. How could I have missed it floating in the martini glass? I joked with him, "Would you like me to scrape it off the top or make you a new one?" He laughed! It would have been a great scene if I had been playing the part of a waitress in a movie opposite Robert De Niro playing a customer. But there were no cameras, no crew, no one coming over to touch up my makeup between takes. I was just a waitress, waiting on Robert De Niro, playing himself. I couldn't stand the thought of being a waitress for another day and decided to go back to school.

I went back to Hunter, this time for a master's degree in elementary education, because one thing I'd learned in the city, living the cliché of the out-of-work actress, was this: you must have a backup plan. But backup plans aren't as exciting or fulfilling as dreams. As I moved away from my dream and became more invested in my backup plan, I became depressed and started drinking more. I could no longer afford the skyrocketing rents in Manhattan and jumped from one bad neighborhood in Brooklyn to another. I spent countless nights barhopping and driving drunk, cruising up and down the Brooklyn-Queens Expressway as if I were riding the Cyclone at Coney Island. I bordered on nonfunctional. I cried everywhere. I was teaching preschool on the east side of Prospect Park at the time. I would show up to work late and hungover. I'd cry on the playground, in the director's office, on the subway to and from school, jogging around Prospect Park in the morning. I cried more than the four-year-olds in my class.

In the fall of 2001, though, I regained some hope. My theater company was doing cabaret now and booking gigs more frequently and at bigger venues. Instead of getting stiffed at Ludlow Bar, we were being offered hundreds of dollars for a three-minute set at Shine, a hot club on West Broadway. There was promise on the romantic front, too. I was playing phone tag with an old friend, Dylan. We had known each other for years, and then one night at a party, after we talked into the wee hours of the morning, he looked me in the eyes and said, "I've never seen you this way before." I knew exactly what he meant. I had never seen *him* this new way either.

Perhaps we were just drunk, or perhaps a shift had actually occurred. But the possibility of it excited me. He was different from any of the other men I'd been interested in before—usually noncommittal, dysfunctional bad boys. Dylan loved his mother but didn't live with her. He was a firefighter and good with kids. With his loyalty to his family, he reminded me of my father. I respected him. He had a thick Queens accent that somehow made it irresistibly charming when he called me "sweetheart" and "baby." And he was a male! I wouldn't have to hide him! I could introduce him to my family! We played phone tag, missing each other while on vacations and not getting messages left with roommates. When we finally touched base, it was early September, and we made a plan to go out for dinner. I was sure that New York was finally about to be mine. I would have the career I dreamed of and a decent man by my side. We could live the dream together. We set our first date for that Tuesday. Tuesday, September 11, 2001.

The house I lived in at the time was in Vinegar Hill, a neighborhood near the Brooklyn Navy Yard between DUMBO and Williamsburg. (My roommates and I called it "Dumbsburg.") It was on the edge of Brooklyn, right across the water from the towers. That morning, our yard gathered a flurry of burnt paper documents. When we discovered the reason for the hours of incessant sirens, we ran around and closed all the windows to relieve ourselves of the stench of burning bodies in the air. I began to panic. Instead of our dinner date, I watched the firefighter death tally on the news go up for three straight days and was convinced that Dylan was dead.

He finally called on the third day, explaining that he'd lost his phone in the rubble. After that, we talked on the phone often. After thinking he was dead for seventy-two hours, I wanted to see him more than I had ever wanted to see anyone. I wanted to hold on and be grounded, but a traumatized man in combat is not a good choice when searching for stability. He worked around the clock at Ground Zero, finding arms and legs and putting them together with other body parts, hoping they weren't parts that belonged to friends he worked with. He went delirious from a combination of sleep deprivation and trauma. He stopped returning calls and started to just spend time with other fire-fighters. He pulled away from his family and his friends outside the department. He could only be with people who understood what he was going through; we could not understand.

He lived, but he was gone. And so was my theater company. The big show we were looking forward to at Shine got canceled with no rain date. It was just blocks away from Ground Zero. They were shutting their doors with no immediate plans to re-open. Trying to find other cabaret work didn't seem to make sense in this new city.

The plug was pulled on my artistic pursuits, my hope for love, and the electricity of the city that once got me high. New York and I crashed and burned at the same time. I went into severe withdrawal, as if I had gone cold turkey too fast. On the outside I was a well-respected preschool teacher with a master's degree. Parents were fighting to get their kids into my class. But if you scratched the surface of this mirage and looked underneath, I was clearly a depressed alcoholic hitting a low I never knew pos-sible. Everyone kept saying, "We will never forget," but forgetting was all I wanted to do. I started drinking during the day and fan-tasizing about suicide.

Despite my emotional state, somehow I managed to hold on to life in New York tightly with both hands for another four years. In 2005, though, I finally unraveled and could not hold on for a moment longer. I was done. I quit my job, sublet my apartment, sold all of my shit on the street, and moved back home.

I never expected to stay in New Paltz. I thought I would return to the city one day. Despite how treacherous the end had been, I was still committed to the city the way I'd been to so many bad lovers. But when I returned home, I could feel myself relax. I could breathe again. I started to get in touch with a side of myself I'd forgotten even existed; I started to sit still. In the country, I was able to get sober. As I detoxified myself from the booze, the dysfunctional relationships, and New York City, I started to hear the voices in my head—the ones that told me how awful I was. The voices of the kids who tormented me at school. The voices fueled by the shame of my childhood secrets. The voices I tried to run away from, first with food, then with booze and sex, and then with New York City. I let them wash over me. I sat and listened without the distractions of crowds and sirens. I found the space to go to the core and reprogram the thoughts I was left with when finally alone.

Once I got myself together, I knew I was in the right place; this wasn't the short break from the city I'd imagined. I bought a house on the river—a worn-down, disgusting little shack I rebuilt from the ground up, in the same way that I was rebuilding myself. We got rehabilitated together. I created a space that could comfort me. In that comfort and safety, I started to find the courage to finally tell the truth. I stopped using people for validation and stayed single for four years, focusing on getting better and reconnecting with my creativity. It now makes perfect sense, that right there, in my living room, I started TMI Project, a nonprofit organization that offers storytelling workshops, helping people unburden themselves of their secrets, using the stage as the platform for telling the truth. My mom came and saw me in one of the performances. Even though I was telling the secrets I had been keeping for a lifetime, when the show was over, she hugged me with tears in her eyes and told me she was proud.

Through this work, I also found real love—with a sober woman who is also an actor. I got a chance to come out to my parents, to my ninety-four-year-old grandmother, and then, onstage, to my entire community. For the first time, I was all of myself with the whole world. I never realized how bad it felt to hide until I got to experience how great it felt to be fully seen. Julie and I are now engaged. And my affair with New York City is over.

HEEDLESS, RESILIENT, GULLIBLE, AND STUPID

Janet Steen

I think some part of me knew I was going to leave New York before I even moved there, and even knew the place, unconsciously, that I would leave it for. It was as though the next chapter were already being written before the current one had had a chance to unfold. But you could not have guessed that from the way I threw myself into New York. And throwing yourself into it is really the only way to do it. So I did that, or tried to, for fifteen years.

You're heedless, resilient, gullible, and stupid at twenty-one. I was all of those things and also deeply enamored of the city's mythology when I moved there, especially its artistic and literary lore—all those suffering artists, the legendary bookstores, the places where writers gathered and drank, the places where they lived and died. This feeling came in no small part from the reverence that my father had shown for books and writers. But that didn't mean that, even in my young enthusiasm, I had illusions of becoming the stuff of legend myself. I was from Pittsburgh, after all, from a very self-effacing family. You didn't dream too big. But I could still stay up late in my railroad apartment writing short stories at a flimsy card table that served as my desk, getting a little loaded on peach schnapps, and feeling as though I were carrying on an illustrious tradition. I could try this thing out for a while.

I had to have three roommates and live in Jersey City at first, but it still counted as living in New York. The Manhattan skyline was right outside my backyard, across the Hudson. "Dazzling" was the word that came to mind. I also had to find a job. Through a friend I found out about a proofreading job at *Esquire* magazine, and I got it before they had time to advertise the job. Tedious work, but there were writers and illustrators and photographers coming in and out of the office, and there were parties and drinks after work. It was all a very smart and normal way to go about things. You got a job and tried to work your way up.

There were three of us young women in the railroad apartment, and one young man. Apparently, he had been accused of raping someone while at his Ivy League college just a couple of years before. I didn't know this until after he had moved out. In the apartment below us were two Frenchmen, and in the apartment above, two young Italian men. Frequently one pair or the other would make dinner for us girls. One of my roommates was narcoleptic and would regularly fall asleep at the dinner table; one time she fell asleep on the escalator in Port Authority bus station. She had a poodle she liked to French-kiss. We were an odd little family. But there was always the skyline to look out at, to dream on. I was smart enough to know that your early time in a big city is something to be greatly sentimental about, and I was, even as it was happening. I had instant nostalgia for a place that I felt was more glamorous than I could really take in.

There were other apartments, other jobs, other roommates and friends. This was the New York of pay telephones that never worked, indecipherable announcements about subway delays, mentally ill street people not shunted away but highly visible, freezing at night under cardboard boxes. At the time you could still go to see double features at the old movie houses. A man once came in and sat down next to me at Thalia Uptown and started masturbating during the 1970s post-Vietnam movie *Cutter's Way*. Not exactly erotic material, but in New York you never knew what was going to happen. Many nights were spent going out to see bands—the Feelies, the Mekons, Camper Van Beethoven, Yo La Tengo—bands that attracted a very white postcollege crowd that could be easily typified. I was perhaps a type: I looked like part of the crowd, but I felt unmoored a lot of the time. Still, in that period New York felt like the only place I could possibly be.

———

BUT BEFORE THIS I HAD TAKEN A ROAD TRIP THE SUMMER I was nineteen, with my sister and my best friend. They were driving me up to a college in Vermont, where I was going to spend two months studying French. I have no idea how we came up with the route we took—I don't think any of us was very good at reading a map. We ended up spending a long time driving on twisty back roads through mountains and valleys somewhere in upstate New York. In my memory there are glistening lakes around almost every turn. And there is a VW bus parked somewhere, and a bunch of hippie-looking people just a little older than I am making their way down to a swimming hole. A lot of the houses look built by hand—they're ramshackle and added on to in makeshift ways. At the time I thought back to a high school project I had done for a history fair. It was titled "The Counterculture" and consisted mainly of a lame, thrown-together cardboard display with pictures of hippie types and antiwar demonstrations, and it was accompanied by a taped narration I did interspersed with bits of Jimi Hendrix, Bob Dylan, and other obvious choices. I looked out the car window and thought, *This must be the counterculture.* I had never really seen it like that before, at least not in that untamed country setting, which made it look all the more appealing. I was too young to have ever been a real hippie, a bit too modest to have ever gotten into free love, but I still liked what I saw.

There were the garden-variety late-twenties depression and the first visits to a dim therapist's office on the Upper West Side. Life was supposed to feel edgy, a little bit off to the side and out of the mainstream, but it seemed less and less so. Nine-to-five jobs were draining and claustrophobic. Then when you didn't have one, you just worried about money. But most people I knew were in the same predicament.

Certain parts of the city still thrilled me, the parts where the buildings were lower and people looked like they were doing something secretive or subterranean. The East Village was where my (requisite musician) boyfriend rented studio space with his friends for band rehearsals. It's where we ate because it was cheap. One friend started writing "manifestos"—Xeroxed statements about the crassness of the music business and mass entertainment, bands that had disappointed him, and various other things he felt like announcing to the world—and pasted them up on telephone poles around the neighborhood. They were often cryptic little antiestablishment messages that eventually got torn off and rained on and pasted over. KILL THE MOVIES AND SET YOURSELVES FREE, one said; another proclaimed, THIS POSTER WILL WRECK YOUR LIFE. For some reason they're some of the things I remember most fondly about early 1990s New York.

But strange things started happening. I broke down crying on the subway coming back from Coney Island one Fourth of July. There was too much humanity out there in one place. I started loathing certain parts of town. I dog-sat for a friend on the Upper East Side for a month and lived in her studio apartment in a doorman building, a place that should've felt swanky and nice but instead demoralized me. All those people down there on the sidewalk, all those things to buy. I couldn't get over the thought that my friend, an older woman, was living out her days in that little box on the seventeenth floor. She was perfectly happy there as far as I knew, but I didn't like to think anyone could end up so alone.

Then another equally odd thing happened. Things started to improve. Through chance I climbed up a few rungs on the ladder and became an actual editor at a magazine. I moved to Brooklyn, the obvious place to live at the time, and later the boyfriend and I found an apartment together with a garden. Things were *falling into place*. Apparently, this could happen if you slogged away in one place long enough.

But back then a subtle but persistent guilt settled over me whenever things were going too well. It was a bland, uninteresting sort of Protestant guilt. Not as dark as Catholic guilt, not as entertaining as the Jewish variety. It was more like a sense that I shouldn't be having too much fun or feel too self-satisfied because there were others out there who weren't feeling as good.

The guilt was altogether tied to my father. He was a man capable of great joy who had tremendous sorrow in him. He and my mother had a troubled marriage but soldiered on, together but emotionally separate. By leaving my hometown, I had, I thought, forsaken them to deal with it on their own. Not that I had ever been able to help, but there was always the illusion that if you were nearby or willing to suffer as well, you were at least providing some sort of company. But instead I had gone off to New York, slightly embarrassed that my ambition had become larger than my parents' ambition had ever been.

———

ON THE WEEKENDS SOMETIMES WE BORROWED A FRIEND'S CAR and drove north, out of the city and into the country. And for the first time since that college road trip, I got that warm countercultural feeling again when I saw the ragged fields and old cars parked next to farmhouses and bungalows, the messy way the women dressed (as opposed to the fashion obsession of New York), the general scruffiness. I liked the way people were just throwing their lives together. I was romanticizing, of course, but that's how I'd always gotten drawn into things.

We bought an old gray Volvo, the most respectable-looking car I'd ever driven, and rented a cabin upstate for the whole summer, using it on weekends. The boyfriend became my husband. We were now in between things—in between the claustrophobia of the city and the expansiveness of the country, in between the subways and the open fields. We were literally stuck in heavy traffic trying to get up there much of the time, the feeling of wanting to escape becoming more and more intense.

We kept renting our apartment in Brooklyn, but we took what money we'd saved and bought a house. Upstate. After we signed all the papers at the bank and made the place officially ours on a beautiful day in June, we went to the empty house and I lay down on the wooden floor of the living room in the middle of the afternoon and fell asleep. I was feeling overwhelmed, nearly depressed, but I always did, at least momentarily, when something monumental happened. And this counted as that, mostly because I knew that New York was fading away.

WE GAVE UP THE APARTMENT IN THE CITY. WE HAD A BABY. And true to form, I was overwhelmed, could barely eat for a while. She was a gorgeous little creature who spent most of her time crying. I sat in the living room of our farmhouse and looked out at the road, at people driving by, going places (there they were, free to come and go as they pleased), and I thought, *I'm really stuck now.* I missed New York painfully. Maybe a loud, frenetic city could get a baby to stop crying more easily than I could. I remembered those years of living in Park Slope—the baby-making capital of New York—and thought of the camaraderie I'd have with all those lactating new mothers who looked just like me, exhausted and pushing forty. I could just stroll down the street and sit in a café, where I'd breast-feed and chat and not be alone. In the country I had to strap the little creature in her car seat and snap it in place in the car before I could do just about anything.

And then, once again, things improved. The creature started to blossom into a funny, beautiful little girl. And we lonely former New Yorkers tended to find one another in the hills and valleys. One friendship seemed to lead easily to another, and many of my new friends had the mordant sense of humor you find in New York, which I had always loved. But there was something different too because they were people who had chosen to leave. And that meant something, more than people realized. It meant they were trading in a certain protection that the status of the city afforded them, and that was something to get used to. They risked a certain ordinary life.

But in subtle ways, life became much richer than ordinary to me, even while things went wrong, even when work got slow and cars broke down and storms knocked our power out. If this was throwing life together the way I'd imagined it, well, it was harder than I'd thought it would be, but it still made some kind of sense. The sweetest moments came during outdoor summer parties, when my little girl and my friends' children ran around in fields as the adults sat and drank and talked. The kids ran themselves ragged until dark, staying out long after the sun had set, sometimes holding glow sticks that made trails of colored light in the distance.

And I did sometimes make it into the city, to see friends, to keep a semblance of a high-powered professional life. But by then I had been gone a while. I took the train down one fall evening to go to a publishing party given at my favorite bookstore, Housing Works, in Soho. The place was packed; it was hard to maneuver around the smart-looking, well-dressed crowd. I felt clumsy and

out of practice. Everywhere around me were faces of people I'd
dealt with in the business at one time or another: writers, editors,
agents, publicists. I'd gone to lunch with these people, assigned
reviews of their books or their authors' books, written articles
myself about some of them. I saw one woman coming toward me,
a woman who had chipped away at me over the years to cover her
authors, who had taken me out for drinks, invited me to numerous events. Her eyes met mine, hovered for just a second, and
then drifted off over my shoulder as she made her way past me. It
was that classic moment of reckoning: I had outlived my useful-
ness to her. I suppose I wasn't all that surprised, although at the
moment it stung, both her disregard for me and the realization
that I wasn't who I used to be. And then, a wave of relief. I went
back to talking to a friend who was a friend beyond the business
of it all, drank some more wine, and took the train back upstate.

———

I WAS SITTING ONCE IN THE LIVING ROOM IN THE HOUSE
where I grew up with my father. This was in the last years of
his life. It was late afternoon, and the light was coming into the
room a bit too harshly. I didn't always like things too bright. I
was home for a visit. We were sitting there talking, probably
about things going on in my life, since my father was so very good
at deflecting attention away from himself. I think I was probably
trying very hard to seem relaxed, although I often wasn't as relaxed as I would've liked. There was so much love between us, but
it was so very hard to acknowledge.

And then, almost out of nowhere, a very direct question from
him. He asked me why I had moved away from the place where
I had grown up. (By now it had been nearly twenty years.) He

posed this question as though it were something he'd been wanting to ask for a very long time and had had to find great will to work up to. And I thought I detected an edge of anger in the question, although it was more likely injury. I think he had long mourned the fact that all his children had moved far away.

I had trouble finding the right words. "I guess I just wanted to see what it would be like to live in New York. I didn't necessarily think I would stay that long," I explained, struggling to make sense of it also for myself. "Things just started happening. And then I just kept . . . staying."

That was the thing about New York. For most people who moved there from a smaller place, the way I did, things were never the same afterward. It was like a great love in your life that you could never forget, whether it had gone sour or not. And my many years there prepared me for wanting something utterly different, a different extreme. It was true that New York lent you a certain toughness that made you think you could handle difficulty in all sorts of forms. Moving to a smaller city just didn't seem to be the answer. I wanted fields and winding roads. I wanted to see bearded guys in old trucks, to sit with an old woman in the general store and talk about how high the creeks had been looking lately. I wanted to walk out my door and not have to face a thousand strangers.

My father didn't say a lot. He looked as though he was trying hard to understand. Essentially, I was telling him I had to find a new place to live my life and that I was never able to come home. I was all grown up then anyway, and he was an old man. I wished I could've stayed and been more help to him, but I had to go, and I never did exactly apologize for that.

GOODBYE, HELLO, GOODBYE . . . HELLO

Carolita Johnson

've left New York three times over a span of twenty-eight years. The first time I was twenty-three and headed to Paris. I returned home eleven years later, worn down by my life there as an illegal alien. The second time I left, at age thirty-five and feeling exploited as an independent contractor in New York, it was to embrace France's employee benefits and national health care as a "legal alien." The next and last time I left the place that we who don't live in New York City call "the city" was five years ago, to flee the rising rent. I landed in Kingston, New York, where the rents recently began rising at an even faster clip than downstate once the big city folk caught the scent of cheap real estate and fresh air at a shorter commute than it takes to get to Coney

Island from Midtown Manhattan by subway. I was fifty when I arrived in Kingston. For five years I lived there as an artist, writer, café employee, and finally, as an artist-in-residence, teaching a course at SUNY New Paltz.

On my second return, eighteen years ago, when I came back to start writing and drawing, I began the way most people do: my sentimental education, the romantic adventures and relationships that formed my emotional intelligence (or lack thereof). Five years ago, I'd been annoyed, writing about my more recent life, that my story would appear to end with me moving in with my partner of fourteen years and, even more of a cliché, getting married. But our life didn't end "happily ever after." We were legally married for exactly three days, and my life continued, not quite so happily ever, after death threw my life a plot twist. Four years ago, I became a widow in a small city a hundred miles away from "all that."

I'd been moving northward ever since my last return, starting with Brooklyn, then across the river to the Lower East Side, to Harlem, and then, with a partner, to Inwood. When he turned sixty-nine, I decided it would be wiser to skip getting priced out of the Bronx in five years, so we made for the Hudson Valley, to Kingston, where I thought we could live unfettered by financial worries into his old age.

In Kingston, I never had to network. Kingston networked me. A nondriver, I walked everywhere and saw people all the time, especially once I got a job at the local café. I've always thought it's utter snobbery to live in a city and not work in it, so I applied for and got a few shifts there within a month, even before I needed the money, which I certainly did, later. When my partner was diagnosed with stage 4 cancer, everyone knew it and kept an eye on us and helped me care for him. When I found myself alone again, I wasn't really alone. Kingston was there for me.

My first apartment as a widow in Kingston was like nothing I'd ever seen before. It was $975 a month. It was built in 1920, rather dilapidated, probably a fire hazard, and was a full block deep, with twenty-foot ceilings. It was divided railroad style into five rooms separated by three sets of walnut pocket doors. A windowed shaft to provide light and air in the middle, darkest room had been removed in my apartment, leaving a semiconcealed trapdoor as a scar in my ceiling through which I could hear my upstairs neighbor sneeze occasionally. There were indoor "windows" and transoms designed to maximize the distribution of daylight, two disused fireplaces, and an ingenious thing called a central vacuum cleaner, which was once operated by plugging a hose into holes in the floors that connected it to a giant vacuum in the basement.

The wonder of it led me to take breaks from weeping and panic attacks by scouring microfilmed newspapers for information about its builder and all the prior residents and businesses that had once occupied it. On a roll, I began to list and research my previous addresses and discovered that all my old apartments in New York City had been turned into luxury rentals, many of which had even been subdivided into at least one more bedroom than I had once had, sometimes two more. The rents had tripled, hair-raisingly. If I hadn't considered it yet, the idea of returning "home" to the city now seemed like a cruel joke. How had it come to this?

The same would soon happen to my new Kingston apartment. Nine months after I found it, the building was sold, and the new owners—fresh transplants from Brooklyn—ended my month-to-month arrangement and more than doubled the rent.

———

I'M A TRUE NEW YORKER. MY PARENTS MET AT ROSELAND, A dance hall that was, until recently, in Manhattan, at 239 West 52nd Street. Four years later I was conceived in an apartment on West 73rd Street, known as the Upper West Side and then born and raised in various parts of Queens.

I bring this up because I know that all recently arrived and incoming New Yorkers like to tell their friends who visit them in, say, Queens, that Queens is New York City, but I'll tell you this much: no one in Manhattan ever said "I'm going to the city" if they were on their way to any of New York's other boroughs. No. Going to the city means you're going to Manhattan, aka "the city."

I don't care what anyone ever taught you about the five boroughs of New York City. The only part of the city that *is* the city is Manhattan. Yeah, I'm from Queens: I'm proud to be a tough kid from Queens who has to watch her language around my more genteel New Yorker friends. I'm not from the city. I know that the city is as exquisitely cruel as it is sublime, and I only like living there as long as I can get away from it whenever I want.

That is not an issue for me right now because the rent is too high for me to live there. But guess what? Kingston was recently named "the Brooklyn of the Hudson Valley," and now the rent is going up there, too. I say "there" instead of "here," because six months into the coronavirus pandemic that began in March of 2020, I left Kingston and returned to Queens, where I am now living with my eighty-five-year-old mother, caring for her a year and a half after my father died.

What with the "citiots" coming to buy a house or two—seriously, I've heard them talking about the "couple of houses" (or even three) they're buying—my former upstairs neighbor (also a woman artist) and I aren't the only tenants I know who have been booted from a building by a new owner. These new owners tend to be people who say things like, "It's gotten *so* expensive in Brooklyn that we moved up here, and, oh my God, we hate to be *those people*, but . . ."

But. They actually *are* "those people." The current tenant of my grand old five-room apartment in the heart of Kingston's "uptown" neighborhood moved there after getting booted from his old duplex apartment across the street by more of "those people." Me, I moved a couple blocks away into a very rundown apartment with a rent closer to pregentrification levels but was denied a lease: I imagine that's because my landlady wouldn't mind selling the building, and can you blame her? She promised not to "screw me over." My goodness, I tried to tell her, it wasn't her I was worried about. It was the potential new owners I feared.

I tried not to think about them. I was there almost three years before leaving at the end of August 2020. The attic—my studio/guest room—sometimes had a faint aroma of hamster, probably because the previous renter had a mouse infestation. I've lived in worse. One of its advantages was its proximity to the bus station: I could get on a bus and be in "the city" in a few hours.

I WOULD GO TO THE CITY ABOUT ONCE A MONTH FOR A LONG weekend to see my friends but also to make sure I didn't lose my edge. New York has a short memory and is changing all the time: I needed to see my editors, my agent, my peers, not to mention my siblings. Luckily, at any one moment I had at least three different friends I could crash with, and I tried to divide my time with each of them equitably so I didn't overstay my welcome anywhere. My custom was to clean their apartments on my way out, figuring I was a virtual, unpaying roommate and it was the least I could do. I have to admit it also made their apartments and, by extension, the city feel like home to me.

By contrast, Kingston is small, and because of this I saw my upstate friends and acquaintances every day, which meant I could work from home but never really be alone. All I had to do was go down the block to the café for a cortado, and everyone was there, no need to make a date and no need to linger—though I often did. The café was practically an extension of my own apartment where I could sit and work, often surrounded by people I loved doing the same.

Most of my friends there were women, indubitable feminists and fiercely individual in contrast to many of my women friends in the city. I think this is related to the low rent. Up there, where rent on a one-bedroom apartment was, until recently, typically only $700 a month and where it remains half as low as city rents, you could toss your misbehaving man out on his ass and still make the rent. Affordable rents put women in a position of strength. I've seen too many women in the city who, out of financial desperation, stay with or delude themselves about men they wouldn't hesitate to leave or read the riot act to if only they had what is known as "fuck you" money. (NB: here the words "men" and "jobs" can be considered interchangeable. More than one kind of toxic situation could be improved by affordable rents.)

WHEN I FOUND MYSELF DOING SPIT-TAKES OVER HOW HIGH
the rent had gone on my vermin-infested dumps of yore, I had
a brilliant idea: I looked up "women's boardinghouses," recalling
the ones I'd seen in old black-and-white movies like *Stage Door*,
where a woman of limited means coming to the big city alone
could rent a room with a bed, a desk, and a bookshelf to live in
safety with her fellow entry-level earners and aspiring artists.

Too late: except for one outlier, they've all become hotels or
luxury versions of their former selves, marketed to highly paid
professionals or interns whose parents ostensibly pay their board.
Women in retail or in the service industry today, who are often
older and single, could never afford these rooms. It's hard to understand why the women's boardinghouse is obsolete now that it
would be more useful than ever.

I see women my age and older lose their jobs while they're
still young enough to work but too old to be rehired at entry
level. Highly paid professionals, they're typically laid off and
replaced by their assistants just before they've finished paying
off their thirty-year mortgages. Single women starting out, or
who have worked for decades barely making their livelihood and
whose rent will soon outpace their income, women returning to
the workforce after taking care of their aging, dying parents or
spouses—they compose a growing demographic that will need a
place to live in safety and a sense of community.

It's a fond pastime of us aging, single women to imagine, often over drinks, our fantasy Golden Girls household, inspired
by that TV series about four older women living their golden
years together. There is one last boardinghouse in the city that
I want to someday try to get into for a year before it joins the
others in extinction. This is not a romantic notion: I want to see

what it's like and how it's run because I think this kind of living arrangement needs to make a comeback, albeit updated for modern womanhood to include all our sisters. In the meantime, though, I am cohabitating in Queens with only one proverbial Golden Girl, my mom. One thing I'm grateful for is that my mother has completely forgotten how much she used to despise me. We watch old movies together in the appallingly cluttered and dusty living room, and they trigger memories of her youth in Ecuador and how, sixty years ago, when she forgot her suitcase in the taxi to the airport and arrived in New York City with nothing, unannounced, and (unlike me) couldn't leave.

In Kingston I could only *just* afford to live alone while living off my writing and drawing. My two shifts at the cafe were a bonus that disappeared with the coronavirus outbreak. Though I missed my young colleagues and the social contact, such exposure could make me a constant danger to my vulnerable friends and family. I could spend the next winter "Zooming" with them from anywhere. Maybe being a true New Yorker is what makes me so willing to sacrifice so much to find meaning in life.

I wonder what will become of Kinsgston. A friend, who has been right about everything regarding this pandemic and its repercussions, predicts that more people from the city than ever will move up there and work remotely, away from the potentially contaminated crowds or buy safe houses there to flee to upon the next pandemic, driving rents up further. He thinks rents will get lower in the city as a consequence, but I think that won't happen until there are laws in place prohibiting landlords from warehousing, keeping apartments empty for years, writing their losses off while they wait for tenants who will pay high rent.

Meanwhile, I have a feeling I'll be back in Manhattan again some day, but how I'll do it remains to be seen. The truth is, I know that wherever I go, there are people with more money right behind me who will price me out within five years or less. Knowing this, I usually take a two-year lease and sign twice before looking to move again. I always look for working-class neighborhoods like the one I grew up in, which, by the time I move out, I have helped gentrify by my very presence there, making me part of the problem. I slink in, and slink out, knowing that where we artists go, the upwardly mobile follow. We're a virus, ourselves. You'll never hear me say "Move to my neighborhood, the rent is so reasonable" again. But I know silence isn't the solution.

If I move back to Manhattan, it will mean I found a way to afford it as easily as the people I used to pave the way for (unlikely!) or, hopefully, that I was part of a change. Perhaps we'll meet at "the Carolita" someday.

For now, though, I am enjoying Queens. My neighborhood has gone from unpleasantly white (I refer to the bigots who bullied me here in the '80s) to mostly Asian and Latinx now, the opposite of what my neighborhood in Kingston was becoming when I left. I've found my local café here, where I write in my journal for a break from cleaning and DIY home repair, and find I'm happy to pass on Manhattan for now. And yeah, I *could* say I'm back in "the city," like the gentrifiers so often say in Queens. But I'm too much of a snob.

THE LOOSENING

Rayhané Sanders

I chose New York. I was seventeen and I had to go to college because that's what comes next. Since I have trouble with commitment, I had applied to over a dozen schools. I said "maybe" and they said "yes," and before I knew it I had a choice to make and I chose New York. I chose it because I couldn't possibly imagine myself in some Lands' End catalog version of college— some northeastern, cozy-by-the-fire campus where everyone knows your name and boys wear boat shoes and blizzards keep you indoors, doing drugs and exchanging invites for summer stays on the Cape. And because my home state of California, which I have since grown to love, seemed at the time like a dry well—as dusty and brown and thirsty for action as its drought-plagued canyons, always catching on fire. I remember once my boyfriend and I driving the 10 east, leaving LA for New York in the middle of the Santa Ana season; the warm winds had set Malibu and the West Valley ablaze, and in the rearview mirror we could see the black smoke pluming, and I thought, eyes fixed east, *Let it burn.*

New York seemed to make some promises I couldn't refuse. I would have anonymity—my walk to class would be accompanied by fellow students but also by East Village junkies and Baltic teenage models and finance sharks in their Italian suits, artists and hustlers, playwrights and bums, drag queens and book editors and the whole of humanity. I liked that. I liked that at any moment I could lose myself in the crowds, disappear from view, blend in and liquefy, cease being available. Something about living in the city—even in a room the size of a broom closet and with a shared bathroom down the hall or, later, in a neighborhood where the burgers were fifteen dollars but my boyfriend got held up at knifepoint at three in the afternoon putting quarters into a washing machine—felt decadent, luxurious even. Everyday things were thrilling. Leaving the house for a pack of cigarettes feels incredible when you do it at three-thirty in the morning, walking down Broadway in a negligee with a coat thrown over it. Meeting friends at the movies feels like a coup—victorious, like somehow you *won*—when instead of parking your car at the mall, you pass under the arch at Washington Square Park, where Harry chose Sally, on your walk over.

Fast as an L train approaching the station, seventeen turned into twenty turned into twenty-five turned into thirty. I remained in love, no doubt about it, but there were hints early on, cracks in the façade, that things in this fast-paced, mile-a-minute city could go from thrilling to dismal faster than you knew.

I remember sitting on my front stoop down by the Hudson River, smoking a cigarette, watching the towers burning and, yes, people jumping, nightmare-disbelief dawning to life, when the first tower just collapsed, one minute there, one minute gone, a free fall of dust and engineering and people and reality . . . all turned to ash. It sounded like one wail, like the whole city screamed at once, a grieving mother, her son dead in her arms. The hairs on my arms stood up. The second tower followed soon after, and my street view, our skyline, was different, just like that. I sat there for a few hours—I couldn't get up, there was no way I was moving—watching all of surviving Wall Street heed Mayor Rudy Giuliani's simple missive and "head north," treading up my street wearing their suits and holding their briefcases, painted, head to toe, in gray, like a zombie apocalypse movie, and it felt then like a giant warning: *Nothing is solid. Everything will change.*

There was the instant disaster, yes, but there would also be a slow burn. My boyfriend and I would break up. I'd get an evil bitch of a boss. I'd watch with balled-up fists as boys who had the same olive skin as my cousins back in Tehran got stopped, their backpacks rifled through, at the subway turnstiles. My subway rides would go from exchanging smiles with a mother and her sweet baby to holding my lower back in pain, weighed down by bags of manuscripts for work, while I reached the whole of my five-foot-two-inch being for a sliver of pole to hold on to and even *more* people—was it possible?!—pushed their way into our cattle car, and I thought, *There's got to be another way.*

Friends started to leave—for Miami and LA and San Francisco and New Orleans and Austin, that millennial mecca. My

God, even Boston. People were leaving for Boston. I started to have dreams in which I'd wake up in Los Angeles, look outside, and realize, with panic, that I had given it all up, that I'd gotten off the merry-go-round after working so hard to find a place on it and that my spot was surely now taken by some younger, fresher new arrival; I had left New York and made a ginormous mistake and ruined everything. I'd wake up in a sweat to the roar and squeal of ambulance sirens and sigh with relief at being safely ensconced in Brooklyn. Then I'd have the same dream in crafty reverse: there I'd be, sitting poolside, skin clear, hair done, rested, bouncing my baby on my knee, talking to some girlfriend about how leaving New York—avoiding a destiny of aging workhorse spinsterdom—was the best thing I could've done for my quality of life, for my future, when suddenly I'd wake up in some outerborough brick-and-steel industrial wasteland, the sky outside cold and dreary, the air toxic, rain rapping on the window. Then I'd wake up for real with a start, unsure of where I was, look outside, and cry, cry, because I was still here.

Things were starting to get to me.

What had once enticed me so much about living here, what had made me say yes and excitedly brought me to the altar—bishop's crook lampposts and cobblestone streets and wrought-iron fire escapes and late-night restaurants and all-night bars and Central Park and the Chrysler Building and Film Forum and summer concerts and the Brooklyn Bridge and flea markets and egg creams and Chinatown and cherry blossom trees and plays and brownstones and rooftop gardens and the Chelsea galleries and Grand Central's Oyster Bar and, my God, *people*, so many people, so interesting and inspirational and available you'd never feel lonely again—all that had started to feel like not enough.

I asked those on their way out why they were leaving—"How could you leave New York? Where do you go from here?"—and they told me they had never pictured themselves staying forever; it'd been nice and now they were done. But I had. I had pictured myself here forever. LA had been a place to leave for grander adventures, bigger horizons, smarter people, and fewer blonds, and New York had been a destination to reach and, once here, a star to follow, the dream always a little ahead, calling out to you, a siren song: this apartment, this job, this promotion, this reservation, this next goal to reach, this next hill to climb. We New Yorkers, we're like little striver-warriors, all of us, swords in hand, slashing dragons as we go. Tired but strong, worn-out but resourceful, resolute, steadfast. Determined to make it.

But I was starting to wonder what "it" really was. What was I proving with all of this? I was spending the equivalent of a mortgage on an eight-by-twelve room in an apartment with three other busy shadows, passing ships in the night, whose names I often forgot, in a half-shady neighborhood where I was woken almost nightly by intoxicated masses pouring out of the bars and piling onto the street for a smoke. If it wasn't them, it was the ambulances or the garbage trucks or the impromptu rap battles. Contenders would actually pick my trash can up over the building gate and use the lid for percussion. I was waking up late for work, not showering (again), rushing to the train that would surely be "delayed due to train traffic ahead of us," elbowing some sleazy man behind me even as the MTA's automated message attested that "a crowded subway is no excuse for sexual misconduct." I was looking older than I was. I was finding gray hairs in numbers. I was gaining weight from sitting at my desk so much—there is no such thing as nine to five in New York. The bags under my eyes, particularly the left one, I couldn't help but notice, were deepening and gaining in folds.

I had come to New York when I was seventeen because—and maybe I was not fully conscious of this then—the city had seemed like a great place to discover who you are. It just seemed that there was a lot to experience here, as if all you had to do was show up and the city would take care of the rest, making sure you got the education, the maturing, the wising-up you needed. Its crowds, the noise, the endlessness of it all, the perpetual motion, felt exciting then—revealing—just the deep end I needed to jump into. There is something unique about New York, some quality, some matchless, pertinent combination of promise and despair, wizardry and counterfeit, abundance and depletion, that stimulates and allows for a reckoning to occur—maybe even forces it. The city pulls back the curtain on who you are; it tests you and shows you what you are made of in a way that has become iconic in our popular culture and with good reason. In thirteen years, the city has kicked my ass and made me strong and served me well.

But thirty is not seventeen. You get older, certain things get satisfied, itches get scratched, and you find yourself wanting new things, new environments, better suited to who you are now, to who you hope to be. For all the construction and subway rate hikes, for all the gentrification and new-neighborhood labeling (DUMBO, BoCoCa, Nolita), New York never fundamentally changes; you do. The city is always here if you need it—one big giant laboratory, aflame with bright lights and tests and trials. And, for the most part, it's young people who need it—the next crop, in from the farms and the 'burbs and the mountains and the beaches. They gear up, slap on their goggles, pull on their rubber gloves, and take a deep breath. They don't know it yet, but they'll be deep-sea divers in no time, plumbing depths they didn't know existed, taking on shapes, moving in rhythms, along lines they couldn't anticipate crossing, let alone navigating. Those who make it, that is.

I left the City of Angels a long time ago to reach out and grab new angels, angels of my own making. To set them myself, hand to flesh, upon my shoulders. LA's angels—its freeways, its smog, its culture of celebrity, its endless summer, its open sky void—would no longer do; they had nothing to offer me. I left thirteen years ago with an engine roaring in my belly and a hungry spark in my eye. I stayed away for a long time; when I would visit, I'd keep my head low, my eyes to the squeaky-clean pavement that had no stories to tell. I'd take note of its inconveniences—but what if I want soba noodles at 3 AM? I'd argue to friends—and steer clear of the beaches, where, I feared, the chant of the ocean might wipe my dreams clean. Back at JFK, off the plane, I'd quicken my pace, as if my legs always moved like that, as if because they did meant that I belonged, meant I was one of the city's own.

I stayed away for a good stretch. Like a good New Yorker, I got busier and busier and spent less and less time on myself—haircuts, exercise, thinking. I shut my eyes with the rest of them on the morning trains. It used to amaze me how commuters could keep a hot cup of coffee sturdy in their hand while they let out a little snore, clearly asleep; how they knew to wake up right before their stop. I became one of them. I was tired, depleted. The engine in my belly got me where I wanted to go, and now everything tasted like battery acid up and down my throat.

One summer, I passed by one of the brownstones I had fawned over when I first moved to Park Slope—Berkeley Place or Carroll Street, I can't remember now—one of those picture-perfect postcard-of-New-York ones, with the red door and the flower window boxes and the curved stone stoop, one of those that was still intact and hadn't been turned into oddly shaped studio apartments to maximize the building's earnings. One family, one lucky family, lived here, stars on their foreheads.

There were kids running up and down the front steps chasing a dog; their feet, shoeless and wet, left prints. The mother was trying to pay a pizza-delivery guy; she reached over with a fistful of cash as a couple of teenagers ducked out of the way, taking the box with them. The front door was open, and I slowed my pace, craning my neck to take a good look inside. The house probably cost a couple million at least—more than I'd ever dreamed of having. The plastic bags I was carrying home from the market had branded red lines into my wrists (I lost circulation blocks ago); moist Band-Aids covered half of my blistered, pulsing feet; the burn between my legs was visceral, my thighs chafed and raw from the constant burn of sweat, the constant friction of walking in 90-plus-degree heat and 90 percent humidity. I was, as usual, exhausted. But as I watched the domestic scene play out before me, peering inside my dream Brooklyn-Barbie home—the apex, the diamond, of the dream itself—something truly amazing happened: I didn't want it. Truth be told, it looked cramped; I could see that the staircase rising from the ground floor was not much wider than my hips, that it would be difficult to carry laundry up and down its steps. The mom looked tired—beaten, actually. I knew that in the back the neighbors' gardens would be squeezing in from either side, rectangular plots rubbing up on each other like sticks of gum. I walked on, stunned by my own feelings, feeling like a traitor, wanting nothing more than to ignore what I just felt—but finding myself unable to.

If we are transplants, we say we came to New York for its "energy," but the truth is, that energy doesn't come from the streets or the stores or the buzzy power-lunch restaurants. It's not here because of the subways or the block parties or the Puerto Rican Day Parade. We brought it here. It's just the collective energy of us—the by-product and the fumes of the ambition we lugged with us when we came. Ambition: our bright bird-dream and our heavy load.

What I realized that afternoon in Park Slope—and many afternoons since—is that I had come here so many moons ago to find out who I was, to qualify, to prove things to myself I didn't even have names for yet, to test my worth. And it occurred to me that I had gotten what I came for—I *had* it, like a quarter in my palm. I understood then that the city—even what we call it honors the mythic site that it is, more symbol than place—had served its purpose: I knew exactly who I was, precisely what I was worth, and it was now time to find a more conducive place to enjoy her.

I said goodbye to New York not because anything got bad or went sour. I didn't have a moment, as Joan Didion did, when I realized that I had "stayed too long at the Fair." I left New York because I wanted more. I wanted space and silence, mountains and sky—the calm to appreciate my life, a life that, I now knew, had already begun and didn't need to "get started." I left New York and returned to LA because I had entered into a new reckoning, a different kind of inventory, and when I wake up to a morning full of rolling fog off the coast and open my eyes to the pink shock of bougainvillea outside my window and take in the smell of eucalyptus that just permeates the air here, medicine in every breath, I know that I am right where I need to be. I said goodbye to all that and left New York because I, like Didion, "am not that young anymore." I just never dreamed what good that would signal, what joy that would mean.

YOU ARE HERE

Hope Edelman

Like so many New York stories, this one begins with real estate.

Picture a four-floor brownstone on the north side of Washington Square Park. A golden number 24 nestles inside a stained-glass panel above the front door. Two high school girls sit on the front steps, eating thick slices of Ray's pizza off paper plates, careful to keep the viscous gold oil from dripping onto their jeans.

It's the fall of 1981, the beginning of their senior year. This morning they took the bus thirty-five miles from suburban Spring Valley into Port Authority and then rode the A train to West Fourth Street. It's a Saturday afternoon, early October, low-hanging sun, thin slice of chill in the air. The leaves are just starting to give it up for the year. The dogs across the street at the

Washington Square dog park yip and chase one another in end-less loops. At the park's central fountain, tight clusters of Rasta musicians rhythmically beat their sticks and drums.

An old woman smothered in layers of wool pilots a grocery cart full of blankets along the sidewalk. She stops in front of the girls and stares at their fat pizza slices. Her hair is dull steel and matted, her eyes a cloudy gray.

"Eat yer vegetables!" she barks.

The girl on the left, the tall one with the sad smile—that's me—is startled into silence. Her mother died three months ago. No one's been paying attention to her vegetable intake since then. She looks at her pizza and wonders, *Do mushrooms count?* But the girl on the right, the delicate one with rippling, russet hair and a splash of freckles across her nose, tips her chin back and laughs. That's Heidi, my best friend, fellow lover of books and words.

The bag lady disappears around the corner. New York City is filled with random, quirky moments like this, chance collisions that just might change your life. This kind of thing never happens in Spring Valley. Spring Valley is strip malls and wine from twist-top bottles, black Trans Ams full of muscled Italian guys shouting *yo!* from the back seats. There's nothing sophisticated about Spring Valley. Real life, vibrant, urban, creative life, starts with a 212. So naturally, Manhattan is where the girls want to be.

We'll be writers here one day, they believe. And why not? They're seventeen. Everything is possible. Heidi says she'll come home to her fabulously handsome husband in their Upper East Side penthouse and kick off her Manolo Blahniks. (Yes, they existed in the '80s.) The other girl has no idea what a Manolo Blahnik is, but it sounds exotic and therefore desirable.

"Perfect," she says.

Her future plans lean more toward a leather messenger bag and a fitted tan trench coat, wooden bookshelves lined with hardcovers, and amber whiskey in cut-glass highballs full of ice. It's decidedly more Lion's Head than Elaine's, though under the trench coat might, *might*, be a little black dress. She's still thinking that part through.

But one thing she knows for sure.

"I'm going to live *here*." She slaps the concrete step at her side. This brownstone has history. This brownstone has permanence and solidity. This brownstone has authenticity. It's a place a real writer would live.

"Right *here*," she repeats.

The girls have no way of knowing that in thirty years, both of them on the West Coast by then, they'll look back on this October day and wonder, *Was anyone ever that young?* And they'll realize with sweet amazement, *Yes, we were.* And they'll marvel that of all the dreams they had that day, of everything that happened later and everything that didn't, my apartment in that brownstone was the one wish that came purely, perfectly true.

———

To get from Spring Valley into Manhattan took me ten years and three thousand miles. The story isn't that unusual, I suppose: suburban kid so enamored with New York she couldn't commit until she felt ready for its risks and rewards. I could have applied to NYU for college, but I knew I lacked the sophistication, the social finesse, the kind of tough exterior Manhattan would demand of me. When my mother died, my sense of stability disappeared along with her. My father was a kind man, a good man, but he relied on Scotch—lots of it—to soften his grief. I chose a college in the Midwest, the one farthest from home that accepted me. I couldn't chance failing in New York yet, or letting the city fail me. It was the only place I knew I belonged. If I couldn't survive there, I would have no place else to go.

After college, an entry-level editorial salary wouldn't cover New York rents, and moving back to my father's somber house was out of the question. I took a magazine job in Knoxville, Tennessee, where $15,000 a year paid for a one-bedroom apartment. Three years later, I was accepted to a graduate nonfiction writing program in Iowa and headed back to the Midwest.

It seems romantically itinerant to me now to have pulled up stakes and moved on as each opportunity arose, but really, it was all part of my grand plan to get back to New York one day. New York was where the real writers were. New York was where all the agents and publishers and magazines worth reading were. New York was where the aspiring writers wanted to be in the 1990s. Well, there and Prague.

There were relationships in Chicago and Knoxville and Iowa City, but none that would have led me back home. And no man could compete, in my mind, with the lure of a summer night in Greenwich Village with the air still warm enough at midnight for sundresses and sandals, streetlights casting a silver glow on sidewalk diners sipping from glasses of dark wine at red-checkered tables, full taxis gliding beneath traffic lights flashing candy-colored cycles from green to yellow to red. All those years when I thought I wanted a man to love me, what I really wanted was the romance of being a writer in New York. I ached for it like a woman pining for an unattainable love.

The writer part came sooner than I'd imagined. For ten years I'd been searching for a book about girls whose mothers had died, wanting to know if the persistent sadness and emptiness I felt was normal. In my last year of graduate school, I decided to write it myself, and in a remarkable twist of luck and fate, the book proposal went to auction in New York on April Fool's Day 1992. The resulting contract finally gave me the stamp of legitimacy I felt I needed to move back. In my mind, I wouldn't be returning to New York as her servant or minion. I'd be meeting her as an equal.

TEN YEARS, TWO DEGREES, SEVEN ADDRESSES, AND A BOOK contract: that's what it took to get me home.

I arrived on the Upper East Side in the summer of 1992 with a freshly printed master's degree, a desktop IBM computer, and seven cartons of books. My first apartment was on East 64th Street between First Avenue and York, a 610 square foot, one-bedroom flat—enormous by New York standards—rent stabilized at $760 per month. My aunt, who'd lived there for twenty years, offered it to me when she left New York. My advance check wouldn't have supported me in Manhattan for the eighteen months I needed to finish the book, and so it was my aunt's generosity, as much as the book contract, that made New York possible for me.

Yorkville was an unlikely neighborhood for me to land in, but my gratitude was immune to geography. Every morning as I walked up First Avenue, I passed a parade of perfectly coiffed ladies in peach and turquoise Chanel suits walking pouffy little dogs named Genevieve and Charlemagne. My short cotton sundress paired with brown motorcycle boots raised eyebrows, but I didn't mind. East Side, West Side, above Houston, below Canal—what did neighborhood matter? The sidewalks I walked on were *New York* sidewalks. I could hardly believe my good fortune.

This was 1992, 1993, a tremendous time to be writing nonfiction in New York. Memoir hunger was rampant. Young writers with personal stories of trauma, loss, or just generic dysfunction were in high demand. It's become cliché to romanticize publishing's glory days of the 1990s, but for many the decade really was a charmed, abundant era. The city was brimming with journalists, essayists, screenwriters, and novelists still able to survive on their craft, boosted by the dot-com boom's new need for paid content. Manhattan was a living flowchart of creatives. For a while I dated a *Daily News* reporter I met at a book party at the Lion's Head. I joined an urban writers' room in Greenwich Village, where I took coffee breaks with office mates whose names had studded my bookshelves for years. That spring I played second base on the National Writers Union softball team. We were flat-out the worst team in the Publishing League, but who could blame us? Stick a bunch of young writers in Central Park at dusk with the 57th Street skyline rising majestically from the trees, and they're not thinking, *Line drive to left field.* They're thinking, *Holy crap. I'm really here.*

What I'm trying to convey is the sense of reverence a working writer could feel in the New York of the early 1990s. The pulse of everyday life in Manhattan felt like the very heartbeat of Western civilization. I never took living there for granted, not for a single day.

And then.

One afternoon in early 1994, with my book finished and in production, I returned home to find an eviction notice taped to my front door. *We've been alerted, unauthorized tenant*—that was its gist. Building management gave me one week to leave. Having already paid that month's rent, I bargained it up to three. Real estate brokers were the only way to find decent apartments in Manhattan. They charged horrendous finder's fees, but then you were done with them. The first broker I called had a one-bedroom available on 14th Street, the northern border of Greenwich Village. We agreed to meet that evening.

When I arrived at his office, a fax was coming through. The broker read it while I waited. I watched his face register mild surprise.

"You mind if we stop here first?" he asked. "It's out of your price range, but it's a brownstone right on Washington Square. They don't come up often. Actually, I've never been in one before."

A brownstone? Washington Square?

"Just out of curiosity," I said, "what's the address?"

He checked the fax. "Number 24."

In his bulky blue parka and tweed cap, the realtor looked more like a high school social studies teacher than a Manhattan broker. If I were to call back the next day to discover he didn't exist, that he'd been an angel come to earth for just one night, I'd believe it.

"How much out of my price range?" I said.

———

THE APARTMENT AT 24 WASHINGTON SQUARE NORTH WAS the back half of the uppermost floor, atop three flights of elegantly carved stairs. Its main room featured two skylights and a kitchen against a wall; the compact bedroom looked out on the Empire State Building. At less than 500 square feet, the space was "cozy" in realtor-speak, and in that peculiar New York fashion, rooms that had once housed lesser servants were now an enviable place to live.

In the three months between move-in and book release day, I started creating my first permanent home. The brownstone's original details, circa 1830s, called out for objects of that era. At an outdoor antique booth near Astor Place, I found an inexpensive walnut hall table. I bought half-price walnut picture frames on Madison Avenue and filled them with photos of my ancestors, hardy immigrants from Czechoslovakia and Ukraine. On frigid February nights, as the radiators clanged and pumped out excess heat, I sat warm and content in my snug cocoon, surrounded by images of the great-grandparents and third cousins who'd helped populate Manhattan's Lower East Side.

This was early 1994. Bill Clinton was in the White House, Rudy Giuliani newly settled in Gracie Mansion on a pledge to clean up New York. A 7.0 earthquake rattled my sister's house in Los Angeles, but in New York I was safe and secure. My days began with a mug of freshly brewed coffee and the *New York Times*. When I came home at night after coffee at Caffe Reggio or a foreign film at the Angelika theater, I'd see the Empire State Building glowing in whatever colors corresponded with that month's holiday, like a joyous, communal beacon.

And then.

My book was released in early May, just before Mother's Day. It launched with a segment on the *Today* show and a *New York Times* review. Which should have been my tip-off.

If I'd known more about publishing, I might have known that a *Today* segment meant to unlist my home phone number in advance. I would have known that a seventeen-city book tour, even in the age of seventeen-city book tours, meant the publisher expected a significant return on investment. I might have known that when the marketing director said, "Fasten your seat belt," she did not mean it in jest.

I thought I'd sell a few thousand copies, including a bulk order from my grandma. Instead, I arrived at bookstores in Charlotte, North Carolina, and Salt Lake City to find hundreds of women standing in the aisles. I'd wonder which writer I'd just missed seeing. Then I started getting a clue.

It was as if an entire culture had woken up to realize early mother loss had never been discussed before and had to be discussed, starting now. The book's publicist fielded more media requests than the calendar could hold. "Make them fit," she said. I tried. I did a *People* magazine shoot outdoors in Central Park in 104-degree heat. When Nicole Brown Simpson died in June, leaving two children behind, I spoke to a magazine reporter from a pay phone at the tow pound on Pier 76 while trying to retrieve my stolen car. The rest of the year went much like that, and the next.

New York was where book publishing and media came together, the hub of the publicity wheel. Editors, producers, news outlets, television networks, national magazines, and speakers' bureaus all radiated from its critical mass. Media-friendly, articulate young women with compelling stories that could move books were golden. (Think Elizabeth Wurtzel. Think Lucy Grealy.) I was grateful for the attention. God, I was grateful. What writer wouldn't be? And because I was so grateful I said yes to everything, all of it. Invitations for fundraisers, keynotes at conferences, appearances at hospices and universities and bookstores to tell my story of mother loss and recovery again and again. As the book climbed the *New York Times* Best Seller List, I basked in the spotlight of attention, with no sense of what it might cost me later.

Because this kind of attention as a memoirist almost always comes at a cost. Telling one's story so frequently and on demand turns the story into a commodity, potentially a very lucrative one. The more handsomely one is compensated for being a screwup who's redeemed, or just for being a screwup, the greater the motivation to (1) remain screwed up, and (2) talk about it to the point of self-obsession. I knew I was in deep trouble about eight months in, at dinner with a group of friends, when I found myself feeling inept and bored when the conversation turned to a subject other than me.

My story became its own organism, separate from me. I added parts to jazz it up, took out anecdotes that fell flat in crowds. I started losing track of what had been embellished and what was actually true. It stopped seeming to matter. Performance mattered. Reviews mattered. Sales figures mattered most of all. After two years, I found myself exhausted in a way I had never known possible, taking pills to combat anxiety attacks that otherwise woke me in a raging panic nearly every night. New York had become a hard place to live—how had I never noticed this before? It was beastly hot in the summers, rude and crowded and horrifically expensive year-round. Getting five bags of groceries home from Balducci's market three blocks away required a Herculean effort. My rent rose to $1,540 a month, leaving me with no wiggle room at all. Somehow, while I was off doing media,

New York had become the quintessential celebrity lover: perfect from a distance, yet maddeningly human up close.

Sometimes I'd think of that seventeen-year-old on the brownstone steps who stated "Right here!" with such clarity and conviction. I'd once thought she lacked a strong sense of self. Only now could I see she'd known exactly who she was and what she wanted. She'd had a belief in herself I now envied. She'd thought she'd be happy only if given enough opportunities to say yes. Only now did I realize that what I really needed was the strength and the discrimination to know how to say no.

"IT'S EASY TO SEE THE BEGINNINGS OF THINGS AND HARDER TO see the ends." That's Joan Didion's well-worn saying, but it's never rung true for me. The first and last scenes of my narratives are always clear to me. The middles are the fuzzy parts. I can tell you in excruciating detail how New York began for me on the steps of a brownstone on Washington Square in 1981, and how it came to an end fifteen years later at a kitchen table on that brownstone's top floor, as I sat alone eating cold takeout noodles for dinner, wondering, *What happened?* But none of this explains how a high school girl who once found exquisite beauty in a city's summer night became a thirty-two-year-old woman who thought palm trees and the Pacific Ocean might be a better plan.

I left New York in the spring of 1997, when a bicoastal relationship took a sharp turn toward marriage. I told the man I was ready to leave New York, which was not untrue. We bought a house high in a canyon on two acres of land. I craved the quiet it offered. I would garden. I would hike. I would, I don't know, bake bread or something. Whatever people who lived in canyons did.

What I really needed, I soon learned, was to leave New York for six months and return refreshed and renewed, but by then it was too late. But let's get back to the brownstone.

When I gave up the brownstone apartment, I wept. For two and a half years, it had been more than my home: it had been a fantasy come to life. Taking my family photos off the wall felt like a betrayal of my younger self, subjecting her to a painful but necessary breakup as she sat glaring at me in grief and incomprehension. At some point I asked a friend to help me pack. I couldn't face the guilt alone.

On my last day in New York, I sat on the brownstone's front steps with a pen and paper for an hour to catalog everything that passed by. I wanted to capture a lasting, written snapshot of what had once felt like the center of the world and in some ways still did. I counted thirty-four taxis, ninety-four pedestrians, eighteen dogs, one scarlet macaw, two policemen, seven Hare Krishnas, one Chabad Mitzvah Mobile trumpeting Hebrew songs, and a woman I'm pretty sure was Diana Ross. Then I read through the list and said a silent goodbye.

I left certain I'd cycle back one day: it didn't seem possible for me to ever break free of New York's gravitational pull. But married life developed its own momentum. In Los Angeles we began having children and my husband started a company and I took a teaching job and, well, there you have it. It's been fifteen years.

California has taught me this: you can take the girl out of New York, but all that accomplishes is taking the girl out of New York. I never planted a garden. And don't get me started about baking bread. My friends call me the Woody Allen of Topanga Canyon. I'm a born apartment dweller, most comfortable in small, crowded rooms. I still have a recurring dream about returning to the brownstone apartment and staring through the keyhole, devastated to see someone else's furniture inside. I spend the rest of the dream searching for the key.

I know the truth: I'm not going back anytime soon. My daughters are children of freeways and wildfires and coyotes, not of subways and summer rain and gray winter slush. New York to them is honking and crowds and relatives they see once a year. But it's something entirely different to me.

To me, New York will always be those three months in the brownstone apartment between move-in day and book release, when it was possible for a motherless seventeen-year-old girl to believe she'd found a secret portal to her future. That wondrous, magical New York was the one I fell in love with, the one that I still pine for. It's the one that got away.

MY MISSPENT YOUTH

Meghan Daum

"**M**y Misspent Youth" was first published in the October 18, 1999, issue of the *New Yorker*.

To read it fourteen years later is to look at a time capsule. There's talk of $18,000 salaries and $1,055 rents for one-bedroom apartments. Tuition at Columbia ran me $20,000 per year; today it's more than twice that much. The fresh-cut flowers I insisted on buying from the Korean grocer surely cost more now than the eight or ten dollars a week I shelled out back then. "My Misspent Youth" is a Manhattan-centric story; instead of experiencing Brooklyn as the center of the literary universe, I haunted the bars of the Lower East Side and coveted an apartment in a grand Edwardian building in Morningside Heights.

The essay had its share of detractors back in its day. Adjectives like "whiny," "entitled," and "shallow" were in heavy rotation.

"Why can't you enjoy things like walking in the park, which is free?" an indignant caller asked me during an interview on WNYC. But its audience seems to have snuck up on it over time. Today, scarcely a week goes by that I do not hear from someone who, upon discovering it in the recesses of the internet or in the 2001 book that bore its name, has felt it to be describing his or her own life, has recognized those foolish, delicious fantasies involving prewar apartments with chipping paint and clanking radiators and grieved alongside me for a version of New York— and, by extension, a version of adulthood, of being human, of being *alive*—that was discontinued long ago and may have, in fact, never been the commodity we like to crack it up to be.

The essay has made me into something of a reluctant advice lady. *Is an MFA worth it? Should I turn down the job in Indianapolis and go to New York? Will I regret it forever if I don't? Will I regret it forever if I do?* I nearly always say yes, *go*. I nearly always say buy your ticket and don't look back—at least not until it's time to look back. Because when you leave, chances are the thing you'll be looking back on for the rest of your life is New York. I have now been gone for more years than I was ever there. I have lived on the midwestern prairies and in the Santa Monica Mountains. I have managed to get out of debt. I have a house, a car, and health insurance. I don't really know my way around Brooklyn. But, still, New York is the foundation. New York is the place I am from, even though I was never from there to begin with.

I got married (to a man who'd lived just blocks away from me in Manhattan, a man I wouldn't meet until we'd both logged thousands of miles hopping from place to place) in Central Park, near the entrance at West 86th Street. It was late October 2009, an unseasonably warm day that, now that I think of it, essentially

marked the ten-year anniversary of my essay's appearance in the
New Yorker. The sky, a cloudless and almost cartoonish shade of
blue, had loosened itself from a night of thunderstorms and held
us in the kind of enormous, intoxicating embrace you can only
get from a perfect New York day. The gargoyles and cornices of
the buildings of Central Park West looked down on us like wise
and crotchety angels. The people on the street cheered us and
ignored us in equal measure. Life wasn't solved or certain or even
especially stable. But it was financially sound for the moment.
Things were as grown-up as they were probably ever going to get.
I carried fresh-cut flowers from the Korean market. Whatever
they cost, they were worth it.

OCTOBER 18, 1999

EARLIER THIS SUMMER I WAS WALKING DOWN WEST END AVE-
nue in Manhattan and remembered, with a sadness that nearly
knocked me off my feet, just why I came to New York seven years
ago and just why I am now about to leave. Certain kinds of buildings seem almost too gorgeous to belong to the actual world, or
at least the present-day world. Given the aluminum siding and
brickface that proliferates throughout most of the United States,
I'm always amazed that massive, ornate residences like 838 West
End Avenue, with its yellow façade and black hieroglyphics, or
310 Riverside Drive, with its gargoyles and cornices, are still
standing and receiving mail delivery and depositing kids in and
out of the front doors like pretty much any domicile anywhere.
When I was growing up in northern New Jersey, just twenty-five
miles away from Manhattan, I had no concept that actual people could live in such places. My first inkling came when I was

seventeen. I walked into an apartment on the Upper West Side of Manhattan and decided, within two minutes, what the controlling force of my life would be.

It was the summer of 1987, and I was in the process of learning how to drive a stick shift. My father is a composer, and he allowed me to drive him to Manhattan in our Plymouth Horizon in order to drop off some lead sheets to a music copyist he worked with. The music copyist lived on West End Avenue and 104th Street, in a modest four-room apartment in a 1920s-era building. The moment the rickety elevator lurched onto the sixth floor and the copyist opened the door, life for me was never the same.

There was nothing particularly fancy about the place. It was a standard prewar with moldings around the ceilings and, most likely, porcelain hexagonal bathroom tiles that were coming loose. Although I'm not sure if there were faded Persian rugs on the floors and NPR humming from the speakers, it was just the sort of place for that. The music copyist and his wife had lived there for almost twenty years, and although rent was the furthest thing from my mind at the time, I can now surmise, based on what they probably earned, that the apartment was rent controlled, perhaps $300 per month. It's now difficult to imagine a time when I didn't walk into someone's apartment and immediately start the income-to-rent ratio calculations. But on that summer night, standing in the living room of this apartment, looking down on the streets whose voluptuous, stony buildings formed the shore to the river that so famously keeps here safely away from there, my life was changed forever. I mean no melodrama in this. From that moment on, everything I did, every decision I made, every college applied to or not applied to, every job taken or not taken, was based on an unwavering determination to live in a prewar, oak-floored apartment on or at least in the immediate vicinity of 104th Street and West End Avenue.

I've always been somebody who exerts a great deal of energy trying to get my realities to match my fantasies, even if the fantasies are made from materials that are no longer manufactured, even if some governmental agency has assessed my aspirations and pronounced them a health hazard. Lately, my New York fantasy has proven a little too retro for my own good. Though I did come to New York immediately after college and lived, believe it or not, within four blocks of 104th Street and West End Avenue, it wasn't until recently that I began to realize that I wasn't having quite as good a time here as I once did. I say this as someone who has had a very, very good time in New York. I say this also as someone who has enjoyed a good deal of professional success here, particularly considering that I am young and committed to a field that is notoriously low paying and unsteady. But low pay and unsteadiness never really bothered me all that much. I've historically been pretty good at getting by on what I have, especially if you apply the increasingly common definition of "getting by," which has more to do with keeping up appearances than keeping things under control. Like a social smoker whose supposedly endearing desire to emulate Marlene Dietrich has landed her in a cancer ward, I have recently woken up to the frightening fallout of my own romantic notions of life in the big city: I am completely over my head in debt. I have not made a life for myself in New York City. I have purchased a life for myself.

As I write this, I owe $7,791 to my Visa card. To be fair (To whom? Myself? Does fairness even come into play when one is trying to live a dream life?), much of those charges are from medical expenses, particularly bills from a series of dental procedures

I needed last year. As a freelance person, I'm responsible for buying my own health insurance, which is $300 per month for basic coverage in New York State. That's far more than I can afford, so I don't have any. Although I try to pay the $339 per quarter charge to keep a hospitalization insurance policy that will cover me if some major disaster befalls, I am often late in paying it and it gets canceled. But lest this begin to sound like a rant about health care, I will say that medical expenses represent only a fraction of my troubles. I need to make an estimated quarterly tax payment next month of $5,400, which is going to be tough because I just recently paid back $3,000 to my boyfriend (now ex) who lent me money to pay last year's taxes, and I still owe $300 to the accountant who prepared the return. My checking account is overdrawn by $1,784. I have no savings, no investments, no pension fund, and no inheritance on the horizon. I have student loans from graduate school amounting to $60,000. I pay $448.83 per month on these loans, installments that cover less than the interest that's accruing on the loan; despite my payments, the $60,000 debt seems to actually be growing with each passing month.

It's tempting to go into a litany of all the things on which I do not spend money. I have no dependents, not even a cat or a fish. I do not have a car. I've owned the same four pairs of shoes for the past three years. Much of the clothing in my closet has been there since the early 1990s, the rare additions usually taking the form of a $16 shirt from Old Navy, a discounted dress from Loehmann's, or a Christmas sweater from my mother. At twenty-nine, it's only been for the last two years that I've lived without roommates. My rent, $1,055 a month for a 400-square-foot apartment, is, as we say in New York City when describing the Holy Grail, below market. I do not own expensive stereo equipment, and even though I own a television I cannot bring myself to spend the $30 a month on cable, which, curiously, I've deemed an indulgence. With one exception, I have not spent money on overseas travel. All of this is true, just as it is true to say that there have been times when I haven't hesitated to buy things for my home—some rugs, a fax machine, a $200 antique lamp. There are even more times— every week, for instance—that I don't hesitate to spend money in a social capacity, $45 on dinner, $20 on drinks. I make long-distance phone calls almost daily with no thought to peak calling hours or dime-a-minute rates. I have a compulsive need to have fresh-cut flowers in my apartment at all times, and I'll spend eight or ten dollars once or twice a week at the Korean market to keep that routine going. This behavior may be careless, but it is also somewhat beside the point. In the grand scheme of things, the consumer items themselves do not factor heavily; it's easier to feel guilt over spending $60 on a blender, as I did last month, than to examine the more elaborate reasons why I reached a point where I found it impossible to live within my means.

Once you're in this kind of debt, and by "kind" I'm talking less about numbers than about something having to do with form, with the brand of the debt, all those bills start not to matter anymore. If I allowed them to matter, I would become so panicked that I wouldn't be able to work, which would only set me back further. I've also noticed that my kind of debt takes a form that many people find easier to swallow than, say, the kind of debt that reflects overt recklessness. I spent money on my education and my career. These are broad categories. There's room here for copious rationalizations, and I'll make full use of them. I live in the most expensive city in the country because I have long believed, and had many people convinced, that my career was dependent upon it. I spend money on martinis and expensive dinners because, as is typical among my species of debtor, I tell myself that martinis and expensive dinners are the entire point—the point of being young, the point of living in New York City, the point of living. In this mind-set, the dollars spent, like the mechanics of a machine no one bothers to understand, become an abstraction, an intangible avenue toward self-expression, a mere vehicle of style.

I grew up in the kind of town that probably comes as close to defining a generalized notion of the American Dream as any. It's an affluent, New Jersey suburb whose main draw is its good public school system. As in many well-to-do suburbs, if you're not in need of K–12 services, there's not much in it for you, and so virtually no one between the ages of eighteen and thirty-five can afford or has reason to live there. The result is that the teenager is king. He sets the cultural and intellectual standard for the community. Moreover, he does so without the benefit of any adult influence other than his parents.

As I try to sort out the origins of my present financial situation, I always come back to the feelings I had as a teenager in the suburbs and the ineffable hankering I felt to access some kind of earthier, more "intellectual" lifestyle. When I was growing up in the 1980s, the cultural hegemony of my world was mired in a 1950s sensibility that came directly out of the parents' nostalgia about their youths. I went to parties in junior high school where we actually danced to *The Big Chill* soundtrack. Kids wore Bermuda shorts and seersucker shirts. Unlike the self-conscious vibe of the world I entered later in college, there was nothing ironic in any of this. We knew no one older than ourselves or younger than our parents—no college or graduate students, no single professionals, barely anyone who worked outside a corporate structure. Therefore, the teen agenda looked a lot like the parental agenda, which was, even though it was the late 1980s, pretty much an Eisenhower-era paradigm: college, work, marriage, return to suburbs. As adolescents we were, for better or worse, the staple crop and chief export of the place. Realtors have been known to drive prospective home buyers throughout the town and point out houses in which kids have gone to Ivy League colleges.

My family was in a unique situation because we lived off of my father's income as a freelance composer. Although I never had the sense that we were poor, I now realize that we must have, at certain times anyway, come pretty close to it. The main reason I never felt poor was that my parents, who had experienced their own kind of lifestyle epiphany when they were first exposed to academic settings, had an aesthetic value system that was less a reflection of having or not having money than with, in our opinion anyway, good taste. Unlike the neighbors, who had expensive wall-to-wall carpet and furniture sets from Seaman's, we had wood floors and Oriental rugs, and I grew up believing that we were superior because of it. Even when I got older and began to run into my financial problems, I never had a conscious desire for a lot of money. I was never interested in being rich. I just wanted to live in a place with oak floors.

In what emerged as the major misconception of the subsequent twelve years, I somehow got the idea that oak floors were located exclusively in New York City. This came chiefly from watching Woody Allen movies. I wanted to live someplace that looked like Mia Farrow's apartment in *Hannah and Her Sisters* (little did I know that it was Mia Farrow's apartment). To me, this kind of space did not connote wealth. These were places where the paint was peeling and the rugs were frayed, places where smart people sat around drinking gin and tonics, having interesting conversations, and living, according to my logic, in an authentic way. As far as I was aware at seventeen, rich was something else entirely. Rich meant monstrous Tudor-style houses in the ritzy section of my town. Rich were the handful of kids who drove BMWs to school. I had the distinct feeling that my orthodontist, whose sprawling ranch house had front steps that were polished in such a way that they looked like they were made of ice, was rich. None of these particular trappings of wealth held my attention. In fact, nothing outside of the movies really held my attention until that night in 1987 when I saw the apartment on 104th Street.

How different the ride down that clanking elevator was from the ride up! Like a lover to whom you suddenly turn one morning and feel nothing but loathing, my relationship to my suburban town went, in the time it took that elevator to descend six floors, from indifference to abhorrence. With all the drama and preciousness of a seventeen-year-old girl, I now realized the pathetic smallness of my world. I now saw the suburbs, as I announced to my father, "for what they really are." The suburb-city alliance was, in my opinion, an unequal partnership between parasite and host, a dynamic permanently tainted by a sense that although the suburbs cannot live without the city, the city would hardly notice if the suburbs were all spontaneously irradiated by a tyrannical dictator of a distant star system.

Worst of all, the suburbs were a place from which escape held little romance. Unlike the kid from the small midwestern or southern town who saves up for bus money to come to the big town, the suburban New Jersey teenager who sits in her bedroom, listening to 1980s Suzanne Vega records and longing for some life that is being vaguely described in the songs—"my name is Luka, I live on the second floor" (could this be on 104th Street?)—doesn't elicit much sympathy. But I persevered, planning my escape through the standard channels: college selection. I'd seen the music copyist's apartment during the summer between my junior and senior years of high school and so applying to college that fall became a matter of picturing the apartment and wondering what kind of college an inhabitant of such an apartment would have attended.

My logic, informed by a combination of college guidebooks and the alma maters of those featured in the *New York Times* wedding announcements, went something like this: Bryn Mawr rather than Gettysburg, Columbia rather than NYU, Wisconsin rather than Texas, Yale rather than Harvard, Vassar rather than Smith. My ranking system had nothing to do with the academic merits of the schools. It was more a game of degrees of separation from Upper West Side houseplants and intellectualism. Somehow, Vassar emerged as the most direct route. After all, Meryl Streep, a girl from suburban New Jersey, had gone there (and later played Woody Allen's ex-wife in *Manhattan*), as well as the Apthorp-dwelling Rachel Samstat in *Heartburn*, a character based on Nora Ephron, a personal role model of mine, not to mention a real-life resident of the Apthorp. I also had some vague notions about getting myself into a position where I could become a writer, and this had something to do with being "artsy." So in a manner particular to restless suburban girls who consider themselves different and unconventional in much the same way that protagonists in young adult novels are portrayed, I was so consumed with going to a particular kind of artsy college and mixing with a particular kind of artsy crowd that I could do nothing during my entire senior year of high school but throw wads of paper into a wastebasket from across the room and say "If I make this shot, I get into Vassar."

I made the shot. I went to Vassar. It was either the best move of my life or the biggest mistake. I'm still not sure which. Though it would be five years until I entered my debt era, my years at Vassar did more than expand my intellect. They expanded my sense of entitlement so much that, by the end, I had no ability to separate myself from the many extremely wealthy people I encountered there. For the record, let me say that a large part of that sense of entitlement has been a very good thing for me. Self-entitlement is a quality that has gotten a bad name for itself, and yet in my opinion, it's one of the best things a student can get out of an education. Much of my success and happiness is a direct result of it. But self-entitlement has also contributed to my downfall, mostly because of my inability to recognize where ambition and chutzpah end and cold, hard cash begins. Like the naïve teenager who thought Mia Farrow's apartment represented the urban version of middle-class digs, I continued to believe throughout college that it wasn't fabulous wealth I was aspiring to, merely hipness.

Though there were lots of different kinds of kids at Vassar, I immediately found the ones who had grown up in Manhattan, and I learned most of what I felt I needed to know by socializing with them. In this way, my education was primarily about becoming fully versed in a certain set of references that, individually, have very little to do with either a canon of knowledge as defined by academia or preparation for the job market. My education had mostly to do with speaking the language of the culturally sophisticated, with having a mastery over a number

of points of cultural trivia ranging from the techniques of Cara-
vaggio to the discography of the Velvet Underground. This
meant being privy to the kind of information that is only learned
from hours spent hanging out with friends in dorm rooms and
is therefore unavailable to those buried in the library trying to
keep their scholarships or working at Stereo World trying to
pay the bills. It is to have heard rumors that Domino's Pizza has
ties to the pro-life movement, that Bob Dylan's mother invented
Wite-Out, and that Jamie Lee Curtis is a hermaphrodite. It is
to never wear nude pantyhose, never smoke menthol cigarettes,
never refer to female friends as "girlfriends," and never listen to
Billy Joel in earnest. It is to know at least two people featured in
the *New York Times* wedding pages on any given Sunday and to
think nothing of putting eighty dollars toward a bridal shower
dinner at a chic restaurant for one of these people. It is to know
that anyone who uses the word "chic" is anything but. It is to
know arugula from iceberg lettuce, Calder from Klimt, Truffaut
from Cassavetes. It is to be secure in one's ability to grasp these
comparisons and weigh one against the other within a fraction
of a second, to know, as my Jewish Manhattanite friends put it,
"from stuff"—to know from real estate, from contemporary fiction, from clothing designers and editors of glossy magazines and
Shakespearean tragedies and skirt lengths. Name-dropping was
my drug of choice, and I inhaled the stuff. By the time graduation
came, I'd earned a degree in English, but that seemed incidental
to my stellar achievements in the field of "from stuff."

I still wanted to be a writer. And with my ever-evolving sense
of entitlement, that seemed more possible than ever. When I
graduated in 1992, I followed a herd of my classmates into Manhattan, many of whom moved back in with their parents on Park

Avenue. I got myself an entry-level job in publishing and, along with a couple of friends, rented a five-room, prewar apartment with chipping paint on 100th Street and Riverside Drive, a mere four blocks from the scene of my 1987 epiphany. I was ecstatic. Such expert marksmanship! Such rich rewards for thorough research and careful planning. My job, as an editorial assistant at a glossy fashion magazine, paid $18,000 a year. The woman who hired me, herself a 1950s-era Vassar graduate, told me that she hoped I had an independent source of income, as I surely wouldn't be able to support myself on my salary. But I did support myself. My roommates, an elementary school teacher who was making $19,000 a year and a film student who worked part-time at a nonprofit arts organization, supported themselves too. We each paid around $550 per month and lived as recent graduates should, eating ramen noodles and ninety-nine-cent White Rose macaroni and cheese.

Looking back, I see those years as a cheap, happy time. It was a time at which a certain kind of poverty was appropriate; anything ritzier would have been embarrassing. Our neighborhood was a place for people who knew the city, for people from the city. Unlike the west seventies and eighties, which I've always experienced as slightly ephemeral, mall-like, and populated by those who've come from elsewhere, the residents of this neighborhood seem to give off a feeling of being very deeply rooted into the ground. It's also a place that has absolutely no investment in fashion. No matter what the decade, there's an odd 1970s quality to the neighborhood. It's a place where you can still find people wearing corduroy blazers, a place that has always made me think of both the television show *Taxi* and the cover of Carole King's *Tapestry* album. Though I was living completely hand to mouth, I loved my neighborhood and looked forward to moving ahead in my career and one day being able to afford my own place in roughly an eight-block radius. From my position at the time, that seemed well within the range of feasibility. It was 1993, I was twenty-three, and I'd received a raise so that I was earning $21,000. I had no idea it was the closest I'd be to financial solvency for at least the next decade.

I'd been told I was lucky to get a job at a magazine—I had, after all, graduated into what was being called the worst job market in twenty years—and even though I had little interest in its subject matter, I didn't dare turn down the position. Within my first week on the job, I found myself immersed in a culture that was concerned entirely with money and celebrity. Socialites sat on the editorial board in order to give input on trends among the extremely wealthy. Editorial assistants who earned $18,000 managed to wear Prada, rent timeshares in the Hamptons, have regular facials, and pay thousands of dollars a year for gym memberships and personal trainers. Many of them lived in doorman buildings in the West Village or Upper East Side, for which their parents helped foot the bill.

THIS WASN'T MY SCENE. I FELT AS FAR AWAY FROM MY *HANNAH and Her Sisters* fantasy as I had in the suburbs. I didn't want to be rich. I just wanted to live in New York and be a writer. Moreover, I wanted to be a writer in New York immediately. After a year of office work, I decided that an MFA program in creative writing would provide the most direct route to literary legitimacy. I applied to exactly one program, Columbia, which, not coincidentally, happened to be located in my neighborhood. It's also the most expensive writing program in the country, a fact I ignored because the students, for the most part, seemed so down-to-earth and modest. Unlike my Prada-wearing, Hamptons-going colleagues from the magazine, Columbia students, in their flannel shirts and roach-infested student housing, seemed as earnest and unrich as I was, and I figured that if they could take out $20,000-a-year loans, so could I. Even as I stayed at Columbia for three years and borrowed more than $60,000 to get my degree, I was told repeatedly, by fellow students, faculty, administrators, and professional writers whose careers I wished to emulate, not to think about the loans. Student loans, after all, were low interest, long term, and far more benign than credit-card debt. Not thinking about them was a skill I quickly developed.

If there is a line of demarcation in this story, a single moment where I crossed the boundary between debtlessness and total financial mayhem, it's the first dollar that I put toward achieving a life that had less to do with overt wealth than with what I perceived as intellectual New York bohemianism. It seems laughable now, but at the time I thought I was taking a step down from the Chanel suits and Manolo Blahniks of my office job. Hanging out at the Cuban coffee shop and traipsing over the syringes and windblown trash of upper Broadway, I was under the impression that I was, in a certain way, slumming. And even though I was having a great time and becoming a better writer, the truth was that the year I entered graduate school was the year I stopped making decisions that were appropriate for my situation and began making a rich person's decisions. Entering this particular graduate program was a rich person's decision. But it's hard to recognize that you're acting like a rich person when you're becoming increasingly poor. Besides, I was never without a job.

I worked for an anthropology professor for $9 an hour. I read manuscripts at $10 a pop for a quack literary agent. I worked at a university press for $10 an hour. Sometimes I called in sick to these jobs and did temp work in Midtown offices for $17 an hour. A couple of times I took out cash advances on my credit cards to pay the rent.

There were a handful of us who were pulling these kinds of stunts. My roommate had maxed out her credit cards in order to finance a student film. I knew several women and even a few men who were actively looking for rich marriage partners to bail them out of their debt. One aspiring novelist I know underwent a series of drug treatments and uncomfortable surgical procedures in order to sell her eggs for $2,500. A couple of promising writers dropped out of the program and left the city. These days, when I talk to the people who left, they give off the sense of having averted a car crash, but by the same token, they wonder if they'd be further along in their careers had they stuck it out. But this question of sticking it out has less to do with MFA programs than with the city in general. Whether or not one is paying $20,000 a year to try to make it as a writer, New York City has become a prohibitively expensive place to live for just about anyone. Although I've devoted a lot of energy to being envious of Columbia classmates whose relatives were picking up the tab for their educations, it's now becoming clear to me that assuming the presence of a personal underwriter is not limited to entry-level jobs at glossy magazines or expensive graduate programs. These days, being a creative person in New York is, in many cases, contingent upon inheriting the means to do it.

But the striver in me never flinched. As I was finishing at Columbia, my writing career was giving off signs that it might actually go somewhere. If I hadn't been doing so well I might have pulled out of the game. I would have gotten a job, started paying my bills, and averted my own impending car crash. Instead, I continued to hedge my bets. I was publishing magazine articles regularly and, after a few months of temping at insurance companies and banks, scored some steady writing gigs that, to my delight, allowed me to work as a full-time freelance writer. After five years and eight different roommates in the 100th Street apartment, I was earning enough money to move to my own place and, more importantly, had garnered enough contacts with established Manhattanites to find myself a two-year sublet in a rent-stabilized apartment. The fact that I got this sublet through a connection from a Columbia professor has always struck me as justification enough for the money I spent to go to school; as we all know by now, the value of a rent-stabilized one-bedroom is equal to if not greater than that of a master's degree or even the sale of a manuscript to a publisher. And though I still had not hit the literary jackpot by producing the best-seller that would pay off my loans and buy me some permanent housing, I still felt I'd come out ahead in the deal.

So it's not that I was sold a complete bill of goods. Things were going well. In 1997 I was twenty-seven, teaching a writing course at NYU, publishing in a variety of national magazines, and earning about $40,000 a year after taxes. (The teaching job, incidentally, paid a paltry $2,500 for an entire semester, but I was too enamored with the idea of being a college teacher to wonder if I could afford to take it.) Neither clueless suburbanite nor corporate, subsidized yuppie, I could finally begin practicing the life I'd spent so long studying for. I had a decent-sized apartment with oak floors and porcelain hexagonal bathroom tiles that were coming loose. Like an honest New Yorker, I even had mice lurking in the kitchen. I bought the rugs and the fax machine. I installed a second telephone line for fax, data purposes.

Soon, however, I had some hefty dental bills that I was forced to charge to Visa. I tried not to think about that too much until I ended up making a few doctor's visits that, being uninsured, I also charged to Visa. When April rolled around, I realized my income was significantly higher that year than any previous year and that I had woefully underestimated what I owed the IRS. Despite a bevy of the typical freelancer's write-offs—haircuts, contact lenses, an $89.99 sonic rodent control device—I was hit with a tax bill of over $20,000. And although the IRS apparently deemed sonic rodent control devices an acceptable deduction, it seemed that I'd earned too much money to be eligible to write off the nearly $7,000 (most of it interest) I'd paid to the student loan agency or the $3,000 in dental bills. Most heartbreaking of all, my accountant proffered some reason that my $60 pledge to WNYC—my Upper West Side tableau couldn't possibly be complete without the NPR coffee mug—was not tax deductible as advertised. In the months it took me to assemble that $20,000, I had to reduce my monthly student loan payments from the suggested $800 per month to the aforementioned $448.83 per month, a reduction that effectively ensured that I wouldn't touch the principal for years. I continued to pay my $1,055 per month rent and made every effort to pay the phone, gas, and electric bills, the American Express bills, and the hospitalization-only medical coverage.

It was around this time that I started having trouble thinking about anything other than how to make a payment on whatever bill was sitting on my desk, most likely weeks overdue, at any given time. I started getting collection calls from Visa, final disconnection notices from the phone company, letters from the gas company saying "Have you forgotten us?" I noticed that I was drinking more than I had in the past, often alone at home where I would sip Sauvignon Blanc at my desk and pretend to write when in fact I'd be working out some kind of desperate math equation on the toolbar calculator, making wild guesses as to when I'd receive some random $800 check from some unreliable accounting department of some slow-paying publication, how long it would take the money to clear into my account, what would be left after I set aside a third of it for taxes, and, finally, which lucky creditor would be the recipient of the cash award. There's nothing like completing one of these calculations, realizing that you've drunk half a bottle of $7.99 wine and feeling more guilt about having spent $7.99 than the fact that you're now too tipsy to work. One night I did a whole bunch of calculations and realized that despite having earned a taxable income of $59,000 in 1998, despite having not gone overboard on classic debtor's paraphernalia like clothes and vacations and stereo equipment, despite having followed the urban striver's guide to success, I was more than $75,000 in the hole.

There are days when my debt seems to be at the center of my being, a cancer that must be treated with the morphine of excuses and rationales and promises to myself that I'm going to come up with the big score—book advance, screenplay deal, Publishers Clearing House prize—and save myself. There are other days when the debt feels like someone else's cancer, a tragedy outside myself, a condemned building next door that I try to avoid walking past. I suppose that's why I'm even able to publicly disclose this information. For me, money has always, truly, been "only money," a petty concern of the shallower classes, a fatuous substitute for more important things like fresh flowers and "meaningful conversations" in the living room. But the days when I can ignore the whole matter are growing further and further apart. My rent-stabilized sublet is about to expire, and I now must find somewhere else to live. I have friends getting rich off the stock market and buying million-dollar houses. I have other friends who are almost as bad off as I am and who compulsively volunteer for relief work in third world countries as a way of forgetting that they can't quite afford to live in the first world.

But New York City, which has a way of making you feel like you're in the third world just seconds after you've thought you conquered all of Western civilization, has never really been part of the rest of the world. In that sense, I suppose it's foolish to believe that one can seek one's fortune, or at least one's sustenance, through rational means. I suppose that part of the city's magical beastliness is the fact that you can show up with the best of intentions, do what's considered to be all the right things, actually achieve some measure of success, and still find yourself caught inside a financial emergency.

I have to be out of my sublet by September 1. Even if I tried to assume control of the lease, the landlord will renovate the apartment and raise the rent to $2,000. I told a friend about this the other day, hoping she would gasp or give me some sort of reaction. Instead she said, "That's cheaper than our place." A two-bedroom apartment down the street rented for $4,500 a month. A studio anywhere in Manhattan or the desirable parts of Brooklyn will go for an average of $1,750. West 104th Street is totally beyond my means. Worse, 104th Street is now beyond the means of most of the people that made me want to live there in the first place. The New York that changed my life on that summer night when I was seventeen simply no longer exists.

Now, having taken all of this apart, I am determined to not put it back together the same way. Several months ago, on a day when the debt anxiety had flared up even more than usual, I arrived at the idea of moving to Lincoln, Nebraska. I'd been to Lincoln on a magazine assignment twice before, met some nice people, and found myself liking it enough to entertain the notion of moving there. But both times I'd discarded the idea of moving there the minute the wheels hit the tarmac at LaGuardia. Surely, I'd never be able to live without twenty-four-hour take-out food and glitzy Russian martini bars. On this latest round of panic, however, I chewed on the idea for a while, decided that it was a good plan, and have pretty much continued to feel that way ever since. I can rent an apartment there for $300 a month. I can rent an entire house, if I want one, for $700. Full coverage health insurance will cost me $66 a month. Apparently, people in Nebraska also listen to NPR, and there are even places to live in Lincoln that have oak floors. Had I known that before, I might have skipped out on this New York thing altogether and spared myself the financial and psychological ordeal. But I'm kind of glad I didn't know because I'm someone who has had a very, very good time here. I'm just leaving the party before the cops break it up.

MINNESOTA NICE

Cheryl Strayed

saw a man get stabbed on a sunny afternoon in the West Village on my twenty-fourth birthday. He didn't die. He didn't even call out for help. He just cursed the man who'd attacked him in a language I could neither understand nor identify while clutching the place on his thigh where the knife had entered it, his palms smeared with blood. I was sitting alone at a little wooden table on the sidewalk across the street, drinking coffee and eating a slice of cake in the warm September sun.

"Someone just stabbed that man," I said loudly to the waiter, who emerged from the café doors moments after the attack.

He turned to glance at him. The injured man remained in the spot where he'd been stabbed, across the narrow street from us on the edge of a small park I didn't know the name of. He'd run there in the moments before the assault, attempting to shield himself with a metal bike rack. In a last-ditch effort he'd tried to lift the entire impossible apparatus, hoping to topple it onto his assailant. He'd hoisted it perhaps two feet before it crashed back onto the pavement with a frightful clatter. In the next instant the knife was in his leg. In spite of the assailant's force, his delivery was almost delicate, the deed done in one elegant jab, as if he were popping a balloon. Then, without a sound, he ran, knife in hand.

That's when the victim cried out in the language I didn't understand and the waiter came outside.

"I wouldn't worry about it," he said to me now, languidly refilling my coffee cup from the pot he carried.

"You wouldn't?" I asked.

Of all the things to worry about, it seemed a man getting stabbed a dozen yards away would be the thing. And yet, how strange it was that it appeared I was the only one who was alarmed—there'd been other witnesses to the stabbing, the dozen or so people who'd been walking along the sidewalk when the clamor began. Some had paused to watch, others had crossed the street to avoid it, but they'd all continued on their way once it was over.

"Hey!" I hollered to the injured man after the waiter went back inside the café. "Do you need help?"

He looked in my direction and shook his head vaguely, then rambled away in a limping fashion as if I'd chased him off, his jeans bloody and torn where he'd been wounded.

I'd been living in New York City for little more than a month by then. I was renting an apartment on Seventh Avenue in Park Slope with the man who was then my husband and waitressing at a place ten blocks away. It was 1992, a time when unknown writers who were married to even more unknown musicians and paid the bills waiting tables could still afford to rent an apartment on Seventh Avenue in Park Slope. On my days off I roved the city like a gleeful tourist, feeling important simply to be there. I went to the tops of the Empire State Building and the Statue of Liberty. I wandered Central Park and the Brooklyn Botanic Garden. I waited in line for nosebleed tickets to the opera and off-Broadway plays. I visited MOMA and the Whitney and the Met. I poked around the East Village and Soho. I hung out at the Strand and CBGBs and strolled meaningfully past the Chelsea Hotel thinking of all the glorious and fucked-up people who'd stayed there.

I am in New York City! I couldn't help but exclaim silently in my head every now and then, country bumpkin from Minnesota that I was. I couldn't keep myself from thinking everything in New York was superior to every other place I'd ever been, which hadn't been all that many places. I was stunned by New York. Its grand parks and museums. Its cozy cobbled streets and dazzlingly bright thoroughfares. Its alternately efficient and appalling subway system. Its endlessly gorgeous women clad in slim pants and killer shoes and interesting coats.

And yet something happened on my way to falling head over heels in love with the place. Maybe it was the man getting stabbed that no one worried about. Or maybe it was bigger than that. The abruptness, the gruffness, the avoid-eye-contact indifference of the crowded subways and streets felt as foreign to me as Japan or Cameroon, as alien to me as Mars. Even the couple who owned the bodega below our apartment greeted my husband and me each day as if we were complete strangers, which is to say they didn't greet us at all, no matter how many times we came in to buy toilet paper or soup, cat food or pasta. They merely took our money and returned our change with gestures so automatic and faces so expressionless they might as well have been robots.

"Do they really not *recognize* us?" I asked my husband on a regular basis, both of us mildly outraged by this tiny thing that grew to feel like the greatest New York City crime of all, to be denied the universal silent acknowledgment of familiarity, the faintest smile, the hint of a nod.

Maybe it was the way my customers at the place where I waited tables always knew I wasn't from there because I was "too nice"—"Minnesota Nice," one group of regulars had nicknamed me—much as I attempted to seem like a harder, cooler, more dazzling thing: a New Yorker.

In the end, I had to realize it was never meant to be. It wasn't New York. It was me. I'd entered the city the way one enters any grand love affair: with no exit plan. I went willing to live there forever, to become one of the women clad in slim pants and killer shoes and interesting coats. I was ready for the city to sweep me into its arms, but instead it held me at a cool distance. And so I left New York the way one leaves a love affair too: because, much as I loved it, I wasn't truly in love. I had no compelling reason to stay.

On a cold afternoon in February, my husband and I loaded our things into a pickup truck that was double-parked on the street on Seventh Avenue, each of us taking turns alternately guarding the truck from would-be thieves and going up and down the stairs with boxes. Past dark, our work done hours later than we'd hoped, we got into the cab with our two cats in their kennels squeezed between us. Just as my husband started the engine, there was a loud rapping on the window a few inches from my head. I turned with a start and saw the man who owned the bodega. The one who'd never once shown us a glimmer of recognition. He was beaming now and holding a bag of tangerines. I stared at him for a moment, startled and uncertain, until he made a motion with his hand for me to roll down the window and I did.

"For you," he said and handed me the tangerines. "Good luck."

SHELTER IN PLACE

Emily Raboteau

> I insisted on the dark city.
> I persisted in the dark city.
>
> —Sheila Maldonado

Everything I want to say about New York City happened one afternoon in J. Hood Wright Park at the start of the lockdown. Not since the children were toddlers had we spent so much time in this park, five blocks to the south of our building in Washington Heights. We needed public spaces during quarantine. We needed trees, fresh air, and the opportunity to gather, even at a distance. Without the respite, we'd have gone mad in the cells of our three-room apartment, my family and I, the bewildering spring of 2020 when the boys turned seven and nine.

The governor and the mayor were in some cockfight about what to name the lockdown and who was running the show. The mayor warned us to shelter in place. The governor thought New Yorkers would riot under such oppressive language. Instead, we were "on pause." So long as we behaved, the parks would remain open. But to me, pandemic time felt fast-forwarded, not paused, even as the days without childcare were long, because the city and our access to it transformed so quickly. No more trips to the public library or the American Museum of Natural History. No more subway rides. The routine was pulled out from under us. When you are forty-three in New York City, raising children, you have already lost the New York that mattered to you at age twenty-three. The loss I am talking about is something else entirely.

Somewhere at the beginning of the curve my college room-mate called from the West Coast to ask if we'd be leaving the city. Where on earth did she think we would go? To my mother's house in New Jersey, she suggested, or to my brother's house down South? I told her, edgily, that we were staying put. We would tough it out, I said, as if New York gave a fuck whether my family personally abandoned it. The truth was, nobody had offered us shelter. Maybe they feared we'd infect them. Had we thought about renting a place in the country for a time, she asked, genuinely concerned—somewhere less congested, at least until the curve flattened? "With what money?" I bristled.

Here's the thing. Before this virus reared its head, we'd sunk all our savings into a down payment on a run-down house in the Bronx, at the end of the 1 line. The plan was to get away from the George Washington Bridge and the nexus of highways whose traffic fumes had given my kids asthma along with a third of the other kids in our zip code. In the midst of this global pandemic, we were somehow going to close on this house, fix it up, and move in. Our jobs were here, uptown, where we were raising our boys, though now, overnight, we were working remotely from the apartment we'd outgrown in which we were now homeschooling. We were committed to New York, like married people with children are committed to each other; we were stuck, without free time or space to admit to regret. "I just think it will be hard, psychologically, to be in the city during this crisis," my college roommate predicted. "So many people are about to die." I resented her in that moment because I knew she was right and because we didn't have the option to leave.

One night in mid-March the super alerted us to shut the windows. He'd heard some story that turned out to be bullshit about helicopters spraying the city with disinfectant. By April half our building had emptied out. Roughly speaking, the white half. As in the rest of the city, income was the strongest predictor of flight. Some of these neighbors handed us their keys before they fled for second homes or vacation towns, asking us to please shove their packages and mail inside their apartment doors. We said we'd see them on the other side, acknowledging the sudden divide between us. The other side was not the cure, since nobody could say with certainty when the vaccine would arrive and this purgatory would end. The other side was anywhere but here, and when we said we'd see them there, we didn't really mean it, because we didn't really believe they were coming back.

CUNY, my employer, was defunded. A quarter of my colleagues were laid off. Several of them died. Our union begged the governor to tax the rich to save the school for the sake of the common good. I was warned to prepare for furlough. I feared my students' welfare. There was talk of turning City College's campus into a bivouac for the hospital's overflow of patients. "Is New York over?" asked my friend Ayana from across the street. She wore a hand-sewn face mask in an African print called "money flies." "No," I told her. "It's too big to fail."

Nevertheless, packages started getting stolen from the lobby. The methadone clinic was closed, the local heroin addicts had nowhere to go, the subway trains were rumored to have become mobile homeless shelters. The line at the food bank snaked around the corner. The *cacerolazo* grew more frenzied each night at 7 PM, like we were rattling the bars of our cages as well as cheering for the essential workers—the nurses, janitors, supers, food deliverers, mail carriers, and bus drivers who had no choice but to risk their lives to give us life. A lady madly banged a stop sign with the handle of her mop, and on the night she didn't show to add that sound to the clanging of empty pots, I assumed the virus got her. The rhythm was off. Subway service was suspended from 1 to 5 AM. The crematoriums ran around the clock. I lost sleep and hair but counted myself lucky to be able to feed my kids.

"This is *hard*," wailed my friend Drema from her front stoop in Harlem after her father died of Covid-19. It took her weeks to find a free funeral home to retrieve his body from the morgue because the death business was so swamped. She'd been a child in the 1970s and claimed this New York felt like that one—the Rotten Apple. Muggings were up. She felt unsafe now letting her preteen daughter walk alone around the block.

On Easter I hid plastic candy-filled eggs in the alleyway near the trash cans. The woman in 65 baked us cornbread and hung it, still warm, on our doorknob. The woman in 63 was taken out on a stretcher, feverish, and put on dialysis. By Mother's Day I was desperate to escape. I tried, along with the rest of New York City, to foster a dog. I thought a dog would reduce our stress, but all the shelter dogs were taken. It was true. Only the biting pit bulls and hopeless medical cases remained. At some point in May, I ransacked empty apartment 34 for children's books after we exhausted our supply. In apartment 61, they'd forgotten to turn off the alarm clock before leaving, and I heard it beeping for three months through the wall, even in my dreams.

My children changed with the abrupt closure of their school. They lost their baby teeth, their tempers, their social lives, their Spanish. The older one, I feared, was growing less cute—not to us, of course, but to others in authority who might, under the wrong circumstances, find him menacing. The changes within the parks were equally abrupt. The playgrounds were locked, the basketball hoops removed, the dog runs closed, the benches roped off with caution tape, police cruising to unevenly enforce the new order. On the surrounding streets of Washington Heights, the immigrant economy vanished overnight. The sidewalk tables of tube socks, knockoff watches, winter hats, and fruit suddenly gone and in their place on the empty sidewalks— discarded blue surgical gloves and piles of dog shit. The mom-and-pop shops shuttered, maybe for good, the signs in the windows of the bodegas required face coverings, the traffic on the George Washington Bridge thinned out, the air turned clear. Down in the subway, without the usual volume of human trash to forage, the rats were said to be eating one another. I hazarded the A train, to bring our taxes to our accountant's Midtown office, and found the near-empty train car to be a time capsule. Its advertisements from the beforetime made no sense in the new reality. An orchid show at the botanical garden? A "degree with a purpose" from Apex Tech? As the death toll mounted, the soundscape changed—sirens, constant ambulance sirens, underscored by birdsong. As food insecurity increased, the kids' basketball coach, who had time on his hands with the league shut down, shifted gears to delivering bags of food to hungry families in the hood. Around the corner, down the block, next door, folks were unable to make rent and doubling up, two families in one-bedrooms, ten, fifteen people, Domingo said. They were growing desperate. He predicted that by June they'd be driven by hunger to riot out in the street. The woman from empty apartment 5 texted from Connecticut to say she was bored. Somewhere near peak week when they were forklifting the dead into refrigerated trucks and digging mass graves in the Bronx, a doctor at the nearby hospital killed herself, unable to take the strain. Meanwhile, the flowers were blooming in the J. Hood Wright, where we dutifully taught the boys to ride their bikes.

ON THE DAY I WANT TO TELL YOU ABOUT, THE WEEPING CHERRY tree was beginning to bud over by the boulders. Through its veil of pink blossoms were visible the towers of the hospital where they'd already run out of beds. Ahmaud Arbery had not yet been shot on his jog. Breonna Taylor had not yet been shot in her bed. George Floyd had not yet been suffocated on the street. We did not yet have the data indicating the virus was disproportionately taking Black and brown lives from the same zip codes plagued by environmental injustice. We had not yet schooled the boys in these inequities nor closed on the house. All those things were on the near horizon. On this gorgeous spring day, the park was full of people trying to stretch out, find solace, breathe, or play, and my boys and I were among them.

The nine-year-old had sent us on a scavenger hunt. Find a bottle cap. A leaf. A rock. A cigarette butt. A flower. I led the seven-year-old toward the cherry tree to pick a bloom. A well-dressed white woman stood beneath its canopy, serenely photographing its branches with the camera of her phone. I thought I understood what she meant to capture: this cherry tree in the time of corona, this unlikely thing of beauty in the midst of the battered city under the shadow of death. As we drew closer, a soccer ball rolled near her feet, nearly kissing her ankle. It belonged to a Dominican kid, brown skinned, like my own. In a flash, the woman's affect changed from peaceful to revolted. "Get away from me!" she screamed at the boy, though it was the ball that approached her, not his body. The boy stopped in his tracks. My boy flinched, too, at the sudden violence in the air. Was he confused by her tone or was he already old enough to get it and all that lay beneath? The boy's mother, who was heavily pregnant, rose from a nearby park bench like an avenging angel.

"Don't you talk to my son like that," she yelled. "He's a child. He's just playing."

"He's too close to me," the white woman claimed. "He's supposed to be six feet away." Her voice was full of panic and blame.

"So move your own damn body six feet. This ain't your house! This is the *park*. He's allowed to play."

Above her mask, the white woman looked displeased to have been addressed so rudely and more than a little afraid but reluctant to back down. "You're teaching him to be disrespectful just like you," she spat.

"Get the fuck outta here or I'ma run you out," said the mother. She meant it, too. The white woman had the good sense to leave.

Surely that white woman felt vulnerable to infection. The pandemic was making people jumpy. But it was also magnifying the deep-seated racial and class tensions already in place, tensions over real estate exploitation, gentrification, who owns the city, who belongs to what neighborhood, who gets pushed out of neighborhoods, what it means to be a good neighbor, who has a right to move freely in public space, and whose freedom of movement is policed. When the white woman retreated without apology or consideration for these factors, I bet she thought, "These people are animals."

Witnessing the fight with my boy, I absolutely took the mother's side. I felt her righteous anger for all the countless times in their young lives my own kids have already been criminalized, in some cases by their own teachers. There was a lesson for me, in the boldness of her advocacy. Normally, I'm much more polite. But if that white woman, who had no comprehension of her own base knee-jerk disrespect, had not had the good sense to leave the park when she did, I would have joined the campaign to oust her. Quite simply, she did not deserve the cherry tree because she did not understand how to share.

———

THERE ARE THOSE FOR WHOM NEW YORK WAS ONLY EVER A playground, and I feel similarly about them. They never deserved it. It is June 2020 as I write this. In New York City, twenty-one thousand people have died, and the spring has given way to a summer of struggle. Just as Domingo predicted, there are rebellions in the streets, here in New York and all over the world.

Home school is now on the art and history of protest. We are in it, marching with the boys. In the middle of Frederick Douglass Boulevard, we paused in a crowd a thousand strong to kneel with our fists raised and then got up to walk the distance. Until the next wave, we are done with sheltering in place. The sirens are less frequent now. The city is in phase one of reopening, on the cusp of phase two. A lot of the storefronts in our hood are still boarded up. It's unclear how the schools will reopen come fall. The ice cream trucks have returned. The tables are back up on the streets, only now the vendors are hawking masks. A guy sells illegal fireworks from the trunk of his car. Every night you can hear them popping off. Calls to 311 are up. The neighbors who had the means to flee have not yet returned. For richer or poorer, better or worse, in sickness and in health, for the love of this hobbled unbeatable city at the epicenter of pandemonium, we stayed. Soon, we will move into the house.

ABOUT THE CONTRIBUTORS

ELISA ALBERT ("Currency") is the author of the novels *After Birth* and *The Book of Dahlia*, the story collection *How This Night Is Different*, and the editor of the anthology *Freud's Blind Spot*. Her fiction and nonfiction have appeared in *Tin House*, the *New York Times*, the *Literary Review*, Longreads, *Bennington Review*, the *Paris Review*, Salon, *Gulf Coast*, *Post Road*, and on NPR. She lives and works in Albany, New York.

CHLOE CALDWELL ("Leaving My Groovy Lifestyle") is the author of the novella *Women* and the essay collections *I'll Tell You in Person* and *Legs Get Led Astray*. Her essays have been published in the *New York Times*, *Buzzfeed*, *Vice*, *Nylon*, and Longreads. She lives in Hudson, New York, with her family.

EMILY CARTER ROIPHE ("Transport") is the author of the story collection *Glory Goes and Gets Some*, which won a Whiting Award. She is currently a freelance writer, living in Albuquerque, New Mexico, with her husband-nurse, Johnnie, and their dog, Comet.

MEGHAN DAUM ("My Misspent Youth") is the author of six books, most recently *The Problem with Everything: My Journey*

Through the New Culture Wars. She has written for the *New Yorker,* the *New York Times Magazine,* the *Atlantic,* and *Vogue,* among other publications. After many years away, she currently lives in New York City again.

MARCY DERMANSKY ("Maybe I Loved You") is the author of the critically acclaimed novels *Very Nice, The Red Car, Bad Marie,* and *Twins.* She has received fellowships from the MacDowell Colony and the Edward F. Albee Foundation. She lives in Montclair, New Jersey, with her daughter. Find out more about Dermansky at her website, marcydermansky.com, or follow her on Twitter and Instagram at @mdermansky.

HOPE EDELMAN ("You Are Here") is the author of eight nonfiction books, including the best-sellers *Motherless Daughters, Motherless Mothers,* and *The Possibility of Everything.* Her essays and articles have appeared in numerous magazines and newspapers, including the *New York Times,* the *Los Angeles Times,* the *Chicago Tribune, Glamour, Self, Real Simple, Writer's Digest,* CNN.com, and *Parade.* She lives in Los Angeles and teaches at the Iowa Summer Writing Festival in Iowa City every summer.

LAUREN ELKIN ("Losing New York") is the author of *Flâneuse: Women Walk the City,* which was a finalist for the PEN/Diamonstein-Spielvogel Award for the Art of the Essay and a *New York Times* Notable Book of 2017. Her next book, *Art Monsters: On Beauty and Excess,* is forthcoming from Farrar, Straus and Giroux. She lives in Paris and Liverpool.

MELISSA FEBOS ("Home") is the author of *Whip Smart, Abandon Me,* and *Girlhood.* The inaugural winner of the Jeanne Córdova Nonfiction Award from LAMBDA Literary, her essays have appeared in the *Believer, McSweeney's Quarterly, Granta, Tin House,* the *New York Times,* and elsewhere. She is an associate professor at the University of Iowa, where she teaches in the Nonfiction Writing Program.

ROXANE GAY ("Strange Lands") splits her time between Los Angeles and New York (for love).

EMILY GOULD ("Russia, with Love") is the author of *And the Heart Says Whatever, Friendship,* and *Perfect Tunes* and is the co-creator of Emily Books. She lives in Brooklyn with her family.

ANN HOOD ("Manhattan, Always Out of Reach") is the author of the best-selling novels *Somewhere Off the Coast of Maine, The Obituary Writer, The Book That Matters Most,* and *The Knitting Circle,* as well as the memoir *Comfort: A Journey Through Grief,* which was a *New York Times* Editor's Choice and chosen as one of the top ten nonfiction books of 2008 by *Entertainment Weekly.* She has won two Pushcart Prizes, two Best American Food Writing Awards, as well as Best American Spiritual Writing and Travel Writing awards. Hood's short stories and essays have appeared in many publications, including *Ploughshares, Tin House, Traveler, Bon Appetit, O, More,* and the *Paris Review.*

DANIELLE A. JACKSON ("Brooklyn Summer") is a writer from Memphis based in Little Rock, Arkansas, whose work has appeared in the *New York Times Book Review, Bookforum,* and *Pitchfork,* among other publications. She is the managing editor at *Oxford American.*

LESLIE JAMISON ("The Assistant's Loft") is the author of *The Recovering, The Empathy Exams, Make It Scream, Make It Burn,* and *The Gin Closet.* She is a contributing writer for the *New York Times Magazine* and directs the graduate nonfiction program at Columbia University.

CAROLITA JOHNSON ("Goodbye, Hello, Goodbye . . . Hello") is a writer, cartoonist, and storyteller and a native New

Yorker, regularly contributing cartoons to the *New Yorker* magazine since 2003 and writing illustrated personal essays for Longreads, among others, about her existence as a woman and artist. She recently returned to her native Queens from Kingston, NY, to care for her mother.

LISA KO ("Fondly, Marie") Lisa Ko is the author of *The Leavers*, which was a 2017 National Book Award for Fiction finalist, won the 2016 PEN/Bellwether Prize for Socially Engaged Fiction, and was a finalist for the 2018 PEN/Hemingway Award. Her writing has appeared in *The Best American Short Stories*, the *New York Times*, the *Believer*, and elsewhere.

ADA LIMÓN ("Eleven True Things"), a current Guggenheim fellow, is the author of five poetry collections, including *The Carrying*, which won the National Book Critics Circle Award for Poetry.

EMILY ST. JOHN MANDEL ("Long Trains Leaving") is the author of five novels, most recently *Station Eleven* and *The Glass Hotel*. She lives in New York City with her family.

LIZA MONROY ("A War Zone for Anyone Looking for Love") is the author of the essay collection *Seeing As Your Shoes Are Soon to Be on Fire*, the novel *Mexican High*, and the memoir *The Marriage Act: The Risk I Took to Keep My Best Friend in America, and What It Taught Us About Love*. She has written for the *New York Times*, the *New York Times Magazine*, the *LA Times*, Longreads, the *Washington Post*, *O*, *Jezebel*, *Salon*, *Marie Claire*, *Newsweek*, *Self*, *Poets & Writers*, and various anthologies. She lives in California.

MARIE MYUNG-OK LEE ("Misfits Fit Here") is the author of the novel *Somebody's Daughter*, the young adult novel *Finding My Voice*, and the forthcoming novel *The Evening Hero, MD: The*

Infinite Futures of Einstein Alfred Nobel Kwok, M.D. Her essays have appeared in the *New York Times*, Slate, Salon, the *Washington Post*, the *Nation*, the *Atlantic*, and the *Paris Review*. She is a staff writer at The Millions and teaches fiction at Columbia University.

MIRA PTACIN ("Homecoming") is author of the acclaimed memoir *Poor Your Soul*, as well as *The In-Betweens: The Spiritualists, Mediums, and Legends of Camp Etna.* She lives on Peaks Island, Maine, with her family and is currently working on her next book. MiraMPtacin.com

EMILY RABOTEAU ("Shelter in Place) is the author of *The Professor's Daughter, Searching for Zion: The Quest for Home in the African Diaspora*, winner of the 2014 American Book Award, and the forthcoming *Caution: Lessons in Survival.* She is a professor of English at the City College of New York.

RAYHANE SANDERS ("The Loosening") is a literary agent and freelance book editor who lives in Los Angeles and loves New York.

ROSIE SCHAAP ("Homemaker") is the author of *Becoming a Sommelier* and *Drinking with Men: A Memoir*, which was named one of 2013's best books by *Library Journal* and NPR. From 2011 to 2017, she was a columnist for the *New York Times Magazine* and has also contributed to *Lucky Peach, Saveur*, and *This American Life.* She teaches creative writing in Fairleigh Dickinson University's MFA program.

DANI SHAPIRO ("My City") is the author of the best-selling memoirs *Inheritance, Still Writing, Devotion*, and *Slow Motion* and five novels, including *Black & White* and *Family History.* Her work has appeared in the *New Yorker, Granta, Tin House, Ploughshares, n+1, Vogue, Elle*, the *New York Times Book Review*, and many other publications. She lives with her family in Litchfield County, Connecticut.

JANET STEEN ("Heedless, Resilient, Gullible, and Stupid") worked in New York City for magazines such as *Esquire*, *Time Out New York*, and *Details*. She edits other people's books and writes essays, fiction, and uncategorizable things. She lives in a hollow in the mountains of upstate New York.

EMMA STRAUB ("Someday, Some Morning, Sometime") is the *New York Times* best-selling author of *All Adults Here*, *Modern Lovers*, *The Vacationers*, *Laura Lamont's Life in Pictures*, and the short story collection *Other People We Married*. Her books have been published in over twenty countries. Straub and her husband own Books Are Magic, an independent bookstore in Brooklyn, New York.

CHERYL STRAYED ("Minnesota Nice") is the author of the number-one *New York Times* best-seller *Wild*, the *New York Times* best-sellers *Tiny Beautiful Things* and *Brave Enough*, and the novel *Torch*. Strayed's writing has appeared in *The Best American Essays*, the *New York Times Magazine*, the *Washington Post Magazine*, *Vogue*, *Allure*, the *Missouri Review*, the *Sun*, The *Rumpus*—where she has written the popular "Dear Sugar" column since 2010—and elsewhere. Strayed's books have been translated into nearly forty languages around the world and have been adapted for both the screen and the stage. Her essays have been published in *The Best American Essays*, the *New York Times*, the *Washington Post Magazine*, *Vogue*, Salon, the *Sun*, *Tin House*, the *New York Times Book Review*, and elsewhere. She lives in Portland, Oregon.

EVA TENUTO ("Crash and Burn") is the cofounder and executive director of TMI Project, a nonprofit organization offering transformative storytelling workshops and performances in which storytellers divulge the TMI parts of their stories that they usually leave out. Since 2010, Tenuto has brought the TMI Project from her living room to a host of performance spaces, high schools, colleges, detention centers, mental health facilities, theaters, and the United Nations. Tenuto is the editor and director of multiple solo shows, one of which was awarded Best Comedic Script of 2014 in the United Solo Festival. Her directorial film debut, *Vicarious Resilience*, a docu short, celebrated its world premiere at the Woodstock Film Festival. Her essays have appeared in assorted anthologies and on Longreads.

REBECCA WOLFF ("So Long, Suckers") is the author of three collections of poetry (*Manderley, Figment*, and *The King*) and a novel, *The Beginners*, as well as numerous pieces of occasional prose. Wolff is the editor of *Fence* and Fence Books and the publisher of The Constant Critic, a site for poetry criticism. She lives with her two children in Hudson, New York, where she is a freelance editor and an alderwoman, working on issues of affordable housing and equity.

ACKNOWLEDGMENTS

HERE'S A LITTLE SECRET: EDITING AN ANTHOLOGY IS A GREAT way to get your name on the cover of a book without having to write the whole damn thing—or even much of it, actually—which is awesome for a writer who has so far been too traumatized by fear to complete a book of her own.

It's also a great way to position yourself among a coterie of writers who are way out of your league. I cannot express enough gratitude to all the great and accomplished authors in this collection who were kind enough to appear here with me. An extra-special thank you to the talented and kindhearted Cheryl Strayed, who made good on her promise to contribute to the collection even though she was in the midst of the craziest year of her life and battling pneumonia.

Deep gratitude goes out to my agent, Mel Flashman; to my editor for the new edition of this book, Claire Potter; my original editor, Laura Mazer; to Brooke Warner, who acquired the book; and Rachel Kramer Bussel, who referred me and gave me some pointers on editing anthologies.

Thanks to my parents, who first brought me to New York City. And to my late grandparents, who took me to the restaurant where I spotted that woman contentedly eating and writing by herself.

If I hadn't met my sweet husband, Brian Macaluso, in 2003, I might never have up and said goodbye to all that two years later. And I couldn't have pulled this together without his love, encouragement, and support.

ABOUT THE EDITOR

© Sylvie Rosokoff

SARI BOTTON ("Real Estate") is a writer and editor living in Kingston, New York. Her writing has appeared in the *New York Times, Harper's Bazaar, Marie Claire, Women's Wear Daily, W,* The Rumpus, The Millions, Catapult, plus other publications and assorted anthologies. She is the former essays editor for Longreads and edited the award-winning anthology *Goodbye to All That: Writers on Loving and Leaving New York* and its *New York Times* best-selling follow-up *Never Can Say Goodbye: Writers on Their Unshakable Love for New York.* She teaches creative nonfiction courses at Catapult and in the MFA program at Bay Path University.